John O'Donoghue

John O'Donoghue was born in north London to Irish parents. He was first sectioned aged sixteen, and spent over a decade in and out of psychiatric hospitals. In 1988 he went to the University of East Anglia, graduating in 1992. From 2000 to 2005 he was Chair of Survivors' Poetry. He lectures in creative writing and lives in Brighton with his wife and four children.

Praise for *Sectioned*

'The humdrum reality of mental illness has rarely been so well conveyed. It's less a story of locked wards than of hostels, soup kitchens, sheltered housing, drug addicts, well-meaning charity workers and relentless poverty. O'Donoghue is honest about his own failings: misfortune is compounded by his capacity to fuck up. What saves him, in part, is poetry: he begins to write as a teenager and through most of his ordeals he keeps it up. *Sectioned* is . . . a vindication of O'Donoghue's faith: psychosis could easily have killed him, or the liquid cosh stunned him into silence, but here he is, against the odds, speaking loud and plain' Blake Morrison, *Guardian*

'*Sectioned* is a beautifully drawn account of his attempts to escape his mental straitjacket . . . The book is punctuated with moments of vibrant humour and a great sense of irony' *Sunday Times*

'Alternately harrowing and blackly comic . . . Crammed with picaresque vignettes' James Morrison, *Guardian*

'O'Donoghue is a shrewd observer of people and places and there is much fascinating material here, especially for anyone interested in mental illness and its treatment . . . His poet's fine eye for detail is a great advantage . . . The book ends with a feeling of potential, of more poems to be composed and a different life to be lived' *Morning Star*

'He pulls no punches . . . *Sectioned* reads as part-novel, part-stream of consciousness as it recounts the writer's harrowing ordeal' *Gay Times*

Sectioned

A Life Interrupted

JOHN O'DONOGHUE

JOHN MURRAY

First published in Great Britain in 2009 by John Murray (Publishers)
An Hachette UK company

First published in paperback in 2009

4

A CIP catalogue record for this title is available from the British Library

ISBN 978-0-7195-2054-9

Typeset in Monotype Bembo by Servis Filmsetting Ltd, Stockport, Cheshire

Printed and bound by Clays Ltd, St Ives plc

John Murray policy is to use papers that are natural, renewable and recyclable products
and made from wood grown in sustainable forests. The logging and manufacturing
processes are expected to conform to the environmental regulations of the country of
origin.

John Murray (Publishers)
338 Euston Road
London NW1 3BH

www.johnmurray.co.uk

for
Buster

Contents

Contents

Introduction

The prayer meeting was held every Thursday after school. I'd get out of lessons and walk down Essex Road to the Smiths' house. My friends in the Christian Union would all be there, some a little ahead, some still to arrive. Mrs Smith would greet us all with an enormous smile. She was small and white-haired, with a daughter and two sons at Arden's, the smart private school up the road from where I lived in Waltham Pond, the hamlet where north-east London runs out into Essex. The rest of the Christian Union were all at the Leyton Senior High Schools, one for boys, the other for girls. We met in the front room where we were given tea and biscuits, and then got down to praising, thanking and beseeching the Lord.

I was raised a Catholic, the son of Irish immigrants, so this was a new world to me. The prayers were all made up for a start, the Grace about the only set prayer we ever said. Our Fathers and Hail Marys didn't figure at the Smiths', but there wasn't a problem: my Catholicism was respected, challenged sometimes, but I was accepted. I had asked Jesus to come into my life. Maybe they thought in time I'd convert; maybe they thought Jesus was enough and denominations old hat and divisive. For there were Baptists, Methodists and Greek Orthodox in the Christian Union as well as Anglicans. C.S. Lewis was more important to us than Calvin or Wesley or the Forty-Nine Articles. C.S. Lewis, the chronicler of *Narnia*, the founder of 'mere Christianity', was our patron saint. We could all identify with him.

My family was like a lot of Irish Catholic families in the 1960s. Above the mantelpiece hung two plates, one of JFK, the other of Pope John XXIII. For my parents, JFK and John XXIII were ushering in a decade that promised the people of the world that temporal and spiritual power was passing to a new generation, that a young President and a modernizing Pope were about to change the planet. And my parents, one off a farm in Kerry, the other the daughter of a sawmill worker from Monaghan, were as keen as any to be a part of this new Holy Roman Empire. I was born into a world that seemed to be changing for the better.

Although my mother disapproved of me going to the local ex-grammar – she'd have been happier if I'd moved on to a Catholic high school – I was eager to reach out and find fellow Christians. The Christian Union had seemed as good a place as any to start.

The Thursday prayer meeting began slowly. Tanesha Ghosh thanked God for His Creation. Jon Griffin prayed for Simon. Graham Stewart praised Jesus for our teachers. The prayers moved around the room, one by one. I felt my turn coming and started rambling. 'Oh God, thank You for all You've done for me ... I'm not very good at praying, but I just wanted to say ... touch me.'

It was an odd request. For it wasn't God I was asking to touch me, it was my fellow members of the Christian Union. Any laying on of hands, though, was short-lived.

Mrs Smith's daughter stood in the doorway. I can remember looking round to see her, hips grinding, staring at me, eyes wide. Immediately someone shouted, 'Oh, my God, get James!' and the next thing I knew I was told not to look and hurried into a back room, disorientated by it all. What was going on? Who was James? What was happening to Mrs Smith's daughter?

I was in a kneeling position when James entered the room. He put his hands on my groin and started to draw up bile from my belly. In a commanding voice, he asked me who I was. Confused, I couldn't answer. He grabbed at my genitals and drew more bile out of me, which I hurled up into a little bin that someone had put in front of me. James – I guessed by now – was the local vicar, and there were other voices in the room, breathless, excited, fearful, all of them asking me who I was. It was like a chant, a mantra.

I had no idea what was going on. I was trapped, held in the room, unable to stop what was happening. Hysteria had broken out. When I'd asked to be touched I'd set something off, and now James was fighting it.

The same question, over and over, as the bile drained out of me: 'Who are you? Who are you? Who are you?' James had his hands on me, drawing up the hot liquid through my body. I began convulsing. Something in me was responding to him. I felt my chest growing into breasts, James putting his hands on them, some instinct in me interacting with his probing, strong, inescapable presence.

James's voice rang through the room. 'Who are you? I command you in the name of Jesus to say who you are!'

'I am Satan,' I said.

Gasps echoed off the four walls. Moans went up around me. James's hands worked harder. All at once, I felt a force from above, white and powerful, push down into me. I saw a crown in my head, whiter on the brilliant white already behind my eyes. Wind blew out of my penis.

I said, 'I am John.'

Again gasps as a kind of awed relaxation entered all of the people in the room. My eyes opened, and I felt calm, purer.

'Look at this,' a friendly voice said.

I looked at the small bin, half full with bile.

There was laughter, as if whatever the bile represented no longer had any hold over me.

I was ushered out to the Smiths' car. Mrs Smith said goodbye to me and her son Dominic offered to drive me back home. But whatever had happened wasn't letting me go. Waves of energy were still throbbing through me, and I was transmitting them to Mrs Smith. But she didn't react. She just carried on as if nothing was happening. But I knew what was happening.

I had been delivered.

But it hadn't worked.

I was still in the grip of the Devil.

PART I

Where Are We From?

I

Claybury, 1975

Smoke is coming out of the wall. Only I can see it, only I know what's going on. Everything is sinking. I am heavy; this chair with its metal frame and fake black leather is heavy; the formica dining table I'm sitting at is so heavy it could have fallen from a dwarf star. Gravity is pressing down on me with a force I can withstand only because my own heaviness acts as a balance to the dark and majestic compression at work in the universe. This is why the smoke is coming out of the wall. This is why only I can see it.

I'd been in Claybury for four months before I was given ECT. I was sixteen. The day I went down for it I was wearing a striped hospital dressing gown and yellow pyjamas. I'd been given the Last Rites, and only came round a day or two before I had my treatments.

Lee, the nurse from Hong Kong, persuaded me to sign the consent form and he took me down. It was a long walk through the corridors of Claybury, the smell of shag tobacco and soggy hospital food hanging thick in the dusty air.

When we arrived Lee left me outside the clinic. I sat with a bunch of long-stay patients in a little waiting area. Quite a few of the long stays looked like they had ECT on a regular basis. One man – white-haired, square-headed, a crimp in his forehead – couldn't stop moving his legs and twitching. His tongue slobbered and his mouth twisted as we waited. He made yearning noises and looked at me.

My turn came. A dark-haired nurse led me through a door and over to an operating table. I lay down and a bright yellow light was shone in my eyes. My psychiatrist, Dr Popper, told me I could say anything before she injected me with muscle relaxant and the electrodes were placed at my temples.

'Is this like a sexual ceremony to you?' I asked. I think I was trying to shock her, to sound like I was up on my Freud. I hadn't read a word of Freud.

'No,' she answered. She was taken aback, and I felt ashamed of myself. 'Now I want you to count down from ten as I give you this injection.'

The needle went into a vein in my hand. I counted. Ten ... nine ... eight ...

When I came round things seemed a little more hard-edged, a little more defined. My thoughts were clearer. I'd woken up in the men's dormitory, in cool sheets, with daylight streaming in through the tall windows.

I got up, found I was still in my pyjamas and put on my dressing gown. I walked slowly, my head banging, past the hospital beds and towards the patients' kitchen. I could see everyone at lunch in the long dining area between the day rooms and the dorms. The big metal cube of the food trolley was halfway down the row of tables and the medicine cabinet was next to it.

'Hello, John,' said Miriam. 'How are you feeling?'

Miriam was a warm, Jewish woman in her fifties, who was suffering from a sluggish thyroid. She told me she fed me before I had the ECT, but I can remember none of this. The immediate period before I had the treatments is lost to me, those memories burnt away.

'I'm ... all right,' I said.

8

'Come and sit down, John. Have something to eat.'

'I don't think I can face anything, Miriam. I feel a bit ... funny.'

But Miriam didn't have time to argue.

'I am the Blessed Virgin Mary!'

A statuesque woman, tall and naked, had stepped out of a darkened side room. Everyone stopped eating to stare. Two male nurses rushed over from the medicine cabinet and bustled her back into the room. A third nurse prepared a needle and hurried down the dining area to help them; there were sounds of a struggle, then silence.

I looked at Miriam's fish and chips. It was the best meal of the week, but I had no appetite.

'What was it like, John?' she asked. 'Did it hurt?'

'I don't know, Miriam. They put me out. I do have a headache. But perhaps I'll be better soon.'

Miriam looked at me, the Jewish mother and the poor sick *goyische* boy.

'I hope so, John,' she said. 'I hope so. Now why don't you have some food? It'll do you good.'

Miriam felt that chicken soup would have me right in no time. But it was going to take a little longer than that.

It's six o'clock. Any second now my father will come through the door, home from work on the railways, a bar of chocolate in his blue jacket. He brings in the cold and the dust, and a masculine smell of oil and putty and grease.

'There, John Boy,' he says, handing me a bar of Cadbury's Dairy Milk. I eat the chocolate and play with the foil wrapper, tearing and rolling and shaping it until I have legs, a tail, a head, a little wiry body. I make dogs and cats, silver and dimpled and shiny.

9

Playing with the little rectangle of foil and making magic animals out of it is almost as good as eating the chocolate.

Hearing my father call me John Boy is best of all.

———

My father has been complaining of a pain in his shoulder. He's been to see the doctor who's prescribed him painkillers. But he seems OK, keeping to his routine of a sleep during the day now he's on nights, and taking it easy in the evening. He never misses *The Val Doonican Show*, and it's good to see him up and enjoying Waterford's most famous son.

My father falls forward. He's on his stomach on the floor in front of us. Suddenly he lets a roar out of him. We turn him over. His eyes are closed and his lips are turning blue.

'Quick, John,' says my mother, 'run and get the doctor.'

The doctor's surgery is in Frances Road, about five minutes away. I sprint down the street, the wind whistling behind me, my heart thumping with every stride I take. But the surgery is shut and there's no doctor there. I run as fast as I can to the police station and ask for a police doctor. But they don't have one either. They phone for an ambulance.

I get back home and tell my mother what's happening.

The ambulance arrives and she goes off with my father. They put him in a metal chair with a red blanket over him. I wait for her to get back. The flat is quiet now. It almost seems as if it all never happened. I say a prayer for my father, that he will come back to us, that he will be all right.

Then my mother is at the door. She lets herself in. I can hear her coming up the stairs. The door opens.

'Well, John,' she says, 'your father is dead.'

Four hours later, exhausted from weeping, I dry my eyes. I have no father. The quiet man I loved is gone, his strength, his stoicism, the Irish he never spoke with us. There is so much about him now that I'll never know.

My mother and I look out on a world that is suddenly bleaker, scarier, emptier.

My father died about a year and a half before my own admission. My mother's grief led to neglect. Neglect of me, neglect of herself. She grew thin and gaunt, a haggard woman whose heart was broken. Food, housework, shopping – none of this mattered any more. She took to wandering the roads, wailing for my father, and I stayed off school to 'look after' her, although I had as little idea of how to look after her as she had of looking after me. I was fourteen, and trying to cope with my own grief.

She was called up by my school to meet the Head and discuss my truancy. She collapsed on his desk, sobbing. I was dazed by it all, ashamed of my inability to provide, confused by my mother's descent into grief and madness.

Neighbours, friends of my mother's, intervened. I think that they – upset and frustrated by my mother's constant tearful calls on them – contacted the social services. They acted quickly. My mother was admitted to Claybury, a large Victorian asylum in Woodford Bridge. I stayed with my mother's friends until she got better.

There's me – aged fourteen – and the young social worker behind her desk.

'So – do you want to be fostered?'

Whipps Cross Hospital suddenly stops and a gigantic hush falls on the place. The bustle and rush goes out of it. It's a big question. If I say no I'll be loyal to my mother, the grief-struck, heartbroken woman who walks the roads wailing. If I say yes I'll betray her. The silence deepens.

'Yes.'

I say the word quietly. It slides out of my mouth like a lie.

I tell myself that if I'm placed into a nice middle-class English home I'll get help with my homework, 'study hard at the books', eat regular meals.

Like my parents, I'm trying to emigrate.

I visit my mother every evening, taking the bus, a new single-decker 235 that goes all the way. My sunny optimism about Claybury's facilities, the football pitches, the extensive grounds – 'It's a schoolboy's paradise!' – doesn't really register with my mother.

'The least you say in these places, the quicker you get out of them,' she says.

Advice that is wasted on me.

'She is having the bit with him.'

An Indian woman is standing in front of Dr Popper, accusing her of having an affair with a doctor who is blushing, sitting a few chairs down from her. Neither is responding. We are having group therapy. But the group is very large: O1 is closed for redecorating and O1 and O2 have been combined. There are about forty patients altogether, plus the staff from the two wards. 'Therapy' is becoming more like a mad cabaret turn. There are just too many patients to properly focus on. Only a stunning performance is going to get any attention.

We're all sat around the walls of the large day room. The size of the group says something about the hospital: it seems to be collapsing in on itself, just like us.

The Indian woman is manic. She used to be one of their own, a psychiatrist, privy to secrets, theirs and ours. Everyone is appalled, appalled and amused. The woman is suffering, but that doesn't stop her embarrassing the most powerful figures in our lives.

'She is having the bit!'

The two doctors sit in stony silence. Dr Popper looks strained. The summer air shimmers in the room, dispelling the thick institutional dust from the choking carpets. The scented breeze stirs memories of outside, of freedom, of escape. But we're afraid of that world, for Claybury, like all institutions, is a kind of Neverland. Here, adulthood and responsibility are postponed by the routines of mealtimes, medication, visiting hours and occupational therapy.

The Indian doctor can go as far as she likes in her ramblings. Her allegations are not what's embarrassing Dr Popper: these are a symptom of her illness, a projection of her speeding, deluded mind. No, it's the fact that a mad shrink is worse than a bent copper, and this woman's madness is a sign that even our doctors are mortal, like us can crack and go crazy.

She's very disturbing.

For all of us.

❧

'Oh, Jesus! Oh, Jesus! Oh, Jesus!'

I keep up my prayer all night. My room is next door to my foster-parents' bedroom. Through the thin walls they can hear me.

'Oh, Jesus! Oh, Jesus! Oh, Jesus!'

I'm in the grip of the Devil.

Through the wall, Ivy sobs. But Frank knows what to do. He goes downstairs and makes a call. Within an hour two doctors have arrived. They try to ask me some questions but all they get is:

'Oh, Jesus! Oh, Jesus! Oh, Jesus!'

Soon the ambulance comes and takes me away.

❦

I see the strands of smoke again. There are faces in it now, evil faces, leering at me. They whisper as I walk towards the day room. The whispering sounds like sticks kindling, catching fire and crackling. But I can't tell anyone. The whispers grow louder, the faces in the smoke laugh as I pass, darkness closing in on me like a starless night.

Mass in the Chapel of the Holy Ghost is over and I have come to see Father Richard, Claybury's Catholic chaplain. He's tall, with a little of Friar Tuck's belly about him, white-haired, powerfully built, aged about sixty. He has a groove on his upper lip – the mark of a patient who sliced him years ago, a scar etched deep into him.

'John XXIII died and went to heaven.'

I had never heard a priest tell me a joke before. I've been brought up to respect the clergy, to believe that they are special, that they're called by God. Father Richard is very much in this mould. I think he's a saintly man, very English in his way, solid, down-to-earth, but devout and holy. We're in the whitewashed room where he goes after he's celebrated Mass, sitting at a table facing one another. He's taken off his vestments and is in his black two-piece clerical suit.

'St Peter meets him at the Pearly Gates.

'"Who are you?" asks St Peter.

'"Who am I?" says John XXIII. "I'm John XXIII."

'"John XXIII?" says St Peter. "I haven't got you down here. What did you do in life?"

'"What did I do? I called the Second Vatican Council!"

'"Wait here," says St Peter. "I'll go and have a word with the Holy Ghost."

14

'St Peter goes inside and finds the Holy Ghost in a back room writing in a large vellum book.

'"Excuse me," says St Peter. "Got one at the Gates who says he's for here."

'"What's his name?" says the Holy Ghost, looking up from his work and casting his fathomless eyes on St Peter.

'"John XXIII."

'"Rings a bell," says the Holy Ghost. "What did he do in life?"

'"Says he called the Second Vatican Council."

'"The Second Vatican Council? Oh, yes ... I know ... forgot to go to that one."'

I laugh – but it's a dark kind of laugh, subversive, disrespectful. I think of the plate we used to have over our mantel of Pope John and I wonder what my parents would make of Father Richard.

The Cookery Group takes place on Tuesday mornings at the far end of the hospital. Claybury is vast and the kitchen is a long way from the ward. There is a painting that hangs in the corridor near O2, a canvas with brightly coloured oblongs overlapping each other, blue, yellow, red, green. There's a large black dot in the bottom right-hand corner, with the words 'YOU ARE HERE!' beside it – a map to show you that you're lost, but not how to find your way out.

We amble down with a couple of nurses and the occupational therapist, and pass some of the long-stay patients on the way. There is one woman I often see in the corridors. She is frail and gaunt, with lank hair and a shapeless dress that once belonged to somebody else. She shuffles along, avoiding eye contact, rubbing her hands as if she was washing them over and over.

Another long-stay patient – a man in a blue cloth cap and the cast-off jacket, shirt and trousers of a stranger – comes up to me and looks as if he is about to speak. But all that comes out of his mouth is air. His lips twist and gurn and his face twitches. I don't know why he's fixated with me. He never approaches anyone else.

At the kitchen we are greeted by the white-coated catering manager who gives Sally, the occupational therapist, a cardboard box of ingredients and some chops in a greaseproof paper parcel. He's wearing a tie like the one I used to wear for school. It's odd to see it on him, a reminder of a life I used to live.

The small kitchen is tucked away from the clank and clamour of the large hospital kitchen and we are ushered towards it by the catering manager. I see for the first time that what has happened to me is all about scale. Something large has happened in my life and it needs a large place to deal with it, to get everything back to a size I can cope with, the size my life was before I was admitted to this place, before things went wrong. I feel a little dizzy thinking about it, the telescoped perspectives.

'Are you OK, John?' asks Sally. 'You look a bit pale.'

'I'm fine,' I hear myself saying.

YOU ARE HERE! I wonder if whoever painted that picture felt like this, as if everything had suddenly got a lot bigger around them. I wonder if they felt that the world inside them was out of synch with the world outside. I wonder if they got over it. I try to focus on what's happening in the Cookery Group.

Miriam takes charge. Sally fades into the background, letting her get on with it. She has me chopping vegetables and peeling potatoes along with the rest while she prepares the meat, some lamb chops, the white rind of their fat like half moons on the greaseproof paper. Miriam does marvellous things with these chops, smothering them with sumptuous flavours and seasonings. She soon has it all under control and we sit down and talk.

'My sons have grown up and left me,' Miriam tells me. We're at a table with a starched white linen tablecloth, the table laid, food smells wafting in the kitchen air.

'I've broken up my home,' I say.

Miriam and I look at each other from either side of our predicament.

'When we get out of here, John, you must come and visit us.'

Miriam can't stop being a mother. But have I stopped being a son? Have I given up the right to be my mother's son? By being somebody else's foster-son? By being Miriam's surrogate? Whose child am I? Has my betrayal brought all of this on me?

Lunch is served. It's the closest we come to home cooking in here.

One day Colin, a dark-haired man with a husky voice and bottle-thick glasses, asks me if I feel like walking down to the White Hart with him for a drink. I quite like Colin. He's an epileptic, scarred from falls and fits, about ten years older than me.

So I say yes and Colin and I set off. We walk down the hill, the traffic flowing by, people going about their daytime business, the routine of the ward behind us. The outside world looks a little strange. It's quicker and busier than I remember. Compared to Claybury's tranquil grounds and the torpor of the corridors it's as if the world is spinning faster outside than it is inside. This is the first time in two months that I've been outside the hospital gates.

We sit drinking silently in the public bar, our illnesses invisible amongst the mid-afternoon boozers. All is going well. But then I lean over. I am losing control of myself, lying at an angle of 90° on the seat, in a very strange space. It's the drugs mixing with the alcohol.

'Get him out of here,' says one of the drinkers to Colin in

disgust. But Colin's got a better idea: he walks out quickly and I'm left dazed and alone.

From the orange curtains of the day room comes a wisp of smoke. It drifts across the patients' lounge like a snake's shadow gliding through the dusty air. It seems to slither and just as suddenly disappears. I thought I was free. But here is the smoke again. And this time there's a smell, matches, burning, sulphur. And the whispers, growing louder and louder as I walk towards the medicine cabinet for medication which isn't working.

My mother has come to visit me. Although she's only fifty-three she's been placed in an old people's home run by nuns in Braintree after she ran away from the first place in Isleworth.

Braintree is a long way away and although the home has done her good – she's put on weight and seems to be getting over my father's death – there is still something desperate about her. I'm shocked that she's sitting here opposite me, ashamed that she should see me here.

'What way are you affected? Can you not move? Can you not speak? What is up with you?' she asks.

I'm too stunned to answer. I was supposed to be the one who would do the caring. I'd visited my mother every weekend – long journeys every time – and it was me who was going to salvage our life, to do well at school, get a decent job, make sure we picked up the pieces. I can't speak. I'm lost. My plan has backfired. Something buckles inside me.

I'm slipping into a world of smoke, and density, and terror.

———

'We've brought you some grapes and a copy of that French magazine you asked for.'

My foster-parents are sitting opposite me in the lounge.

Frank and Ivy, two middle-aged Cockneys, uneasy in this huge room. She takes out the fruit and the latest edition of *Paris Match* and places them on the coffee table in front of me. I should be sitting my O levels, but I haven't studied anything since I came here. My hope of getting a CSE Grade 1 in Maths has gone for good. At least I might be able to keep my hand in at French.

'The boys send their love.'

'Thanks,' I murmur.

'Well ... how are they treating you?'

I think of the groups, the medication, the ECT.

'Fine,' I say. 'Just fine.'

'I couldn't get wet, you see.'

Sophie is telling us about her weekend. She seems smaller than she usually is, sunk in herself somehow, as if she was being gnawed at from the inside, was looking inward to coax whatever was eating her away to stop. She's blonde and frail and very young, early twenties I think, but now almost like a child. The small group – about six of us – sit on the same black chairs they have in the dining room, heavy, repressive, all straight edges. There's hardly any comfort in them. Sophie is upset, smoking languidly and telling us about what happened when she went home on weekend leave.

'I don't know why, I just couldn't.'

She starts gently weeping, tears at first, then sobs. There is a terrible feeling of dread, of tension, mixed with a kind of numbed pity for her. A woman to my right starts shaking, her body rocking backwards and forwards, her left leg suddenly hopping up and down. I can feel waves of misery and terror circulating in the room, as if the poison in our minds has been let out and is suffocating us.

'The group seems to be having problems focusing,' says Dr Popper.

Silence, but not calm, slowly settles and deepens. The woman beside me is still shaking, although not as much, and her leg has stopped its jackhammering. The silence grows, and with it the tension.

She finally snaps.

'She couldn't get wet! Don't you understand?'

She is standing now. I don't know what they're talking about, but it's very upsetting for Sophie, who is still quietly weeping.

'She couldn't fuck! Is that what it is, Sophie?'

But Sophie is still crying, head down, and can't – or won't – reply.

There is a young Greek woman sitting opposite me. She wears a black veil and looks bewildered. This is because she doesn't speak English, but she has to come to the groups otherwise she would lie in bed all day and her depression would get worse.

Dr Popper lets the silence run, even though the woman is standing over Sophie now, bending down to comfort her.

'What's the matter, Sophie? It's OK, love, it's happened to me, it's nothing to be ashamed of – I'm sure you love your boyfriend.'

Sophie looks up, her eyes full of hatred.

'You stupid, silly bitch,' she screams. 'You don't understand, do you? It wasn't my boyfriend I was trying to fuck!'

The night light is red. It's left on all night in the dormitory, and reminds me of the light by the altar at Mass. But this light is kind of scary; there is an evil glow to it. I've been aware of evil ever since I came in here, of a presence watching me, waiting for me. I watch it all night till finally I fall asleep.

The white van is waiting. My mother eventually comes down the stairs and out of the front door. She looks sick, not like before, more sober somehow. She realizes now what I've done. She's composed, dignified, not making a fuss. The driver opens the back doors of the van and my mother moves towards them. He takes her arm as she approaches and helps her up. As she steps on to the duckboards, he puts his hand on her back and gives her a shove. Then he slams the door shut and walks round to the front. He gets in and drives off. I stand on the pavement, blinking. I've broken up our home. My mother is gone, off to nuns who will care for her. And I'm off as well. But not to my new foster-parents. It's all over in seconds.

I arrive at the vicarage with my social worker a few days before Christmas. It'll soon be 1975. My foster-parents are away at their son's but have told social services they'll take me in the New Year. Meanwhile, I've been fixed up with the vicar of St John's, Leytonstone, and his family.

The door of the vicarage opens and a smart woman in her early forties stands before us.

'Hello! You must be John?'

'Hello,' I say shyly.

'Come in, come in,' she says.

We all walk into the vicarage. I have never been in a vicarage before. I've been in a presbytery, the time my parents moved from Hackney to Leyton. They'd introduced themselves to Canon Harnett, the parish priest of St Joseph's. I could see that my father warmed to Canon Harnett – they had the same kind of husky Kerry accent, a clannishness my mother, a Monaghan woman, was subtly excluded from. I think of them all, so careful over my upbringing, so far now from where I stand.

The vicarage is big. I have never been in such a big house. We walk through the hallway to the living room. Sofas and a coffee table and a tall window give a sense of ease and comfort. A blond boy a few years younger than me and a girl a few years older are relaxing on the sofas.

'This is John, everyone. Remember we spoke about John? He'll be staying with us over Christmas until his new foster-parents come back from their son's. Say hello, you two.'

The children of the house smile and say hello, and I say hello back.

'Right, John, we've got a room sorted out for you upstairs, so why don't you come with me?'

My social worker stays in the living room while I go upstairs with the vicar's wife. She shows me into a room on the first landing.

The room is large and it's the first time I've ever had one to myself. She leaves me and I put my bag on the floor beside the bed. I think of my bed at home, the bed I shared with my mother as a child, the prayers I'd say every night at the foot of it. I feel lost here, amongst these strangers. And I think of my mother, and how we never said goodbye.

I've been given a diary for Christmas. It's a handsome present, with dark blue leather binding and gold leaf on the edges of each page. When it's closed it looks like my mother's missal. I open it and write under 1 January: 'Mum—'

'John!' Ivy calls me from downstairs.

I close the diary, put it away in my bedside cabinet, and walk down to the kitchen. This is the first time I've ever been in my foster-parents' place, the first time I've ever met them. Two weeks ago I was in a vicarage. It seems like another planet now. Frank and Ivy live in a small two-bedroom council flat in Waltham Pond. It's the only council property in the area, a small low-rise block near the Windmill pub. It actually seems a lot smaller than our own flat. I've been told that my mother has made plans to sell the property, although I've never thought of it as 'property'. This is the word my social worker uses. My mother needs the proceeds to pay the nuns who are looking after her. She has white hair and a lined face, but it will be odd to see her in an old people's home. I will have to go and visit once a week. It's quite a journey from Waltham Pond to Isleworth. It will take up most of my Sundays.

'Now, John, what do you want to call us?'

I've thought about this.

'Do you mind if I call you Frank and Ivy?'

Frank smiles, big horse teeth just like my father's grinning at me.

'Not at all, John. I told you he wouldn't want to call us Mum and Dad,' he says to Ivy. She looks disappointed, but I can't call them what they're not.

'What we do,' she says, 'is we have a little rota. If you and Frank share the washing-up, I'll cook, shop, clean, do all the rest. Apart from the odd bit of housework, like hoovering and dusting. I have a little cleaning job I do three mornings a week, but that hardly wears me out! I'm sure you helped around the house when you were at home, didn't you?'

I hardly lifted a finger at home, even when I stayed away from school to look after my mother.

'I did a bit,' I say.

'I'm sure you did,' she says. 'Now I'm just making one of my concoctions – egg and ham pie. I hope you like egg and ham pie! What do you eat, John? Are you a bit of a fussy eater? Or will you eat anything?'

I can't eat eggs, not since my mother put a raw one in my bottle when I was a baby. But I might be able to eat them in an egg and ham pie.

'I'll eat anything,' I say.

23

'Good,' says Ivy. 'Well, I expect you'll want to watch a bit of telly?'

I think of the diary upstairs. I would sooner write down what's been happening to me, about breaking up with my mother and her going to the nuns, me coming here, Christmas in the vicarage, Frank and Ivy and the way things have turned out, see if I can make sense of it all. But I know that it would look rude to hide myself away on my first night with them.

'Yes,' I say. 'Do you know what's on?'

The whispering is following me. And here come the wisps of smoke, drifting from the walls. They circle my legs, twist their way up towards my belly. They're all over me, and the whispering is louder now. In a bid for release, I squat-jump down the ward from the dining area to the dorms, leaping with all my force, bounding towards freedom and relief. A noise like thunder roars in my ear each time I land. I am as mad as all hell.

Claybury stretches from Woodford Bridge right down to Ilford and beyond, 235 acres of grounds, football pitches and buildings, with a little white Georgian manor house tucked away in the heart of the rolling landscape. The genteel folk who owned the estate lived here before it became an asylum. These days the manor house is used as offices.

We walk the grounds as often as occupational therapy allows. It's the best therapy of all, free from the drama of the small groups, the tedium of the ward, the claustrophobic atmosphere that can suddenly roll in like fog. This afternoon a small party led by Bob, a young bearded occupational therapist, and Veronica, a student nurse out of uniform, is going for a stroll through Claybury's rolling acres.

Spring has come to England, and as we head away from the

large, ominous Victorian buildings the bleakness of winter in the asylum is starting to fade a little in the mild April sunlight. Like us, the year is recovering.

Bob and Veronica are up ahead. I'm with Jean-Paul and Cathy. He's a handsome Frenchman in his late twenties, and she's a pretty white woman in her mid-thirties who suffers with diabetes and depression. There are a few more patients behind us, all quietly enjoying the walk. The pace is slow, steady, and we're soon on a path leading deeper into the grounds, past manicured lawns and hedgerows to sunlit meadows, daisies dotting the green, a slight breeze blowing, wisps of cloud in the pale blue sky.

A squirrel suddenly darts out across the clearing. I watch it stop, sit up on its haunches, look at us and hold up its little paws, miniature fairy hands, as if it was about to box. Jean-Paul and Cathy laugh, and I smile.

'It's all right, fella,' says Bob, coming towards the squirrel. 'We're friends.'

He takes some peanuts out of his jeans' pocket and scatters them on the grass. The squirrel rushes forward, picks one of them up and starts to unpeel the shell with quick, flickering nimbleness.

'Come on,' says Bob, walking on. 'There's something up here I want to show you all.'

We come to the top of a hill. Below us, as far as the eye can see, house after house stretches away. Here and there new London Transport buses, boxy and awkward, lumber through the distant streets below. They look like Dinky Toys from up here.

'Where are we?' asks Cathy.

'Looking down on Barking,' says Bob.

'Is this what you wanted to show us?' I ask.

'Yeah,' says Bob. 'Over there is where this place ends and

the outside begins. Take a look, folks. Soon you'll be leaving Claybury behind and returning to the world.'

I look down at Barking. The streets all have the same sand-coloured houses. There's something dismal about them some-how. I think of Frank and Ivy, of their council flat, of going back to them. And I realize that life on the outside will be hard, will never be the same again. I think of what has changed, of all that has happened, of the road I have come and can't turn back on, my father going to Petticoat Lane for the Christmas turkey, bringing it home under his coat, him handing it over to my mother. I think of him coming in from work, of that bar of chocolate and playing with the foil, of him asking my mother to put her hand down his back and rub the dust of the day off him. Our life has gone. It went with him when he died. I might be the man of the house, but I am not a man. I couldn't keep us together. I broke us up. And now the house is gone too, and my mother with it.

And I suddenly realize that I actually prefer it here, prefer the routines, the occupational therapy, the groups and doctors and nurses and food trollies, the long-stay patients, the chaplains and the grounds, to whatever might lie beyond. Here I have found a kind of consolation, some measure of security.

We turn and make our way back to the ward.

26

II
Leyton Senior High School for Boys, 1976

I'm back at last. It has been a long time, almost twelve months. Nearly everyone I know has either moved up a year or left. It's going to be odd, especially after where I've been, after all that's happened.

I take a deep breath and walk through the school gates. Knots of schoolboys in ones and twos, bunches and small gangs, wearing black blazers and grey trousers, white shirts and striped school ties, pass me on their way to the main building. Teachers are getting out of a few cars parked by the rosebeds. I recognize some of them: Martin Jackson, Philip Brown, Norman Darker. There are some new faces too. A pair of attractive young women step out of a Mini. They're in their mid-twenties, one blonde, one brunette, their short skirts a complete contrast to the suits of the male teachers. It feels strange to be here. There's a lot to catch up.

The school bell rings and I go in.

The sign on the door reads 'School Counsellor'. I knock and wait. Footsteps approach and the door opens.

'John? Hello. How are you?'

Mr Thomas lets me into his office. There are posters on the wall by the window with big bright pictures of flowers and wise sayings: 'Every journey begins with one small step'; 'Give a man a fish and he will eat for a day. Teach him how to fish and he will eat for a lifetime'. Mr Thomas sits at his desk. I sit facing him.

'I'm fine, thanks,' I say.

Mr Thomas was a spin bowler in his youth and played cricket for his village in Lancashire. He's a tall man in his fifties with a burly chest and kind, hazel eyes. His Lancashire accent has softened, but there's something granite about him all the same, as if he was born hard and never weakened.

'I want you to know that you can see me as often as you like, talk about whatever you like. I know you've had a rough time of it lately, but look, there are people – and I'm one of them – who are here to help.'

'Thanks,' I say. 'There is one thing.'

'What, John? What do you want me to do?'

'Can you get me out of Double Maths on Friday?'

'Hello. Remember me?'

I'm passing by reception on my way to lessons. A fair-haired lad about my own age in steel-rimmed glasses and Dunlop Greens is standing just across from me by the Head's office. I can't remember him at all.

'I'm Jacqui's cousin. She asked me to say hello. I came to visit her a few times in Claybury.'

My memory has a few holes in it – a legacy of ECT.

'How is Jacqui?' I ask.

'She's fine. My aunt – Pam – she says hello too. Do you play tennis?'

'I do,' I say.

'Let's have a game then. The name's John.'

'Advantage me,' I say. 'So's mine.'

We laugh.

'Meet me at lunchtime,' he says. 'We can scrounge a couple of rackets from the PE Department. What are you taking this year?'

'English, French and resit Maths. What are you taking?'

'English and History,' he says. 'Mr Brown and Miss Galloway. She's new. Have you seen her?'

'I think I spotted her this morning. Are you waiting to see Mr Carson?' I ask.

'Yeah,' he says. 'I want to start a Debating Society.'

'Oh, yes? Why's that?'

'Just to stir things up a bit.'

The door to the Head's office opens. Mr Carson stands framed in the doorway, smiling. He welcomes John inside and closes the door after him.

'How've you been getting on?' asks Mr Thomas.

'Well, I'm still going to Double Maths on Friday.'

Mr Thomas laughs. His room is just the same, the posters, the chairs, the gentle reassurance.

'Nothing I can do about that, I'm afraid. But are you making friends? I should think a lot of your old pals have left by now, haven't they?'

'To be honest I never had a lot in the first place.'

I'd been at the local Catholic school, Cardinal Wiseman Junior High. When a couple of my friends had chosen to go to the County High, I followed suit. Now they've moved on.

'Isn't there anyone you're a bit pally with?'

'Well, there is one lad.'

'Who's that?'

'His name's John.'

'And how have you got to know him?'

'His cousin was in Claybury with me.'

'I see,' says Mr Thomas. He pauses. Out of the window rain has started to fall, spattering the school gates, the rosebeds, the teachers' cars.

'And how are things at home?' he asks at last.

I think about us living together when my father was alive. I think of him calling me 'John Boy', of his husky Kerry accent, his small, tough hands.

'Fine,' I say quietly.

He picks up a book from his desk.

'You might like to read this,' he says.

He hands me a paperback, a Pelican with a dark blue cover. I look at the title. *Dibs In Search of Self.*

The bell rings for the next period. I take the book, thank Mr Thomas and rush off to Double Maths.

John strums a few chords on his electric guitar and I watch the way his fingers move up and down the fretboard. We sit at either end of his bed, the latest edition of the *Record Mirror* on the floor. John reviews for them, singles, gigs, albums. Now he's just done his first interview – The Dead Boys. It's the major feature in this week's issue and John's name is on the front cover. He's always going down to the Bridge House in Canning Town, where punk bands hang out. He's bought Captain Sensible a drink, stood next to Joe Strummer in the toilets, sneered at Patrik Fitzgerald.

'You any good at singing?' he says.

'I'm useless,' I say.

'Jacqui said you write poetry. What about a poem?'

'I haven't got any with me,' I say.

'Haven't you got any off by heart?'

'OK,' I say. 'There is one.'

I start reciting from memory.

> For years he'd been baptizing my cool white
> Lemonade with the seeping blackness of
> Stout, a broad man, somehow summery – sight
> For sore eyes – in his gentle gangster suit, love
> Double-breasted and shy, me stood outside
> On the pavement, freckling in the sunshine.

And after, when he had drunk his last, died
On Saturday, buried and gone, I'd pine
For pints with him, remembering the first
I'd had, a Guinness by the Ha'penny Bridge,
A man then with a man's desperate thirst,
Him smiling, us sat in by the passage,
Watch me sup in the pub's boozy shade,
That stout sweeter than any lemonade.

John looks at me through his steel-rimmed glasses. The mood in the room has shifted, a sootfall of sadness where before we'd been larking about and having a laugh.

'I got stood outside the pub when I was a kid too,' he says at last. 'The Lion and Key. Where did your old man use to drink?'

'Same place as yours,' I say. 'The Lion and Key. And the Coach and Horses, and sometimes the Three Blackbirds. I'd stand there waiting for him. He'd come out of the pub and pour some of his Guinness into my glass of lemonade. "There now, John Boy," he'd say.'

John gets up.

'See what you think of this,' he says. He takes an LP from his collection on the shelf over his bed, slips it out of the sleeve, and walks over to the turntable by the far wall.

It's *Blood on the Tracks*, Bob Dylan. The needle hisses and 'Tangled Up In Blue' fills the room.

There is a knock at the door.

'Would you boys like a sandwich?'

It's John's mum.

'Yes, please,' says John.

'Cheese and pickle?' she says.

'All right for you?' says John.

I nod.

She smiles at us.

'Good to see you boys enjoying yourselves,' she says, and walks out again.

'John! It's your mother for you.'

Ivy hands me the phone and stands in the doorway of the small kitchen.

'Hello, Mum,' I say.

'Are you coming to see me?' she asks.

'Of course,' I say. 'I'll be up on Sunday.'

'And how are they looking after you?'

'Fine,' I say.

Ivy is still listening in the doorway of the kitchen.

'Are they feeding you?'

'Yes,' I say.

'And are you studying hard at the books?'

'Yes,' I say again.

'And are you going to Mass like a good boy?'

'Yes,' I say a third time.

The line goes quiet. I can hear the long distance between us, empty, vast.

'Well, I'd better go now,' she says. 'I'll be looking out for you.'

'Goodbye,' I say.

I lay the phone in the cradle.

Ivy moves into the kitchen and puts the kettle on.

I walk along James Lane, thinking back to the outpatients' appointment I've just come from. It was strange being back in Whipps Cross. This was where the social worker asked me if I wanted to be fostered. What if I'd said no? I wonder. How would things be now?

Dr Popper talked to me about what had happened in Claybury. She says I had psychotic depression. The voices, the delusions, the hallucinations – these are all symptoms of the illness. When I became catatonic, she decided to give me ECT.

I think about what she's said as I walk down the long narrow lane. There are doors that lead into the back gardens of houses either side of me. Some of the back gardens have trees in them, and a cold wind blows through their branches. I turn up the collar of my blazer and put my hands in my pockets.

I'm not sure what it all means. I think I went into Claybury because of what happened at the Smiths. But what can I say? It's very difficult to talk about. If what they did was supposed to save me, why did I become so ill?

I think about Dr Popper, about her smiling at me in her consulting room, her calm composed gaze. She asked me if I had any questions.

'No, Doctor,' I said. 'No questions.'

I turn into Essex Road and walk quickly towards the school gates.

The school has settled into a comfortable late afternoon hush when I enter Mr Thomas's office.

'How are you?' he asks.

'I've nearly finished *Dibs*,' I tell him. The book is about a little boy who goes to see a therapist once a week, about the playroom where they meet, about his way back into happiness.

'Good,' he says. 'What do you think of it?'

'I've been reading it on the journey up to my mum,' I say and think of the coming weekend. Ivy has got me a job with Barry, the local greengrocer, and I'll be going out with him to do the deliveries after school. Then there'll be homework in the local library on Saturday morning, *The Generation Game* on Frank and Ivy's colour television in the evening, and 11.30 Mass on Sunday. By lunchtime I'll be setting off to see my mother. I wonder how she's getting on.

'I like it. Especially the bit when he's older and he sticks up for his friend.'

Towards the end of the book, Dibs's therapist hears about him ten years after they used to meet. A schoolfriend has been accused of cheating in an exam and expelled from school. Dibs writes a letter in support of his friend – the disturbed little boy at the beginning of the book grows into someone intelligent, articulate, together, on top of his life and not at its mercy.

'And how are you getting on with John?'

'Fine,' I say. 'He's organizing a Debating Society.'

'And what's the first motion before the House?' asks Mr Thomas.

'There's been a petition going around, about abolishing the school uniform. A lad we both know, Billy. He's got a lot of support. John's going to debate with him. And I'm seconding the motion.'

'And why are you wanting to argue for the uniform?' asks Mr Thomas. 'I'm sure it's not the popular option.'

'Devilment, as much as anything,' I say.

Mr Thomas grins. 'Will it get you out of Double Maths?'

'We'd have to seriously overrun for that to happen. I'll never get out of Double Maths,' I say. 'Not even if the Debating Society gets Maths abolished altogether.'

'That's the spirit,' he chuckles. 'Treat all of this as a game. You'll enjoy life much more if you do. Now, let's see if I can't arrange our next meeting for a time that might be more convenient. When did you say you have Double Maths?'

'So are you for this poxy uniform or ain't you?'

Billy, all fourteen stone of him, enters the Sixth Form

Common Room like a bear with blisters. We turn round from the noticeboard. John has just pinned up a sheet of paper which reads 'Debating Society: Mon lunchtime, 12.15 p.m.–12.45 p.m.'. We stand facing Billy. He comes towards us, close now, breathing heavily, sweating.

I look at John. John looks at me. He speaks first.

'I'm against a lot of things, Bill. The Queen and her stupid Silver Jubilee. Emerson, Lake *and* Palmer. West Ham nicking all of the O's best players. But uniform? I can think of better things to get worked up about.'

The Sixth Form Common Room looks out on to the rosebeds near the teachers' parked cars. A thin, bleary light illuminates the windows, the leaves on the trees starting to turn slowly in the autumn sunshine. Desks are laid out in rows as if this is another class, but nobody does any work at them. Boys sit on the desktops, or up on the backs of chairs, reading the *Sun*, or talking about football, telly, Page 3. Small sports hold-alls – Adidas, Puma, Gola – clog up the aisles and half-eaten sandwiches and Mars Bar wrappers are strewn across the desks. From one corner Abba's 'Money, Money, Money' is blasting out of the hi-fi.

'Seventy-five per cent of this school want to abolish the uniform,' says Billy. 'They've signed my petition.'

'Yeah, and a hundred per cent want to abolish homework,' says John. 'That's why I think both sides of the argument need to be heard.'

'Well, the School Committee's meeting in five minutes. It's the first item on the agenda.'

'Haven't you heard, Billy?' says John.

'Heard what?' asks Billy.

'The Head's postponing the Committee Meeting. He wants a proper debate first.'

Billy looks sick.

'Bill,' says John, 'we all know you don't like the uniform. But what are you proposing the school puts in its place?'

'Whatever we like!' cries Billy.

'Oh yeah?' says John.

'Yeah!' says Billy.

'Then you might as well stay at home,' says John. 'Don't you see, you wally? This place might not be what it once was, but take away the uniform and that's the Grammar School, the County High, gone for good. The Old Boys like Frank Muir and Derek Jacobi would never forgive you. You get shot of it, wipe history from the slate, start with Year Zero, and what have you got? Anarchy in the UK.'

'I thought you liked all of that?'

'Billy, old son, let's get one thing straight here. I may be a journalist. I may work for the *Record Mirror*. But I only report on what I see. Doesn't mean I actually have to like it. That's why it's called *Mirror*. I write about what's going on, what's kicking off.'

Billy frowns. John's running rings round him. I start laughing. What is Martin Jackson, the Head of English, always saying? 'Democracy means that fifteen idiots have the right to tell five geniuses how to live.' John thinks Billy is on the side of the Idiots. He says he makes Gerald Ford look like Gore Vidal.

'Liking the music doesn't mean I'm into the politics, though,' continues John. 'Anarchy isn't going to sort out this country. It won't sort out the National Front. And it won't help the kids at this school. I'll tell you what. You come up with a motion on the Queen's Jubilee, get a petition going to stop all that crap, and I'll cover it in my next piece. No hard feelings, mate, but I've got better things to think about.'

'So this debate,' says Billy. 'Your mind's made up already then?'

The hi-fi is on to 'SOS'. John and I take this as the signal to clap our hands in time like a couple of football hooligans. Billy gets the message and walks towards the door in a king-size huff. He stops and turns around.

'You're wrong, the pair of you!' he shouts. 'You arrogant arseholes! You know nothing about this place!'

A blast of jeering and raspberries rips through the air. Billy's face flushes bright red and he shoots out of the door. The room breaks up into laughter. 'Anarchy in the UK' slices around the room like gunfire. Two kids start pogoing, hands on each other's shoulders.

'You don't believe all that, do you, John?' I ask him. 'About the uniform, this place's glory days?'

''Course not,' says John. 'Just can't bear seeing a prat like Bill trying to start the coup. It could all end in disaster. Even worse: it could end in triumph!'

We both laugh.

'Thank God it's Friday,' says John. 'You up to much this weekend?'

'I caught my leg in the chain of the bike.'

It's Sunday afternoon and I'm visiting my mother in Braintree. She's telling me about the long white stitched scar that runs along her calf like a great seam. I've wondered for years about that scar, how she got it, the story it told. We are out sitting on a bench in the sunny garden of the old people's home.

My mother and I haven't had much say about what's happened to us. We can't undo what I've set in motion. We have both become wards of the State, subject to Care Orders, under the full jurisdiction of the law. My new social worker, with her Renault 5 and her big black diary, her jeans, her granddad shirt, her short hair and her leather jacket told me this not long after she took over from her predecessor, the one who arranged for me to be fostered. I'm not sure what it all means. But it makes me feel that there are things going on I'm not aware of or have no control over. It feels like I'm underwater, submerged.

'You see it there?'

My mother holds up her leg and runs her finger along the scar.

'Well, the leg burst open. The chain had bit deep and the blood was pouring out of me. The doctor was sent for. I held a towel up to it to stop the blood, but it was coming out of me in buckets. But they couldn't find the doctor – he wasn't at home, he wasn't in his surgery, he wasn't in the pub. It turned out that there was a big conference on up at the hospital and he was at that. Every doctor in the county was at it. Not a one of them within ten miles of me. They had to telephone the hospital from the priest's house. He was the first to arrive, Father Casey. He rode out to me on his bike, riding as if God Himself was after him. I remember him arriving, the dust rising up, him clatter-ing the bike down on to the road and running over to me. He gave me Extreme Unction, the blood seeping out of me all the while into the towel. Sure I was getting weak with it. Finally, didn't the doctor arrive at last. He came in an ambulance from the hospital. He took out a needle from his bag, a huge needle it was, as long as a knitting needle, like something a fisherman would use to sew up his nets. Well, I passed clean out when I saw it. I think it was a mercy for me, for I felt no pain, no pain at all. And that's how I got this scar.'

The bus winds through the green fields of Essex, away from Braintree, towards Colchester. I look out of the window and think of my mother. What kind of life is she having in that place? What does she think of me, the son she sees once a week, the son who arranged to have her taken away? I open *Dibs* and read.

It's a passage about him and his mother. Dibs is saying good-bye to his therapist. His mother stands waiting for him, outside in the hall. Dibs runs towards her, flings his arms round her, and tells her that he loves her. The mother and the therapist are both surprised by his sudden outburst of affection. His mother takes his hand, tears in her eyes, and they walk off.

I close the book and look out the window. The bus takes me further and further away, the lonesome drone of its engine humming in my ears, my mother far behind me.

A letter comes from Braintree. I open it on the bus to school.

The Convent
10 Heath Road
Braintree
Essex

Dear John,

I hope you are taking care of yourself and being a good boy. The weather here has been good since you came. The little cleaner Clare was asking after you – do you have a notion of her? I think she might have one of you. I'm seeing the doctor later today – my blood pressure is high and he's going to see about increasing the tablets. A lady here says she has a pile of magazines for you next time you come up. They're the ones you get with the *Sunday Times*. She's an educated woman her-self – but then I was no dunce either. Are you studying much? Your social worker tells me you want to be a writer – well, make sure you write me the odd letter. I like to get them and it's nice to see your handwriting when the nuns are giving out the post. But could you try and make your scribbles a bit clearer? You seem to scrawl in a language all your own.

Sister Mary is calling me – I think the doctor must be here.

Take care of yourself,

love from,

Mum xxx

She sends me a letter once a week. I keep them in a shoebox under my bed. Sometimes, when I am missing her, I take them out and read them, one by one, until I've read them all.

And then I read them again.

The Art assistant is putting away the paint pots and brushes, the pencils and the lumps of clay on the benches. The lesson has ended and I've been sent over to the Head of Art. He's heard I write poetry and has asked to see me. I think he wants to know if I'm any good. He wears a brown grocer's coat and stands behind a desk in the Art room, looking at some of the drawings done by the last class. I've heard that the Art assistant is called Chloe. She's only about eighteen and still at Art college, when she's not working part-time at the school. She's dark and plump and pretty and I can't quite take my eyes off her. She sees me looking and smiles at me and I can feel myself blushing.

'You asked to see me, sir?'

'I did?'

The Head of Art is still looking at the drawings on his desk.

'Yes, sir. Mr Brown sent me. About my poetry, sir.'

He snaps out of his vague looking-at-art trance and says, 'Oh, yes, yes of course. Well – are you a Big Ender or a Little Ender?'

'I don't eat eggs, sir.'

'So you know what I'm referring to?'

'*Gulliver's Travels*, sir.'

'At least you're well read. Do you know what I mean by a Big Ender or a Little Ender? In poetic terms?'

I haven't got a clue. I start to think the Head of Art is round the bend.

'No, sir.'

'Can't you guess?'

Two options, either/or. Big End/Little End. Suddenly I get a glimmer.

'Do you mean whether I rhyme my poems or not, sir?'

'Splendid! Splendid!' he cries. 'Exactly right!'

'I tend to rhyme, sir.'

'"Irish poets, learn your trade/Sing whatever is well made." That's by one of your countrymen.'

'Yeats, sir?'

'My, you *are* well read. Now – what about a poem? Do you have one?'

'Not with me, sir.'

'Come, come. You must have one you know by heart?'

I think about the one I'd recited for John, about my father. I notice that Chloe is listening, still quietly collecting the art materials from the previous class. I wonder what she would like. She seems to be smiling to herself as the Head of Art and I play out our little scene.

'I do have one, sir.'

I start reciting a poem about sadness and joy, about how I feel sometimes.

> Drunk on sunshine the butterfly
>   staggers through light and shade
> wearing a golden cape the sky
>   has thoughtfully made.
>
> O how I wish that sober I
>   on such a day as this
> could lollop like a butterfly
>   aerial with bliss.

The Head of Art has his head cocked to one side. It's as if he's weighing the sound of each word, each syllable.

'Do you have more like that?' he says at last.

'Yes, sir. Quite a few.'

'Well, Chloe,' he says, 'what do you make of our young poet?'

She looks up from her collecting.

'I think he's smashing,' she says.

We smile at each other and I wonder how I can see her again.

I walk down the corridor on the ground floor of the main building. My free period is nearly up. The bell will go soon and school will be over.

'Calling it a day?'

It's John, coming out of the toilet.

'Might as well,' I say. 'You?'

'Why not?'

We walk towards the front entrance.

'Guess what?' says John.

'Go on,' I say.

'I'm off to a party.'

'Oh?' I ask. 'Whose?'

'Miss Galloway's.'

'A teacher's party?'

'Keep your voice down!' hisses John. 'Yes, a teacher's party. I'm hoping to be teacher's pet. I think she fancies me. Oh – and she wants me to bring a mate.'

'Anyone in particular?' I ask.

'As a matter of fact ...' he says.

'Not Billy?'

John laughs. 'No, actually. You. She's good mates with the Art assistant. Chloe. I think you've struck lucky.'

Music is coming from the end of the street. It's dark, and the lights from curtained lounges and first-floor windows look like an advent calendar as we walk along the tree-lined pavement.

We've brought a few cans of Carlsberg, and we're wondering what to expect. It feels very wayward, going to a teachers' party.

'I just hope they don't give me a detention,' says John, grinning.

'As long as we're not expelled we'll be all right,' I say.

We've come to the house where the music is thumping. The muffled, thudding bass line of 'Brown Sugar' by the Rolling Stones bumps through the walls. The door is slightly open and a sliver of light lines the door frame. From inside we can hear a hubbub of people talking, laughing, glasses clinking. We look at each other, then John pushes the door and we walk in.

The hallway is lined with men in granddad shirts and jeans, a few of them wearing John Lennon specs, and girls not much older than us in flowery dresses, one still wearing her afghan coat. We push past them, the darkened living room full of writhing bodies, dancing and moving to the music. 'Brown Sugar' fades out and the opening chords of 'Whole Lotta Love' grind through the house. We make our way to the kitchen at the end of the hall. Sue Galloway is chatting to a bearded man in jeans and red lumberjack shirt. His dark hair is short, his eyes blue.

'Durkheim got it all wrong,' he says in a harsh Scottish accent. 'The reason why Protestants kill themselves more than Catholics is because Catholicism is a medieval religion. Protestants believe in Providence and damn all else. And if Providence is against you, then what odds about your eternal reward? You were never one of the Elect in the first place.'

John brushes past Miss Galloway to put his cans of Carlsberg on the table behind her. She turns round, and sees me.

'Hello!' she says. 'Is John with you?'

'I'm right here,' he says.

'Come with me,' she says, turning, smiling, taking his hand. She pulls him through the crowded kitchen towards the music.

The Scotsman with the beard and short hair looks at me. He doesn't seem too impressed; 10 cc are crooning 'The Wall Street Shuffle' from the living room.

The Scotsman and I stand in awkward silence.

'Do you know much about Durkheim?' he asks at last.

Chloe comes into the kitchen. She's on her own and sees me. At last my chance has come.

'Darling,' I say, 'I thought you'd never get here! Please excuse me,' I say to the Scotsman. 'They're playing our song.'

From the living room comes Hawkwind's 'Silver Machine'. I grab Chloe's hand and lead her towards it.

'Thank God for that,' I say, starting to dance. Everyone around us is shaking themselves in the weirdest set of moves I've ever seen, like they're trying to get nits out of their hair.

Chloe smiles.

'You are forward,' she says. 'Come here.'

Chloe has me up against the wall. She leans forward and kisses me. My head swims and I am dizzy from her soft lips, the tip of her tongue.

She moves back and looks at me. She's a bit tiddly, her blue eyes shiny and her face glowing. The walls are throbbing with 'Layla' by Derek and the Dominos, and I'm throbbing too. Chloe shuts her eyes and leans into me again. The music whooshes through me and I am lost in her kiss.

'I hear you won the debate?'

Mr Brown stands in the kitchen holding a glass of red wine. Chloe is in the hall, waiting for me. I'm still reeling from our clinches, and what I've had to drink. But I need another Carlsberg. And she wants more wine.

'Well, it was John who won it, really,' I say, picking up a

can from the table of drink. There's a bottle of Mateus Rosé by a big tin of Watneys Party 7. I pour some wine into Chloe's glass.

'You did us all a favour winning that debate,' says Mr Brown. 'If you hadn't, I think you'd all be coming to school like a bunch of scruffs.'

I'm a little stupefied now. Have I heard right?

'You mean the Head was worried about Billy winning?' I say.

'Yes,' says Mr Brown. 'Very worried. He was in a very tricky position. It's quite hard to argue with a petition signed by seventy-five per cent of the school. In fact, there were quite a lot of teachers who'd signed the petition as well. You did us all a big favour.'

I stumble into the hall. It looks like the whole thing was a set-up.

Up ahead, Chloe has her coat on. A tall blond man is taking her towards the door.

'Chloe!' I call.

They look round. The tall blond man glares at me.

Chloe blows me a kiss, mouths, 'Sorry,' and turns to go.

'She's keen on you,' says John.

It's 4 a.m. and we're walking back to his place. The night is big and dark and the stars look like they could turn to snow. I'm sober now, and starting to feel the cold.

'Not as keen as she is on her boyfriend.'

'Has she got one?' says John.

'She left with him,' I say.

We walk on in silence.

The lights from the front rooms and upstairs windows of the houses are out now and the streets are deserted. It's the early hours of Sunday and I feel guilty. I won't be seeing my mother today. I'll tell her on the phone from John's, and try to make it up to her somehow. But that's not all I'm feeling guilty about.

'What about you?' I ask. 'How did you get on with Miss Galloway?'

'Well, we won't be going steady,' says John, and gives me a wink.

I think of Mr Brown, and the slogan John says he's seen scrawled on the toilet walls at the Bridge House.

Never Trust A Hippy.

We turn into his road and I wonder what Chloe is doing and start to shiver. We get to John's house and he turns his key in the lock.

We go inside and he shuts the door.

III

Claybury, 1977

'You're depressed, John. It will pass. But it's going to take a while. Until it lifts, look around. Think about personal relationships: that's what life is all about.'

I had not expected to be back. Dr Popper speaks across a gulf. It is the distance between my depression and her own well-being. For I'm in the depths now, somewhere way out beyond the realms of melancholy and dejection. I feel like I have become an object, that I have turned to wood, that I'm mired in my own inertia. Even a sigh brings no relief, and the great salt tears I've just shed, here in this consulting room on my doctor's desk, mean nothing either, bring no release from the misery I'm peering out from.

It's my first day back in Claybury. I am too low to care.

I'm anxious about my O levels. I've convinced myself that I'm not going to do well. The Smiths seem my only hope. As I stand at their door, waves of sadness and anxiety crash around me. Mrs Smith welcomes me with her usual huge smile. Whatever has happened in her back room is never spoken of – it's too big to ever discuss. I still come to the Thursday prayer meetings but now life is taking me far from God and Bible Study and C.S. Lewis.

My foster-parents encourage me to get a job as it will 'occupy my mind' and I work for Barry the greengrocer, delivering orders on Friday evenings to posh houses in Waltham Pond and serving in the shop on Saturdays. Then I work in pubs, the Prince of Wales in Chagford, and the George in North Waltham. I also return to Claybury at least once a week to visit people I know who are still patients. And on Sundays I visit my mother. So homework is done when I can fit it in, or else it's skimped. And there are the poems, which come before everything. I write them after school, in the red Silvine exercise books I keep in my bedside cabinet. But now I realize I've left my revision too late and I'm doing badly in my exams.

Mrs Smith lays her hands on me in her living room and prays with me. But it's no good – I'm sinking. My plans to rescue my mother, to pass my exams and get a good job will all come to nothing.

A large black tunnel beckons and I walk like a zombie towards it.

My GP looks over his spectacles at me.

'Would you like to go back into hospital, John?'

I've come to see him at his morning surgery. I always feel worse in the mornings. I can't see the point of getting up, can't see the point of anything. Frank and Ivy don't know I'm here. They know something is wrong – I stay in my room most evenings, and I've withdrawn so far into myself it's as if I've become invisible. Part of this withdrawal is shame. I can't bear to let anyone see me when I'm like this. If I hide away, wait until I'm better, then I can come out of my room. But I just seem to be falling deeper and deeper into pain. The times when I'm OK, when I'm well, when I'm myself – they now seem lost to me. They're a total contrast to this other me, this sad, quiet, pathetic boy.

Silently I nod.

Claybury's grounds are sunny today, and we have walked as far as this clearing, where Catherine has halted, and is now holding me, looking into my eyes. Catherine is lovely. She's got dark hair and a voluptuous figure, always in jeans and Indian shirts. I think sometimes that she dresses like a tomboy to hide her femininity, but if anything she looks even more attractive in her Levi's and chemises.

'Don't you understand, dear boy? I'm trying to seduce you.'

'If we did anything,' I say slowly, 'you would have to have a baby.'

'I skip sometimes,' she says.

I don't understand what she means. She takes my silence for obstinacy.

'Can't you see, dear boy? I'm missing my sexual intercourse!'

Catherine suddenly sweeps away, throwing out her arms as she goes.

'How does it feel to be in love with the most beautiful person in the world?'

I am a little bewildered, a little overwhelmed. I like Catherine. But I don't think I am in love with her.

She walks off and I follow behind, like a shadow she has cast.

'You're a manic depressive, John.'

Dr Popper is telling me about my treatment. She wants to put me on Lithium. She says Lithium will stabilize my moods and make me better. But I wonder about this. Perhaps my extremes of emotion are a reaction to the events of my life. For three years I have been battling forces outside my control. Can a drug help with events I couldn't prevent? Bereavement? My mother's breakdown? My abandonment of her? Being fostered? My own breakdown? Surely what I need can't just come out of a pill.

'We'll start you on it this evening. You'll need to have your blood monitored regularly. Lithium can be quite toxic. But it's also very effective in helping manic depressives. And from what we can gather, it runs in your family.'

My mother told me about her father, a fiddler who lost the use of the ring finger on his left hand. It happened in an accident at the sawmill in Monaghan. But he still played, doubling over the dead finger on to his middle finger, moving this strange-looking claw up and down the violin strings, playing jigs and reels just as well as he ever did. People would come from miles around to see him. But one night, said my mother, he got up and tried to cut his ear off. He was hearing voices. I wonder if my mother has heard voices too.

Is that what it means to be a manic depressive? To go up and down and hear voices? But what about schizophrenics? I thought they heard voices? I leave Dr Popper feeling confused. I'm not psychotic this time, I'm depressed. But I think I have reason to be. I see now why my mother was so sceptical about psychiatrists. They think my problems are all in my head.

Since I have been sectioned I have been given a lot of drugs. I have taken, for instance, Stelazine, both the little flat round blue pills and the capsules with tiny blue and yellow particles inside. This stops psychosis, Lee the nurse from Hong Kong tells me, but I'm not psychotic. I don't understand why they give it to me. Perhaps it's because they gave me Stelazine last time. The main problem with it is the side effects. It can lock your jaw and make your joints stiff if you don't take Kemadrine, which counteracts the side effects of Stelazine. But Kemadrine has side effects too, and leaves you with a very dry mouth and a 'spacey' feeling. That's when the Stelazine isn't 'bombing' you, making you lethargic and heavy. It's like a house of cards, one drug building on another, all of them rickety. Every drug has its side effects; the drugs that counteract the side effects have their own side effects in turn. Take one away, and the house of cards collapses.

Largactyl is another strange drug. Its main effect is sedative, the 'liquid cosh' as Eddie calls it. Eddie is a Cockney who has brown sauce with his dinner and sounds like he might have been in prison. He calls Claybury a 'low-security unit' and the nurses 'screws in drag'. He hates Largactyl. It's got side effects too, which is what he complains about to anyone who'll listen, but he's kept on it for weeks. The most obvious side effect is the Largactyl Tan: Eddie gets burnt if he goes out in the sun for even a few minutes. The drug makes you sensitive to sunshine. Eddie starts to look like a Desert Rat. The drug also brings on Largactyl Belly, a dome-like stomach, which perhaps comes from it slowing you down so much. What with the Tan and the Belly, a lot of long stays look like fat Arabs. Eddie doesn't want to get like them.

There's one final, really odd side effect of the drug. It can make women produce breast milk. 'I wouldn't feed it to a pig,' says Eddie.

I wonder if he knows anything about Lithium.

'And how did that make you feel?'

The Free Church chaplain is delicately probing.

'It made me feel ... sad ... I suppose.'

Valerie is talking about her son. He is nine. Her son likes to rub his penis up and down on the carpet. He says it makes it tingle. But Valerie is worried about this. She is worried that her son is losing his innocence.

'You know, it may be that Simon is acting out something.'

'What do you mean?' asks Valerie.

She is a mousy-haired woman in her thirties, dressed in a short black cardigan, white blouse and black jeans. Her legs are crossed and she swings one sandalled foot back and forth as she talks, like a metronome.

'Well,' says the chaplain, 'Simon could be acting out something going on in your marriage that he's aware of, which perhaps disturbs him?'

'You mean in our sex lives?'

I wonder what it's like to have a marriage, a family, a sex life. Most people I've met in Claybury seem to be here because of some problem with their family.

'Possibly,' says the chaplain. He is dark-haired, around the same age as Valerie. His group is optional but there are still about ten of us, just under half of the ward.

'It could be that he gets comfort from what he's been doing. Perhaps he's feeling anxious about something. Or it could be that he's trying to attract your attention, to be provocative, and that this is a way he knows he can do it. Do you think he has any cause for anxiety, or any greater need for your attention than usual?'

Valerie pauses. She looks like she is thinking, not about Simon and what it is he might be 'acting out', more as if she's deciding whether to trust us or not.

'I think my husband,' she says at last, 'may be ... may be ... interfering with him.'

And she breaks down, her sobs all you can hear.

The chaplain rises and comes over to her. He puts his arm round her.

'I know that was hard,' he says. 'You were very brave to share that with us.'

Valerie gradually stops sobbing. The group sits in complete silence.

Eventually the chaplain says, 'How do other people feel

about what we've just heard?' He is sitting on the wooden arm of Valerie's armchair, looking out at us.

Silence.

What response can there be?

But the chaplain cannot let us rest in silence. This is a silence that needs filling.

'Rachel, what about you?'

Rachel, dark hair, shy, early twenties, has nothing to say. She looks very uncomfortable.

'Eddie?' says the chaplain.

But Eddie doesn't get a chance to respond.

'You cannot conduct this group!' roars Julian. 'A little bit of Valerie here, diminuendo on the strings, then *sotto voce* bring in Rachel as you give a wave of your baton, then up, up to a crescendo with Eddie on brass! These are people's *feelings* you're dealing with, for God's sake!'

Julian's rage is frightening.

The silence has been filled.

Completely.

'It's for God's sake I run the group,' says the chaplain quietly. He is bristling at Julian's accusation, on the defensive.

'No, it's not!' roars Julian. 'It's for your own bloody egotistical greed!'

By now Julian's roaring has attracted the attention of Don, the large West Indian charge nurse.

He pushes open the heavy doors to the day room and says, 'Everything all right here, Reverend?'

'No, it's bloody not all right!' shouts Julian, and stands up.

Julian is very tall too, taller even than Don, but Don is stronger. Julian is a journalist and a poet, and has had a big row with his editor. He thinks his editor is out to get him, and this has made him manic, and his mania is in full swing.

'Would you like to leave the group, Julian?' asks Don gently.

Although there is kindness in Don's soft West Indian voice, there is also something else, some reminder of the consequences of Julian's actions, what they can lead to.

'You bloody clergymen are all the bloody same!'

The chaplain doesn't flinch.

'I should bloody know! My father was a vicar, and he was just the bloody same as you! Sanctimonious prick!'

Julian comes towards the chaplain, six feet three of anger on the brink of violence. Don steps forward quickly and takes him by the arm, and Julian lets himself be led away, his anger gentled just in time. I can see more nurses through the wired windows of the day room's doors, gathering outside. Don and Julian leave and find a table to sit at in the dining area. The group settles back into its unease.

After a while the chaplain says, 'We've been focusing on families quite a lot this morning. Families seem to offer us both security and a threat. Security because the family builds the nest; a threat because that nest can be a stifling – even a dangerous – place to be. Next week I think we could look at this a little further.'

He stands up and the group is over. I get up slowly. I feel heavy, weighed down, as depressed as ever.

I see the chaplain walk past Julian in the dining area and out of the ward.

'Sky pilots,' says Eddie. 'Worse than bloody trick cyclists. Take my advice, son. Steer well clear of the lot of 'em. Otherwise they'll screw you right up.'

I think of Father Richard, of Dr Popper. Perhaps Eddie's right. Perhaps I should steer well clear of them. But at the moment I don't really have a choice.

'They're in the park, it's getting dark, and they're listening to the sound of counting down from ten to one!'

Jimmy is playing us his song. Julian and I are on our beds in the men's dorm, listening. Jimmy is about twenty-five, a van driver who plays the guitar and writes songs.

'One for the delectable Catherine, I think, Jimmy. Very Small Faces. Do you like them?' Julian is still a little manic. The drugs are stabilizing him but you can still sense his anger underneath the sedation.

'What, 'Itchycoo Park', you mean?'

Jimmy lays his guitar on his bed. It's evening now, not long until dinner is up.

'Yeah, that's it.' Julian trills the chorus. 'Very hard to make it nowadays, though, Jimmy. I think singer-songwriters are on the way out.'

Jimmy's song is quite simple. I think it's about people trying not to lose their tempers. Julian has told me that depression is anger turned inwards. He may be right. But I don't feel angry – just very down.

'I learned a long time ago,' says Julian, 'that the work of words would never sustain me. That's why I became a journal-ist. I write prose for my bread and butter, and out of poetry I get to eat a little cake every now and then.'

I've never met a poet before. Julian has read me his work, and it sounds very good. I write poems too, poems that try to make sense of my father's death. I've filled three exercise books and I'm still going, although the newer poems are not about my father – they're about this place.

'So when do you write?' asks Jimmy. 'I can only write if I'm feeling a bit depressed. I've got to have the Blues to do it.'

'I'm the complete opposite,' says Julian. 'I can only write on the upswing, rising high on the flight of ideas. I may go mad occasionally – and I was completely bonkers this time – but if I was as sane as the man in the street I'd never write a line.'

'What about you, John?' asks Jimmy.

55

'What about me?'

'You know. When do you write?'

'I write when the mood takes me,' I say. 'Sad or glad, fine. It's the middle bit that's hard.'

'I think that's called "reality",' says Julian. 'Of which human-kind cannot bear very much. It's best avoided. If you do feel the Muse calling you, John, be prepared. Your life will be one of almost total resistance.'

'Resistance, Julian? To what?'

'To reality! Ask Jimmy. What do you musicians call it? "Straight time"! The Muse is cruel, John. She wants you to be dedicated to her and her alone. We're not made for straight time; it sets up too much inner conflict in us. So the loony bin is no disgrace. Look at John Clare, Ivor Gurney, Sylvia Plath, Robert Lowell. Just one word of advice: *le poète maudit* may be fine for Frenchies, Yanks, even you Paddies, but we prefer our poets these days to be as respectable and dull as any middle-ranking civil servant. Look at the popularity of Larkin. If you want to get ahead, cultivate his ordinariness. If you want to be admitted to the Pantheon do exactly the opposite. Live as if every penny was made for giving away, and every day was your last. As the Arabs say, life is like a banana: you either grab it in your hand, or have it shoved up your arse. The life of a poet may be poverty-struck, but there are greater rewards than mere money.'

Jimmy gives me a wink and picks up his guitar again. Julian is very persuasive. Perhaps I could be a journalist, like him. That might give me time to write as well. Perhaps I can find a future that will work.

I'm interested in doing A level Sociology. Claybury is a good example of a closed society, of deviancy and power elites, of the total institution. I write down some thoughts about the ward. They might be useful for when I go back to school.

The Ward

The ward is divided into three groups: the doctors, the nurses and the nursing assistants. There's also the cleaner, Marie, a young Irishwoman, who's about six months' pregnant and works like a navvy. She's had two miscarriages already, but she mops and washes pots and pans in the ward's kitchen six days a week, a whirlwind of work. Some of the other patients are afraid she'll miscarry again, but she scrubs and polishes as if pregnancy is the least of her worries. She has no say in running the ward, no power to speak of, like an untouchable. But we'd all be lost without her.

The patients are a fourth distinct group, separate from the staff. We're 'under section', or else here voluntarily. The law defines us, limits us. But this doesn't mean that because we're removed from society, because we need 'asylum', we're no longer human, that we're not part of society. We *are* removed though, temporary outcasts, and this is the difference between us and the staff.

It's the nurses who act as buffers to the outside world, who stand between us and where we've come from. They work on the front line between 'Out There' and 'In Here', and I always mix freely with them, like I once mixed with the people beyond Claybury's gates. Other patients – Eddie for instance – treat the nurses with a kind of amused old sweat's contempt.

But of course they're here to do more than just care for us: they're also here to keep us locked up, to make sure we're away from the world until we're better, we're safe. Then we might be allowed back. Otherwise, if we're here longer than a year, we become long stays. After a year, patients are taken off the admission wards and put on the long-stay wards. The admission wards might hold about twenty people, men and women, all told. The long-stay wards are not mixed, and they have a lot more people on them, up to forty or more, the beds in the dorms all squeezed together to fit them in. It must be hellish. Julian told me that the last time he was admitted he ended up on the long-stay ward. Perhaps this explains why he is so angry in here, and so docile. He knows what's waiting for him if he doesn't toe the line.

The Nurses

Most of the nurses are only a little older than me. They're adults, just, over twenty-one most of them, but still 'students', as I am myself. I'm treated well by them and Claybury is actually a kind of college, a place where I've come to meet other young people, people far more mature than my friends at school, with their silly voices, their love of Derek and Clive, their obsession with football and music. Of course, as well as my peers, or my nearly peers, I also meet the odd 'professor', like Julian, or Father Richard, or Dr Popper. Not quite sure what I'm learning, but if I ever get to university I think it will be a little like this place.

The nurses, though, unlike my schoolfriends, have 'professional responsibilities', and can't get as close to us patients as we're allowed to get to each other. Relationships between nurses and patients are a complete no-no. One nurse told me they can be prosecuted for having sex with us. We are 'vulnerable', and any nurse who has a sexual relationship with a patient would be accused of taking advantage. They would end up in serious trouble. None of them has ever bothered me, though, unlike a few of the patients.

I like the nurses on our ward, and I often play table tennis with them, or go to their social club, which no one else does. I can talk to them in ways I can't talk to Julian, Catherine or Jimmy. I think this is because although they wear uniforms, they're closer to me in age. And they listen, they don't go on and on about themselves, or act unpredictably. The nurses on O2 are OK.

The Nurses: Who's Who

Don the charge nurse. He's from Jamaica, intelligent, strong, kind.

Sue, the staff nurse. She's from the Philippines; sometimes on Sundays cooks Filipino food for us.

The student nurses. Lee from Hong Kong; Rahul from India; and Siobhan from Ireland.

Class / Race / Gender

The ward's staff groups divide up along certain lines. The nurses are *all* from overseas. At least, the ones on O2 are. The doctors, on the other hand, are all white and British. There are divisions amongst the doctors, though: Dr Popper is very senior, quite distant sometimes; her junior colleague is about fifteen years younger than her, and there are one or two other male doctors who also attend the ward meetings and the groups, and seem even more junior, in training perhaps.

The doctors, I've noticed, have a different sense of hierarchy compared to the nurses. The nurses are closer to one another than the shrinks, regardless of rank. They're friendlier, warmer to one another, not as starchy. The doctors, on the other hand, seem far more distant when they interact, more formal. I've seen their dining room when I was walking in the grounds with Catherine. We looked in through a window round the back of the main building. White linen everywhere, and the gleam of silver and glassware. It looked posh, like a restaurant. We also see the doctors a lot less than the nurses. They come for the morning group therapy sessions, then they're gone for the day. Maybe the reason the nurses seem closer to one another is that most of the nurses are women. Perhaps women in general are naturally warmer than men, less competitive, nicer.

The Nursing Assistants

The nursing assistants, finally, are a much rarer bunch, at the bottom of the pecking order. There's only one on our ward, Nick, a long-haired bloke about a year older than me who spends most of his time sitting in the day room reading books: Hesse, Rilke, Borges. He seems more alienated even than I am. And I'm supposed to be depressed. Although this, as I say, is lifting ... at last ...

It is a lovely late autumn day, just turning into evening. I have been at Claybury for three months. My depression is receding, the darkness giving way to a kind of dusk, and I am walking in the grounds which I have come to know so well. It's a different world out here, away from the groups, the meals, the medication. It's good to be out in the open, where nothing is analyzed and everything is free.

I think about the day's events. Just before lunch Lee suddenly sprinted the length of the ward from one day room to another – about twenty yards – and grabbed Valerie's arms. She'd just put her fist through the glass window of the door at the far end of the dining room. It happened so fast I wasn't sure what was going on. He held her arms tight and she broke down. She was about to cut her wrists on the jagged glass when he secured her.

The shock of sudden violence and the awareness that I am in a place where people are suffering so badly they want to kill themselves has shaken me. I shouldn't be here. But where else is there?

As I walk through the grounds, round the back of the main building and away into the deep green acres of Claybury, the sun starts to dip towards the horizon. I look back, the main building looming over me like a great dark castle, barred windows high up on the walls, the wards settling down for suppertime in a medicated lull. The grounds are tinged with late evening gold, the glades striped with shadow and light, the bushes and trees, the paths and trails gilded with amber. The sun is setting, and the sky is full of gorgeous red and purple tints. It's as if I've travelled to another planet.

I come to the old manor house. It's a white circular Georgian building, used now as offices, pillars supporting the roof. As I walk past its Regency elegance I can hear voices coming from behind it. It sounds like gasping, like someone is being attacked.

There's no one in the building. Everyone must have gone home. I tread very carefully, making my way by inches round to the back. The noises are louder now, coming from behind a hedgerow that runs the length of the small meadow ahead of me.

I walk slowly, stealthily down to the hedgerow. I see a small rock on the ground and pick it up, just in case. I peer over the hedgerow.

At first I'm not sure what it is I'm looking at. There's a man, I think, although his shape is indistinct. He has a woman pinned to the ground. She is moaning as he assaults her, but he isn't hitting her. He's ramming himself at her, swearing now, getting more and more ferocious. I move as quietly as I dare towards them.

Suddenly, he looks up. He must have heard me and I panic. I get ready to run at him, to brain him with the rock while I have the chance, to rescue the woman. But then I see his face.

It's Jimmy.

The woman under him is Catherine.

She's saying, 'Don't stop, don't stop, I'm nearly there!'

I turn and walk away.

'How are you getting on with the Lithium?'

I have been taking Lithium now for nearly three months. It's horrible to swallow, large and white and round, almost the size of an ice hockey puck. I gag every time I have to swallow it.

'I'm getting on fine,' I say. Dr Popper's consulting room has a Gauguin print hanging on the wall, one he painted in Tahiti. '*D'où venons nous? Que sommes nous? Où allons nous?*' Where are we from? What are we? Where are we going? Those mysterious words are inscribed in the top left-hand corner. I wonder why he painted the Tahitian landscape blue. The colour lends the figures in the painting a mystical quality. They're like people who have not yet been discovered, the tribe who know all of humanity's secrets, the answers to all of our questions. And this knowledge seems to have set them free, to have liberated them.

'No side effects?'

'Well … ' I pause.

'Yes?'

'I feel … kind of neutered by it. As if my brain has turned to stone. It's slowed down a lot.'

'Could still be the effects of depression, John. Sometimes, depression can seem to lift, but there can be an undertow to it, a drag still on the brain's functions, which can take a while to recede once the period of low mood has passed. Do you think this might be what's going on?'

'I'm not sure,' I say.

But I am sure. Lithium threatens to freeze my mind. I hate it. I'm going to spit it out when they give me it again.

'Let's see if we can reduce the dosage, shall we?' says Dr Popper.

I think about the way doctors speak. Why do they always say, 'We'? I have no choice in the matter. I've been sectioned.

'I'm aware that you have your A levels to think about, John. This is no place for you. We need to start reorientating you back to the world outside Claybury. How did your leave go?'

I've started going to my foster-parents at the weekends. I'm grateful to them for sticking by me. I've been with them three years now.

'The weekend went fine.'

I'm heeding my mother's advice. I've started saying just enough to give my doctors confidence in me. I'm not sure, though, where I want to be. Claybury is an attractive alternative to life outside in so many ways. For all the shocks, the suffering, the sense of incarceration, I like it here. Catherine, Julian, Jimmy – these are people I've made friends with. Ivy, Frank, my schoolmates – I like them, but they belong to another life. They're not part of this hidden, secret world. Most of all, I feel safe in Claybury.

'We're also very aware,' says Dr Popper, 'how easy it is to get institutionalized here. You'll soon realize, though, John, that you can't avoid your responsibilities. And chief amongst these is your responsibility to yourself. You can either get overwhelmed by your illness, and all that it can bring, or you can fight it. And the best way to do that is to make a life outside here. So when you go home next weekend, think about what I've said. See some friends, get out and about, don't let yourself become introspective. Thinking about yourself and your situation will do you no good, no good whatsoever.'

She smiles broadly at me, her neatly cut blonde hair contrasting with her electric-blue eyes, her gleaming teeth bared in a gesture that's friendly and intimidating at the same time. Julian has a term for this look: he calls it 'the Beams'. Dr Popper is giving me 'the Beams'. This is what she does, Julian reckons, when she thinks your time is nearly up.

I leave the consulting room. I hope my time isn't up. I'm not sure I am ready to leave, not just yet. Suddenly I feel very scared. I walk down the corridor to the dorm. The clock seems to be ticking a little louder and I can hear it all the way to my bed. It ticks away my time. I cannot fight it.

Soon I will be discharged.

IV

Ballinode, 1978

'Well, John, your mother is buried.'

I stop and let my kitbag down. My aunt stands in front of the grey gates, just the same as she ever was, large, red-faced, dark-haired, apron on, sleeves rolled up, slightly bow-legged as if from the weight of her labours, from raising six children and running the house. The taxi drones off into the distance and we are left alone on the sunlit road.

'Johnny tried to phone you, but he couldn't get any reply. What happened? Were you away or what?'

I thought of the telegram that arrived the Friday before: 'Mother dead. Funeral Sunday. Come home.' When my foster-mother had caught me crying she'd said, 'Oh don't, you'll start me off,' so I'd bitten back the tears and felt only a numbness, a resentment, where grief should have been. My social worker said it might take a few days to sort out a travel warrant, and anyway, they couldn't make all the arrangements in Ireland so quickly – there'd be a post-mortem, surely, just like there had been after my father's death.

So I'd gone away with my foster-parents for the weekend, and to school on the Monday, none of it mattering at all, sleepwalking through the week. And now I was here and it was all over.

'There's only her ring left. Come into the house till I show you.'

I follow Auntie Lizzie through the gates, past the front

garden and down the gravel path to the back yard, the big red corrugated shed still there, the sawhorse with a pile of sticks by it. A few old bikes lean up against the stippled white wall of the privy and a thin rope line hung with washing stretches between the house and the shed. I look down to the river beyond the rambling back garden and think of the walks my mother used to take us on, my six cousins and me. We'd all collect sticks up Clentoe Lane, the image of her dappled in sunlight up ahead, the happy summers we shared. I'm nineteen and now Ballinode will never be the same again.

Auntie Lizzie lifts the latch to the back door and I follow her in. It's over five years since I've been here and my eyes flick hungrily around the room. To the left a scullery, the long front room ahead, windows at either end, pale blue lino on the floor, the walls painted light green. A range faces the middle of the room with a mantel above. The only ornaments are two fiddles mounted either side of an old photograph of my grandparents. Doors either end lead off to bedrooms. About halfway up the room, facing the range, is a red settee, with a picture of the Sacred Heart and a small red lamp above, its filament in the shape of a white cross. There's a table and chairs as you come in at the back door. The only sound comes from the small grandfather clock at the far end of the room. The smell of baking – scones, wheaten and soda bread – fills the room.

'Where is everyone?' I ask. I let down my kitbag by the side of the table and sit on one of the chairs facing into the room.

'The Fleadh Ceol is on and Tommy is away at Jimmy's Bar playing the fiddle. The rest have gone up to see him.'

There is a drawer in the table and my aunt pulls it open. She rummages around inside and holds up a small object: my mother's ring.

'Here,' she says, 'put this on.'

I take the thin gold band from her and fit it on the third finger of my left hand.

'No! Not that hand,' says my aunt. 'Sure that's the finger your *own* wedding ring would go on. Take it off and put it on the other hand.'

I take it off and slide it up my finger. It fits perfectly.

'Did you have a good crossing?'

Auntie Lizzie moves over to the range. She takes a lid off the top of it with a short lifter sticking out of the metal cover and I suddenly see an inferno of flames burning away inside the range. She pulls out a fag from behind her ear, lights it off the fire and pops the lid back.

She turns to look at me, the fag in the corner of her mouth.

'Fine,' I say. 'Fine.'

'Will you take a cup of tea?'

'Yes, please,' I say.

She goes out into the kitchen to put the kettle on.

I realize I sound like an Englishman. I'd catch the accent quickly as a boy, speaking like my cousins within days of arrival. But I've been away so long that now I don't feel comfortable trying to lapse into a brogue. I'm too self-conscious. It's like coming home a stranger. I hear the kettle whistling and Auntie Lizzie brings in a cup of tea.

'Now,' says Auntie Lizzie, handing it to me.

'Are you not having a cup yourself?' I ask.

'I'm only just after one,' she says.

She goes over and sits on the settee, and takes a puff of her fag. Silence slowly fills the room. I can hear the clock ticking, each mechanical knock of the pendulum getting louder and louder.

'Was there a good turnout?' I ask at last.

'There was,' she says. 'The mourners took Noel for yourself though. They all came up to him to say they were sorry for his trouble. Must have been near 200 at it. Tommy put a bit in the

Northern Standard about her. Here, I have it somewhere. Let me get it for you.'

She ups and bustles about, looking under the TV, on the mantel, in the drawer of the table, but can't find it.

'That's strange,' she says. 'Tommy must've put it away somewhere. He should be back soon, but you know him of old. He'll be playing that fiddle and working up a thirst. And sure he took your mother's death hard. That's both of his sisters gone now.'

I don't know what to say. Silence creeps into the room again, like gas seeping under the doors.

Suddenly there are feet crunching on the gravel outside.

'Now,' says my aunt. 'Here's them home.'

The back door opens and there are Matt, Evelyn and Anna, my cousins.

'Well, John,' says Matt, breezing in. 'So where were you?'

The girls follow him and they all stand in front of the range.

'I was away for the weekend,' I say.

'My God!' says Matt. 'Sure Johnny was phoning you the whole time! Where did you go?'

'Southend,' I say. 'With my foster-parents. To see their son and his wife.'

'And did you not think you had a funeral to go to?' asks Matt.

'I thought it would be this weekend,' I reply, 'that there'd be a post-mortem.'

'Ach, not at all. Well, we'll go out to the grave in the morning. You must be very sad?'

'I'm not sure what I feel,' I say. 'I'm kind of tired.'

I'd come over on the boat. The long journey took about a day and a half, London to Holyhead, a night crossing, then the train up from Dublin.

'Well, look,' says Matt, 'I'm seeing Eileen tonight. Come out with me and we'll cheer you up. If ever a man needed a few pints, John Kevin, I'd say it was you.'

'Thanks, Matt. Uh – is there somewhere I could lie down?'

Auntie Lizzie stands up.

'Come on and we'll put you in Johnny's room. He's working tonight. You'll have the bed to yourself.'

I pick up my kitbag and follow her to a door leading off to the right.

'Now,' she says, 'take your ease there, John. I'll call you when I have the dinner ready.'

I thank her and she closes the door. I lay my kitbag up against the wall and sit on the large brass bed. I look at the ring on my finger, the dull gold of it, and turn it round a few times. Outside, I can hear the clock ticking. Then it starts to rain, and I get under the eiderdown and between the sheets. And at last I sleep.

'So what's she like, your girlfriend?' I ask Matt.

He changes gear and the car cruises forward down the rain-swept country road. Darkness has fallen and the moon hangs low in the sky, a great luminous hole in the night. Matt dips his head-lights as a van appears from round a corner and speeds past.

'She's a bit of a doll,' says Matt. 'Her sister's not bad either, if you like them with puppy fat. They're both working as nurses. There's only them at home now, and the mother. The father died when they were children – Eileen was ten and Patricia eight. She's the baby, Patricia, and they all call her Chusha.'

Up ahead I can see the lights of Monaghan Town rising to meet us. Uncle Tommy is still at the Fleadh Ceol, and I think of my mother, of the times she played the violin herself at family gatherings, of the ring on her finger flashing as she went faster and faster, so quick I used to think she might bow the fiddle into flames.

'Come on, boy,' he announces. 'We're here.'

I blink my dreamy eyes. We're parked on the Diamond, near the Four Seasons Hotel and Matt is getting out of the car. The rain is monsooning down and I follow him quickly up the steps, through the large glass doors and into the plush lobby of the hotel. Thick creamy carpet spreads out before us, gilt mirrors glimmer and landscape paintings adorn the walls. The heating is up and I feel the brush of luxury for the first time since I set off.

Matt strides towards the reception desk.

'I'm meeting my fiancée, Miss Eileen Cunningham, here this evening. Her sister, Patricia, will be joining us. Is there any message for me?'

The girl behind reception gives Matt an old-fashioned look, a little up-from-under pout that sets off her red hair and freckles.

'Matt Murphy, would you stop putting on airs and graces and go on into the bar like any decent fella? And who's this solemn young curate you're out with?'

'Well, Sheila,' says Matt by way of salute, 'this is my first cousin John Kevin. He'll be hearing confessions this evening if you have anything troubling your conscience.'

'As long as he doesn't give long penances. Pleased to meet you, Father John.'

'Hello,' I say.

'Will you pop in for a drink later, Sheila?' says Matt.

'And join you and Miss Cunningham? I think Eileen would sooner knock me down than let you buy me a drink, Matt.'

'Perhaps you're right,' he says. 'She's not in yet, is she?'

'Am I my sister's keeper? How would I know? I've not seen

her, but then unlike you boys, I've been working this evening. I'll see you again, I'm sure. And Father John – you have very lonesome eyes.'

I give her a lonesome smile and Matt pulls me towards the Four Seasons Bar.

'Who was that?' I ask.

'That's Sheila Shaughnessy,' says Matt. 'We were at the Tech together. A game girl, if you know what I mean. But as tough as a boxer any day. Many's the thump I've had from her, I can tell you.'

We go into the bar. There's a long counter with clusters of beer pumps dotted along it, bottles of upside-down spirits in optics behind. A young dark-haired barman in white shirt and black trousers is drying a glass with a linen tea towel. A few early evening drinkers are scattered at tables around the room.

Matt approaches the bar, with me a little behind him.

'Well, Matt,' says the barman. 'What'll you have?'

'Two Harp Lager,' says Matt. 'How are you keeping, Jim?'

'The same.'

'Much news?'

'Divil the bit. Quiet all around.'

'This here's my cousin,' says Matt. 'From London, England.'

'Well,' says Jim. 'How are you?'

'Fine, thanks,' I say.

Jim puts the pints on the bar in front of us. Matt pays and we make our way to a table.

'He doesn't give much away,' I say.

'Sure Jim talks just like a telegram,' says Matt. 'He's a Cavan boy, where they're too mean to speak. We're lucky he didn't charge us by the word.'

'Sounds like he has the makings of a great barman,' I say.

The doors open. A blonde girl, hands thrust into the pockets of a black coat belted at her waist, stands framed in the doorway, taking in the room. She smiles when she sees Matt and comes over.

'Well, Eileen,' he says, and stands up to greet her.

'Well, Matt,' she says.

Her coat is glistening with flecks of rain, as if the stars had fallen on her, and her cheeks are blushing with the cold. Matt draws back a chair and she sits down.

'Are you not going to introduce me to your friend?' she says.

'This is John Kevin, Eileen. My cousin, from London, England.'

She places the coat carefully on the back of the chair and turns to me.

'I'm very sorry about your poor mother, John. It was a mercy for her in the end, you know?'

'Thank you,' I say.

'What'll you have, Eileen?' asks Matt.

'I'll just take a mineral, Matt. A red lemonade'll be fine.'

Matt gets up and goes off to the bar.

'What did you mean, Eileen?' I ask. 'About it being a mercy for my mother?'

'Matt! Would you ever get me one!'

Eileen and I both turn towards the door.

'Chusha!' cries Matt. 'What are you having?'

'Ach, just whatever Eileen's having herself!'

The drinkers all turn back to their pints, and Patricia joins our table. She is dressed in the same belted black coat as Eileen, and I realize these are nurses' coats. But whereas Eileen is buttoned up, Patricia is looser, larger, full of beans. When she throws off her coat I can see that Patricia is plump and buxom, with large blue eyes and gold-tinted auburn hair. Her accent,

I notice, is also slightly American. She's like a young Maureen O'Hara.

'So did you get off early, Chusha?' asks Eileen.

'I did of course,' she says.

'And how did you manage that?'

'I told Sister that Mammy would be on her own tonight as you were out courting and that she was failed badly since her fall.'

'And she let you go?'

'How could she refuse me?'

I laugh at her impudence.

'Oh, I'm sorry,' says Eileen. 'Chusha – this is Matt's cousin from London, England.'

'Are you John Kevin?'

'I am.'

'I'm sorry about your mother,' she says, her huge blue eyes on me, the sparkle all gone from them. She's just about to say something more when Matt calls over from the bar.

'Hey! You Cockney scut! Come and help me with these drinks!'

'Excuse me,' I say. 'I think Matt needs a hand.'

I smile at them and go to help.

'I just wanted to get you over here to see what you thought,' whispers Matt.

'About what?' I whisper back.

'About the girls!'

Matt sounds as if he's lost his voice and is trying to shout with what's left.

'They're very nice,' I murmur.

'God!' says Matt. 'When did you get to be so English?'

'That must have been when I was born there,' I say.

He looks as if he is about to say something. Then he thinks better of it.

'Come on,' he says. 'I think Chusha has a notion of you already. Or is it the other way round?'

He winks at me and starts gathering up his share of the drinks. I take mine and we rejoin the sisters.

'Are you boys going to the disco here tonight?' asks Patricia.

'If you're taking us,' says Matt, grinning.

'Now how would us poor nurses be able to afford two tickets to the disco?'

'I'll buy the tickets for the disco,' I say.

Matt gives me a look.

'We were going there anyway,' he says. 'At least, Eileen and me were. Chusha was supposed to be working, but she's too fly for that.'

'I'm not a bit fly,' she says. 'I'm just in need of a bit of distraction. You try taking temperatures and emptying bedpans all day.'

'It's got to be easier than filling them,' says Matt. 'I couldn't do that all day.'

'Matt, would you quit!' cries Eileen.

'Well, can I buy you a ticket for the disco, Chusha?' I ask.

'I thought you'd never ask,' she says.

'I told you she was fly,' says Matt.

'Boy, do I want to let off some steam tonight!' she says. 'I could drink this bar dry.'

'Chusha, would you behave yourself!' says Eileen. 'Sure are you not keeping your Confirmation vow?'

'What's that?' I ask.

'After we've made our Confirmation, we all promise not to drink until we're twenty-one.'

'We don't *all* promise,' says Matt. 'I didn't.'

'And I had my fingers crossed behind my back,' says Patricia.

74

We all laugh.

'What would you like to try, then?' I ask.

'Get her a pint of Guinness,' says Matt. 'Sure what else could she want?'

'Matt, a pint's far too much for her!' says Eileen.

'Ach, it won't do her any harm,' says Matt.

'I'm game,' says Patrica. 'I'm ready for anything.'

'I'll get it,' I say.

I get up, go over to the bar and order the drink. The barman pours me a pint and waits for it to settle. The bar starts to fill up. A group of smart young men and their girlfriends bring the cold night air in with them. The girls settle at a table in the centre of the room, while their boyfriends come up to the bar. On an impulse I say, 'Make that two pints of Guinness.'

The barman shifts the settling Guinness out from under the tap and pours another into a second glass. Behind him I can hear Patricia laughing, and I wonder what the disco will be like. Monaghan Town is a different place altogether from London – light years away from the life I've left behind. In fact Ireland itself is like another world. The Irish have their own language, their own sports, their own money – even their own national drink: black, creamy stout, cold, delicious and as dark as the night sky.

'There you are,' says Jim, and places the two pints of Guinness on the counter. I pay the barman and pocket the change. Patricia is still laughing as I take the drinks over to the table.

'Here,' I say. 'I got two pints.'

'I thought you were drinking lager?' says Matt.

'I was,' I say. 'Till I had a little brainwave.'

I turn to Patricia.

'I bet you I can down my pint quicker than you can down yours.'

She doesn't bat an eyelid.

'You're on,' she says.

We both go for our glasses.

'Hold on, you two!' cries Matt. 'You need to do this right. I'll be referee. OK – put your glasses down and only pick them up again after I count to three.'

We put our pints down and eye each other like gunslingers.

'The first one to empty their vessel,' says Matt, 'and slam their glass back down on the table is the winner.'

'And what's the prize for winning?' asks Patricia.

'A kiss if I win,' I say.

'Ah, but what if I win?' she says.

'I don't know,' I say. 'What would you like?'

'That you dance like John Travolta in the disco.'

'I always do,' I say.

We grin like gladiators.

'Right,' says Matt. 'Are you ready?'

We both nod.

'OK,' says Matt. 'After three. One … two … three!'

We snatch up our glasses and start to gollop down the stout. It feels cold and bitter in my mouth, oozing down my throat. I'm sure I'm winning, swallowing like a fish, like a school of fishes, and I can see the glass emptying, the suds of it stuck to the sides as I swallow down the black liquid, just a few briny mouthfuls to go. But as I'm about to have the last of it I hear a sudden crack on the table.

'We have a winner!' crows Matt. 'Making her debut in the Four Seasons All Comers Contest, from Castleblayney, County Monaghan, ladies and gentlemen, I give you – Miss Patricia Cunningham!'

Patricia has a creamy moustache and a huge smile on her face. She looks flushed and pretty and eminently kissable.

I am in love.

*

'There,' says Johnny. 'There's your mother.'

I look down at the grave. There is no headstone, no cross. My mother lies in the earth with no marker to say she's there.

Johnny is my eldest cousin, six feet tall, handsome and wild as the wind over the drumlins. He stands next to me at the graveside. The rest of the family are by Uncle Tommy's Beetle, waiting for us.

I wipe a tear from my eye.

'Come on,' says Johnny. 'Mass is starting.'

After the disco Patricia told me she'd be in Dundalk the following Sunday. I thought a lot about her as the week passed. At last Sunday came and we met by the beach.

'How do you think you'll do in your exams?'

The day is warm and sunny, and the waves are lapping on to the strand. Patricia and I walk along the sandy shore. A mile of beach stretches away before us, the sea a rippling sheet of blue-green dazzle. Above, the sky is huge and cloudless; the only sound is the waves rising and falling and the soft sift of sand as we walk.

'I'm not sure how I'll do,' I say.

I had taken my A levels the week my foster-parents went on holiday. They wouldn't let me stay in the flat on my own so my social worker arranged for me to go into Claybury. I caught the bus every morning, the same one I caught when I used to visit my mother, the 235. It dropped me a few streets from the school gates. And every evening I tried to revise on the ward.

'Will you go to university?'

'I will if I get the grades,' I say.

We walk on, the sun golden and warm, a few rocks ahead of us along the shoreline. In my coat pocket I have a little box. I put my hand in my pocket and bring it out.

'Patricia,' I say. 'There's something I want to ask you.'

I hold up the little heart-shaped box for her to see. It is covered in red velvet, and I spring it open. Inside is a gold Claddagh ring, a fleck of green Connemara stone set in a heart held by two hands.

'Would you be my girl?' I say.

Patricia blushes and nods. I fit it on and we kiss. The sea whispers our names, and a light wind carries them away.

The heat is going out of the day and the sun is declining in the sky. We've come to a little bay at the far end of the beach and I lay my raincoat on the sand. We sit side by side and look out to sea.

'I saw your mother a few times before she died,' says Patricia.

She looks straight ahead and speaks softly.

'Matt took us over to see her in Newbliss, the other end of the county. It wasn't much of a place, John. It was like a cowshed. I couldn't believe the state of it.'

The waves fall in white sprays of foam on to the beach. A trio of seagulls rises and dives into the light of early evening. Their cries echo through the air and carry out to sea.

'She wasn't well. She told us she'd fainted a couple of times. Blood pressure, she said. Her place was a mess, stuff everywhere, dishes stacked up in the sink, food going off in the kitchen. I think she wasn't taking her tablets. Sure she had enough bottles of pills to stock a chemist's – maybe she got confused. One time Matt drove us all into town to do some shopping. Didn't she wet the floor of the shop. 'Hey, missus,' says the store manager, 'you can't be doing that in here.' 'Sure it'll keep down the dust,' says she, quick as a flash. She was a great woman, your mother. She'd make us all laugh, even when they took her into hospital.'

I think of the letter my mother sent me from Newbliss. She

asked was I coming over to see her. I'd been working for the St Vincent de Paul Society, mowing old ladies' lawns, running errands for pensioners, visiting people in hospital. I asked them if they could help. They said they would. So I wrote over and told her I was coming. But their help didn't come in time.

'In the hospital she started to improve a bit. There was one lad who was coming in to see his granny and they'd moved your mother's bed. We were all visiting her, and he said, 'I see they have you up against the wall today, Mrs O'Donoghue.' 'This isn't the first wall ever I was up against,' she said. She had us all in fits. Even the nurses were laughing.'

The sun is sinking into the sea, and the sky is red and violet and purple. A light wind blows in off the waves. The gulls' wings catch the light as they wheel in the sky.

'It all happened very quickly after that,' says Patricia. 'She started to fail, to lose weight, to age. She looked sort of helpless in that hospital bed, as if she was lost, as if she'd given up. She kept asking after you, would you be over. We said of course you would. But there was a look in her eye, a dull look. 'He'll never come,' she said. 'Never.'

'And then we got the news.'

In the sky, a pale moon has risen. The waves ripple to the shore, and in the west the sun is setting. Patricia takes my hand and I turn to her. She holds me in her arms and tries to comfort me. The night is drawing in now and the gulls are flying out to sea, away from the shore and the waves, away from Patricia and me, from the beach and the rocks and the town behind us. They look like they are flying into the sun.

V

Friern, 1979

The three of us stand in a row. The other two look fit, one taller than me, more muscled, bronzed and reddened, short cropped blond hair, the other taller as well, but skinnier, paler, hair black and lank, every inch a runner. We nod in recognition and then sprint off as fast as we can. I start well, but as we come round the small box of Halliwick House the other two pull away on me. We head off for the main building, the morning already hot and sunny. The hard ground is dry and sandy, the bushes like tinder. I'm trailing as we get on to the path, stretches of lawn and grounds beyond, no one else around this early. I can see the wards off to our right, linked by the longest corridor in north-west Europe, a low tunnel with a whitewashed vaulted ceiling. A small fleet of cars is parked in front of the hospital, and a green Mini Moke towing a trailer comes up behind me and overtakes. Two men in donkey jackets are riding up front, two long stays sat on the back of the trailer. They pass the runners up ahead, and I follow behind.

We arrive at the main entrance, me ten yards from them now, long, stone-lipped swathes of grass leading up to the building like the grand avenue of a stately home. We keep going, a few office workers starting to arrive, and I watch the runners disappear round the back, puffing hard, and kick away after them for the final stretch.

*

Back on the ward I look in the mirror and think of all that's happened. The mirror is a blank slate. I can write whatever I like on it. I can be a different person. I can start all over again.

~──~

The queue for the film stretches down Haverstock Hill. It's Visconti's *Ludwig*, which Jamie wants to see.

'Let's go for a drink,' I say. 'We can come back for the next showing.'

'OK,' says Jamie. We both work together in Ryman's in Brewer Street, Soho. It's the only job I can find after leaving school – sales assistant. I earn £33 a week after tax and insurance. Frank and Ivy charge me £16 board and lodging, and my fares for the week are £7. My money goes nowhere. Frank and Ivy have been good to me, but I can't stay with them forever. The allowance they get for looking after me has finished. I feel that there's no point in me being there, and there's no incentive for them to keep me. And my mother's death hangs heavy in their small flat, awkward, taboo, something no one can speak about but which goes through our minds all the time. Ivy's wary eyes, Frank's cackles and gags – they say more than any words.

As we get to the George across the road from the cinema, I spot a newsagent's.

'Hold on, Jamie,' I say. 'Let's have a look at the notices.'

Jamie is looking for accommodation too. I scan the postcards on the noticeboard. One catches my eye: 'Flat to rent. Suit Young Professionals'. There's a phone number, which I get Jamie to take down. We ring it from the phone box outside the pub. A Scottish woman comes on the other end.

'Yes,' says Jamie, 'we're both hoping to develop careers in retail management ... Next Tuesday evening?'

I nod.

'We'll be there.'

Jamie gets off the phone, and we go into the pub, elated. 'Young Professionals!' We laugh at the phrase over our pints of Younger's Tartan. Two weeks later we move in.

❧

'You're fast, boy, but you're not as fast as me.'

I'm in the queue for the patients' canteen, upstairs in Halliwick House. The unit went up in the fifties, a small cube of a building, well away from the main hospital, with two wards and a lounge on the ground floor. Upstairs there's a games room, office, the patients' canteen and two more wards. The floors of the halls between the wards are made of mottled dark brown cork and there's a gloomy dimness to the lighting. It's as if the flooring absorbs the light and radiates back darkness in return. Halliwick House is much more compact than Claybury and O2, as if it's trying to be on a human scale. But it's still an institution.

'Going again tomorrow?' I ask him. The queue moves forward and we move forward with it. He's one of the runners from this morning, still in his t-shirt and shorts, tall, muscular, with the heavy eyelids and husky, slightly slurred voice of the sedated.

'Depends if these horse pills kick in or not.'

'Where's the other lad?' I ask.

'I think he's on Ward 21.'

Ward 21 is in the main hospital. The wards in Halliwick House are all named after trees: Cedar, Ash, Oak, Beech. There are rumours that ten years ago Vivian Stanshall got into the bed Spike Milligan was getting out of. Perhaps it was private then.

The doors open and the queue lurches forward.

'What's your name?' I ask.

'Joe,' he says. 'The Fastest Living Nutter in North London.'

I grin and we follow the queue in for lunch.

*

Malcolm is chairing the Patients' Meeting.

'There have been a lot of complaints about the food. How many people are as disgusted by it as I am?'

The meeting is in the lounge on the ground floor. This is a long, large saloon, with a big Persian carpet covering the parquet floor. The French windows have their tall yellow curtains pulled across and outside darkness has fallen. Around the wood-panelled walls are a collection of about twenty high-backed armchairs, and the patients sit on these, some in dressing gowns and pyjamas, some in their own clothes. There are a few nurses also, coming to the end of their shift. It is about seven thirty.

'Yeah, I wouldn't feed that muck to a pig.' Maxie Reilly, a small fat Cork man, is simmering with rage and frustration. The drugs can't completely quieten him. He's out of his chair and pacing up and down in front of us.

'Why can't they feed us properly in this place? I'll tell you why. It's because we don't exist in here. We've got no fucking rights. I'd like to smash the whole fucking place up.'

Maxie is starting to get seriously angry now. His face is red and he's not really looking at anyone. All he can see is splintering furniture, shattering windows. Maxie is dangerous.

'Sit down, Maxie,' says Malcolm.

Malcolm, a slim, blond hippy in his early forties with a desiccated look about him, is wearing a striped hospital dressing gown and pale yellow pyjamas. This is to prevent him running away. He's sedated too, but that doesn't slow him down either. He peers out at the world through rimless spectacles.

Maxie stops. He looks at Malcolm.

'Until all of you learn that I am the Christ, you will not enter my Kingdom.' Malcolm stands and opens his arms into the shape of a cross. 'For I was hungry, and you gave me to eat; I was thirsty, and you gave me to drink; I was a stranger, and you took me in; naked, and you covered me; sick, and you visited me; I was in prison, and you came to me. What you do to the least of my brothers, you do to me.'

Maxie walks up to Malcolm. All eyes are on them.

'If you're Christ, Malcolm,' says Maxie, 'tell me this. Why didn't you answer my prayers about my missus and kids? Why have they all been taken away from me?'

Malcolm peers at Maxie through his glasses.

'Because you sinned against the Holy Ghost,' says Malcolm.

Maxie's face turns crimson. He draws back his fist and bangs Malcolm full in the face. The nurses jump up and restrain Maxie before he can do any more damage.

Malcolm stands his ground, then slowly, sorrowfully, he turns the other cheek. Maxie is led away, shouting, ranting at Malcolm.

The meeting breaks up. I go up to Malcolm and tell him he's not Christ. He looks at me through his specs. Before I can react he punches me, exactly the same blow Maxie dealt him. A young Irish nurse sees what he's done. She comes over and asks if I'm all right. I tell her I'm fine, but I'm glaring at Malcolm. He pulls his robe together like Moses and goes off to the ward.

'Do you want to talk about it?' she asks.

'Not really,' I say. 'I might be hurting now, but I'll be OK in the morning. Malcolm, though – he's going to be cracked for a long time. I don't know whether to laugh or cry.'

We go back to the ward, to cocoa and the TV lounge. I wonder when they'll let me out of here. I hope it won't be much longer.

I load my gear into the white van. After four years I'm leaving my foster-parents. The van is standing in the road outside the small block of flats. Jamie asks is that everything. I nod. We're off to Hampstead. We've been given the tenancy on a ground-floor flat on South Hill Park Road, two minutes from the Heath. I get in the van and don't look back.

The music blares, jazzy and crude. A pale green light shines off the walls of the small room. The Presence is behind me, watching. The table is white-topped, the chair hard-edged. If I turn around, The Presence will make the music blare louder, the light shine brighter. I have to keep writing. The Presence watches over my shoulder. And The Fire. The Fire is waiting.

Julia is an anorexic. I've never heard the word before. It means that she won't eat. She's kept in a side room on Oak Ward and a nurse sits with her. Julia is beautiful, blonde and blue-eyed, and about twenty. For someone who has been starving herself she's not at all thin. They must have been fattening her up before I got here. I call in to pay a visit. Her nurse, a dark-haired girl of about the same age, is sat on a chair by Julia's bed. Julia sits on top of the bedclothes, reading. Her nurse looks up as I stand in the doorway of the room.

'Hello,' I say. 'My name's John. I think I saw you at the meeting last night. I was just wondering if you fancied going for a walk?'

The grounds of Friern are not as big as Claybury's. Friern Barnet Road runs past the perimeter wall, and Halliwick House stands perhaps twenty feet from the traffic and bustle. We may be in an asylum but there's not the same sense of removal here. We're not folded into England like we were in Claybury. But where else is there for us to go?

'Would that be all right?' Julia asks her nurse.

'As long as I come with you, it shouldn't be a problem.'

Julia and her nurse get up to go when a figure comes up behind me. I turn round. It's Joe, my running pal.

'Can I come?'

'Why not?' says Julia.

Julia's nurse pops along the corridor to the office to let them know we're going out, and when she comes back we all set off. We come out into the hall. It's just been buffed, the smell of polish thick in the air, the dark brown gloom suffused with the waxy aroma. Outside the day is sunny and fresh and we set off, following more or less the path I'd followed the other morning with Joe and the runner from Ward 21.

'Great weather,' says Joe, 'although I'll have to watch it. I'm going to fry in this sun if I don't cover up a bit more.'

We pass another party out for a walk, about six long-stay patients, all men, in loose-fitting sports jackets and black slacks, the thin laces of their shoes variously tied or flapping about loose. A young nurse walks beside them. Our nurse says hello to their nurse and we all say hello in turn to the long stays.

One of them comes up to Julia. He starts looking fondly into her eyes. He has a cow's lick of black hair falling to one side and dark five o'clock shadow. His lips are dry and his skin is flaky and cracked in places. He's as gentle as a Labrador, and Julia for a moment is bemused by his attention.

'Come on, Roger,' says his nurse. 'Would you stop making eyes and leave these people in peace?'

'Goodbye, Pretty Lady,' says Roger, smiling sadly, and he walks off to catch up with his nurse and the rest of the long stays.

'I wonder how long he's been here?' asks Joe.

'Poor man,' says Julia. 'What kind of life is this for him?'

We walk on and come to the Orchard Club, a place round the back of the main hospital selling tea, coffee and other refreshments.

Julia treats us all to drinks, and I have lemon squash. I think about Roger, the long-stay patient. There's something lost about him, as if he's been forgotten, thrown away. As if his life has come to an end.

A flat in Hampstead – we can hardly believe our luck. The Heath is literally just around the corner, and we're on the ground floor. The previous tenants went to the council and had a fair rent set. We pay £11 a week each. At first, everything is fine. But soon the differences between us start to show. Jamie's parents are expats and he was educated abroad. He's into classical music, goes to concerts and all of the latest exhibitions, and knows how to cook. I like music and art as well, but I don't know half as much as Jamie.

I've left Ryman's and now I'm working for the Post Office, sorting mail in the City. Jamie's moved on from Ryman's too and has got a good job in a financial institution. He's moving up into a nice safe middle-class world with prospects. I'm moving down, into a world almost exclusively of men in donkey jackets and overalls. As I work Late Turn, Jamie and I don't see much of each other. It's just as well.

The Art Hut is not too far from Halliwick House. It's a small grey building, like an artist's studio. Nick the occupational therapist is there every day. He's quite a bit older than me, in his forties, with clay on his hands, a paint-streaked overshirt, and a roll-up constantly on the go. He's always helpful, always willing to get paints and sugar paper for everyone who comes through the doors. The routine on the ward isn't like Claybury. There are no groups for a start, nowhere to explore what's led us to Halliwick. There's no set occupational therapy programme either, so I just go to the Art Hut most mornings and hang out there. It's less claustrophobic than the ward.

This morning I'm talking to Nick about *Taxi Driver*, the movie I saw in Kilburn a week before I was sectioned.

'What about the bit where he's walking down the road, and he's in the middle of New York, but he looks like he's a million miles away?'

Nick grins his wry grin.

'A bit like James Dean,' he says. 'On that poster. 'Boulevard of Broken Dreams'.'

It's an image that goes through my mind often in Friern. I feel like I've gone that road many times, alone, alienated, all of London around me, and all of it completely indifferent.

I don't do any drawing or painting in the Art Hut. But I do write. And I write in the Quiet Room on Oak Ward, on the metal table, away from it all. The scenes in *Taxi Driver* – Travis Bickle writing in his diary, the music raucous and jazzy, the camera coming over his shoulder – run through my disturbed mind. There's something that haunts me in that room. And the writing doesn't stop – it's a compulsion, the words, the lines, the images, tumbling out of me. It's as if I'm trying to function as my mind skitters away from me. The writing is who I am – it's my attempt to pull back my sanity from the lure of psychosis. It's my way of holding on to my identity.

I'm writing a poem about the conversation of inanimate objects. My senses are hyped and my mind is racing. I feel loose, disconnected, as if I'm made of mercury, of quicksilver. Phrases tumble through my mind, and I scribble them down as quickly as I can. Sometimes I'm so fast it feels as if I'm racing towards disintegration, as if I'm suddenly thinking at the speed of light, way ahead of any physical ability to keep up with my wits. Then it seems as if my body lacks the same faster-than-light drive as my thoughts and buckles under the exhilaration of my speeding, teeming, scheming mind. It's like feeling your skin peel away from you, as if you've suddenly turned molten and you can no longer accommodate this manic acceleration, this rocket lifting off inside you.

Then the Largactyl kicks in, and I manage to get a bit calmer. But the writing is the biggest help. I need an outlet for my thoughts, I need to catch them before they're gone, I need to write them down before my head is a swarm of ideas. I write blank sonnets, fourteen lines done quickly on whatever paper I can beg from the office. I file everything in a manila folder. These are my worksheets. I've got a lot of them – I write at least one poem a day in Friern.

'There's a lot of people who are high at the moment,' I say to Nick. 'Do you know Joe? And Lucky Luke?' Lucky Luke comes from Cedar Ward, opposite us on the ground floor. We call him Lucky Luke, Joe and me, because we're sorry for him. He's so manic he can't stop talking, his eyelids drooping, sedated, his dry mouth motoring, a froth of spit forming at the corners of his lips as he mumbles on, desperately churning out words as if stopping might kill him.

'What goes up must come down,' says Nick with a sardonic grin.

A line comes into my head. I turn back to the blank page, and start writing again.

———

I leave the Post Office and get a job in the Royal Free Hospital just down the road in Hampstead. I want to be a porter, but because I've worked for the Royal Mail the head porter puts me in the post room. After the grey nylon bib and braces of the Post Office, the donkey jacket and black and brown enamel badge, the Royal Free kit me out in much lighter gear: a pale blue cotton smock top and matching tight trousers, with a white t-shirt with R F HOSPITAL printed in blue letters on the chest. I wear my porter's uniform with thin black canvas shoes I've bought from a Chinese martial arts shop in Kentish Town. Gone is the big floor of the sorting office, the continual drinking, the short commute to the City, the winter. I've got a local job and walk to work in order to sort and deliver post to the wards and departments of the hospital, running up and down fourteen flights of stairs, along the corridors and across the road to the clinical epidemiologists in Pond Street. Spring is here and Hampstead is blooming.

Summer on the ward is bringing out the lovebirds.

Sean is about twenty-three. He was in a bedsit in Camden Town but started hearing voices and has been sectioned. He has curly black hair and wears a green tracksuit and Adidas trainers. He looks a bit like a footballer, like Lou Macari or Kevin Keegan. There are rumours that he had a trial for a First Division club, but got fouled so badly by the full back marking him he had to give up playing. He's very quiet, which I think is because of the drugs they give him, but this hasn't stopped him attracting a girlfriend, a young Swedish woman from Ash Ward. They go around all the time hand in hand. They are devoted sweethearts. I'm not so lucky.

'Will you fuck me?'

Antonia, a large black African girl, clambers into my bed. I've never slept with a girl before and I don't know what to do. She's very brisk, something I never expected women to be. She's also very well spoken, and this too is disconcerting.

Before I know what's happening, she has pulled off her top, reached below the bedclothes and has her hand down my trousers. It's all too much.

'Oh, John!' she moans. 'You could have waited!'

And with that, she's up and off, her top pulled back on, her hand wiped on the back of her skirt, ambling away with her large handbag to find someone else who can satisfy her. It's all over in a minute. I've never felt so foolish in my life.

'I snogged him.'

I'm in Julia's room. She's telling me about Joe, my old running partner. I feel crestfallen. I like Julia myself, but I've never told her, never tried to make any kind of move.

'What do you like about him?' I ask quietly.

'His muscles,' she says.

It seems I've got Julia wrong. I smile weakly and say I've got to go.

But there's nowhere really I can go.

The young Irish nurse, the one who asked me was I all right when Malcolm hit me, is very nice. She's plump with long brown hair, chestnut-streaked, and has that similar American-sounding accent I liked so much in Patricia.

I see her nearly every day. Her Irishness, and the fact she's about the same age as me, draws me to her.

I've written her a poem which she's read. Chris, the blond charge nurse, is talking to her in the office. I'm outside and I can hear every word.

'You know relationships with patients are a non-starter. He could ruin your whole career. You're going to have to decide: is it going to be nursing or him?'

I turn away. I know we'll never get beyond the stripes of her uniform. They're bars that keep her locked into her role and me locked out. I'm a patient, someone who has been diagnosed with an illness that keeps me from her. If ever I felt like the rest of humanity, the great army of the well, this moment brings home to me my essential difference. I've never seen myself as unusual compared to anyone else. I've just had a few more knocks, perhaps. And I know that there are plenty worse off than me. But I walk away from the office feeling crushed.

———

'What about Patricia?' asks John Knight.

We're on the Heath at my twenty-first birthday party. Jamie is in Harrogate visiting his mother. He's left me the flat in case I want to take people back. It's a shame he's not here, but we've not been getting on for some time.

There are a few more friends round the picnic blanket: John — another John — who works with me in the post room. He's in his forties, a stocky man who smokes liquorice roll-ups and has sideburns and a 'tache. Then there's Imelda and Ken, Lorna and Paul, and Imelda's sister, Maeve. I'd met Lorna through mutual friends and we've been close ever since, two only children in a world of brothers and sisters. Lorna's like me, I think. She needs time to herself; she has an Irish mother who suffers with her health. And she writes. Paul is Lorna's boyfriend, and Imelda and Ken are their friends.

'Patricia?' I say. I think of Monaghan, of my mother in her grave across the Irish Sea. 'Well, I wrote to her, but she never really wrote back to me. And anyway, what good would I be to her? I can barely support myself, never mind a girlfriend.'

John points to my t-shirt, the one I wear for work with R F HOSPITAL on the chest.

'Look,' he says. '"Released From Hospital"!'

I grin and raise a glass.

'To absent friends,' I say.

*

It's midnight, Saturday. I put on the donkey jacket and Gannex cap I've bought in Camden Town. I let myself out of the flat and start off down the road. I'm going for a walk. A long walk. Up Downshire Hill, along Hampstead Lane, towards Hendon and the outer suburbs of north-west London. I walk into the wee small hours, till the dawn starts to lighten the sky. It's as if I'm looking for someone, someone who's not there, someone who's gone into the night. Someone who's come in from work in a blue boiler suit and tweed cap with a bar of chocolate for me. Someone I'm trying to find.

—⦁—

The music is louder now, the light colder. The Presence is here, looking over my shoulder as I write. The words fall into lines, ordered and logical. The Universe has patterns which I trace in these lines. The lines come quickly, and all the while The Presence watches, watches and waits. Waits for The Fire.

Oak Ward is settling down for the evening. The cocoa has been made and we've all taken it in the TV lounge. It washes down our night medication, which is the stuff that really puts us out. I'm not on Mogadon, but I can remember taking it when I was first admitted. It totally zonked me.

I walk down the little corridor leading from the TV lounge to the office. There's a toilet just beyond this and I need to go. A Rasta girl stands in the corridor, talking to the charge nurse who's on tonight, a Nigerian nurse I've not seen before. Maybe he's from the agency.

Sean comes out of the toilet just as I'm about five steps from the office. He goes up to the charge nurse and in one quick movement launches himself at his neck, both hands around him, squeezing as hard as he can. They fall to the floor. Sean squeezes and squeezes and the nurse yells for help. The Rasta girl looks up at me and starts screaming at me to get Sean off.

'He's strangling him!' she shouts at me. 'Don't just stand there — do something!'

A nurse from Cedar Ward comes belting across and into the corridor. Sean is still choking the charge nurse with all his strength. But the nurse from Cedar Ward pulls him off and leads Sean away. As suddenly as he attacked the charge nurse, just as suddenly Sean is calm and under control. But the charge nurse is breathing hard and rubbing at his neck. His eyes are wild and red. The Rasta girl looks at me sharply. She thinks I should have helped the charge nurse. But I was so shocked I couldn't move. Now I go up to the charge nurse.

'Are you all right?' I ask.

'He tried to kill me!' gasps the charge nurse. 'What is wrong with him?'

'He hears voices,' I say.

The Rasta girl is disgusted with me. She takes the charge nurse into the office and shuts the door.

I go to the toilet and look in the mirror.

This is not who I wanted to be.

It's been a tough six months. Jamie and I have hardly spoken a word to each other. I decide to move out of the flat. I end up in Conway House, a hostel run by the Church for young Irish labourers in Kilburn. I walk to work and I walk back, exhausting myself.

I've been assigned a social worker. He's arranged for me to go and have a look at a therapeutic community in Hilltop Grange, near where I was fostered in Waltham Pond. It's strange to be travelling on buses and tubes on my own. It's as if Friern is a city, a place you never have to leave, with its own government, its own landmarks, its own amenities. I haven't really been away from it for six months. It's a city of the mad, but the mad seem far more at peace than the society that's put us here. I still remember the Winter of Discontent. Rubbish in the streets, the dead left unburied, pickets everywhere. Mrs Thatcher has been elected and Labour are gone. She looks like Matron bustling on to the ward to sort out all the malingerers.

But I can't go back to the nine to five, the rent on time, the job for life. It's not what I want. I might only be qualified for menial work with my three O levels and Elementary Swimming Certificate but poetry has me now. Sometimes I teem with words, get caught up in the flight of ideas, and then I go into that Quiet Room or the Art Hut and write. I can't do that if I have to get to work at 8 a.m., sort the post, climb fourteen flights of stairs, deliver to the departments on my round, and come home exhausted at 6 p.m. to a flatmate who loathes me or an empty set of rooms or a hostel full of navvies and clergy.

What did Julian say?

Resistance.

That's what I have to do.

Resist.

It won't be easy. But then I'm used to life not being easy.

I take the lift to Nicol Ward. It's the psychiatric unit in the Royal Free, modern, clinical, clean. I get out of the lift and walk past reception into the day room. No one stops me – I'm wearing my porter's uniform, the thin blue smock top and trousers, the white t-shirt with R F HOSPITAL in blue letters on the chest.

I can't go back to Conway House. There's nothing homely or comforting about living there. I thought I'd be amongst my own in Kilburn, that I'd feel like I did when I visited Ireland as a child every summer, that there'd be warmth and kindness and love. But I live in a harsh male world of grim streets, dingy pubs, and dead-end jobs. There's no way out. I'm trapped.

I stand in the middle of the day room and start shouting and moving the palm of my hand rapidly towards the right side of my forehead and away again, like David Bowie weirdly saluting on the cover of *Heroes*. I know what I'm doing, but I don't care.

'Day in, day out, day in, day out!' I shout, over and over, my palm flying backwards and forwards against my forehead. I feel like I'm punching every clock that's ever started my working day, that I'm sorting every letter I've ever delivered, that I'm climbing every staircase I've ever hauled myself up. And in the middle of it all, I know I'm as sane as the nurse coming towards me to see what's going on. I know how mad people act, and I want to be with them again. Sooner the madhouse than a life I can't take any more.

The nurse talks soothingly to me but I continue my rant until she goes off and gets a male nurse. I know what this means. They're thinking of using force to shut me up. I calm down a bit and let myself be led into a large side room. Patients and visitors are looking at me but I don't give a monkey's. I'm free now. I don't have to put up with being me any more.

The room has a large opaque window in it and I know what this means as well. It's a two-way mirror, and they're watching me. So I take a blanket off the trolley I'm lying on and cover the window with it. Then I take all my clothes off and wait for someone to come through the door.

I don't have to wait long.

'What is your name?'

I tell the doctor who I am. He asks me to put my clothes back on and as I do so I tell him that I can't take it any more, that I'm cracked. I tell him about Conway House and the walk to work, about all the stairs I left myself on, the corridors that never seem to end, the days that are all the same, the exhaustion I feel.

He looks at me. I could just be someone who wants it easy, three squares a day and a roof over my head, and no sweat getting it. But you've got to be desperate to pull a stunt like mine. Who in their right mind wants to go into the loony bin?

He sizes me up.

'All right, John,' he says at last. 'We'll get you admitted to Friern.'

He makes a phone call and a male nurse comes and takes me down to a waiting car. On the way I feel a kind of happy bleakness. We arrive and I tell myself that here I can start over again. Here, I can be somebody different. I've been given a chance. And I'm going to take it.

✦

Sean's gone.

Chris tells us what happened.

'At 5 a.m. this morning, a car was waiting for us with a police escort. I took Sean to Broadmoor. I had to tell him where we were going on the way. It's the hardest thing I've ever had to do. I can still remember the look on his face.'

I think of Sean, and of Joe, of the runner we raced around Friern, of Julia, and Maxie, Malcolm, and Antonia. I think of the nurses, of the Rasta girl and the long stays. And I think of the voices, and The Presence, of the music and the green light and The Fire.

And I realize that our conditions aren't signposts on the way from recovery to health, or interesting alternative states of mind, or a defence against a reality we can no longer bear.

Being mad isn't like having a broken leg. Broken minds, broken hearts – sometimes these can't mend. Or perhaps they're made worse by the very cures prescribed for them. And I realize that to be who I want to be isn't going to be easy. I carry a stigma now, a diagnosis, a destiny that isn't mine but which has been assigned to me. I'm marked by events, by comments from others and files I have no right to see, by a history of court orders and sections and reports. I have to be careful.

For outside Friern there are billets like Broadmoor.

And I realize that the State is not always a place of refuge and protection.

Sometimes the State is out to get you.

PART II

What Are We?

VI

Grovelands House, 1980

I stand outside an enormous gravel-fronted house, taking in the tall gables, the imposing Edwardian edifice of wings and ivy-covered walls. I've come a long way, right across London. The house reminds me of the vicarage I was placed in before I went to my foster-parents. Except that it's even bigger, a huge middle-class mansion. But the people living here aren't a vicar and his family – this is a halfway house, and I'm halfway to somewhere beyond the ward and the patients' canteen, the lounge and the grounds. After all the months of waiting, at last I'm returning to the world.

I stand at the front door and ring the bell. The door opens slowly.

'Hello! You must be John. Come in. We've been expecting you!'

A fresh-faced girl with short dark hair, wearing blue jeans and a dark green cardigan leads me through the gloomy hallway into a large room with French windows at one end and a view out on to the leafy suburban street at the other. About twenty people sit round on shabby sofas and lumpy armchairs, drinking cups of tea and smoking.

'Sit down, John.'

The fresh-faced girl indicates a vacant armchair.

'Welcome to Grovelands House. My name is Zoe Walker, and I work here. Now we're just going to ask you a few questions and when we're finished, if you have any you'd like to ask us, feel free. Who'd like to start?'

'Tell us about yourself.'

I don't hear where the voice comes from. It could be any one of them. I look down and start talking to the floor.

'I've been in Friern for the past five months—'

'I can't hear you. Can you speak up, please.'

'I've been in Friern for the past five months—'

'There's no need to shout.'

This isn't going well.

'What skills do you feel you could bring to the house?'

Skills? I don't really have any.

'I'm good with my hands. I made a drawing board and set square when I was a schoolboy and looked after a cow on a commune I visited as a teenager. It was only a school trip, but it showed me I had a liking for growing things and being connected to nature.'

It sounds lame, but at least it's true. No one warned me about 'skills' though. Another patient at Friern came here, but she said it was too intense for her. It's a therapeutic community, and to me therapy has a comforting ring to it, like care. I like the sound of it. And I like the look of it. I want to be here.

'What brought you into hospital?'

This from a woman in her thirties, tea in one hand, fag in the other, her face lined and her blonde hair lank. She looks as if she's come up a few hard roads.

I tell her about my parents, about being fostered, about Claybury and Friern.

Her gaze softens, and she says, 'Sounds like you've had a tough time.'

A respectful silence falls across the room.

Then a short bearded man, carelessly dressed in a shirt

too big for him and fawn trousers badly in need of an iron, looks thoughtfully at his cupped hands before asking, 'Do you feel you can make the necessary commitment to the House?'

What does that mean? What is the necessary commitment?

'Yes, I do,' I say. 'I think I'm ready.'

Again they all fall silent. The interview is coming to an end.

'Well,' says Zoe, 'is there anything you'd like to ask us?'

I look around the room. It's the kind of house I imagined my foster-parents would live in. In fact, it's even better than I imagined. And what's more, there's company and a programme of groups and projects. If they accept me I can stay here for eighteen months. That should be long enough.

'If I came here, would I have my own room, or would I have to share?'

'To start off with, you'd be sharing,' says Zoe. 'But after a while, yes, you would get a room to yourself.'

'And what about work?'

'Again, that's something we tend to defer until near the end of your time with us. Everyone who comes here is encouraged to work on themselves. We have a good relationship with the local GP and you'll have no trouble registering with him. Then you can start getting sickness benefit.'

'I see,' I say. 'Well, that's about it, I guess.'

'OK,' she says. 'If you could wait outside, we're now going to discuss your application. We'll call you in and let you know what our decision is when we've finished.'

I rise slowly and walk over to the door leading into the dining room. I open it and feel all the eyes in the room boring into my back. Have I charmed them into taking me? Through the door there's a long table and more windows which let in bright sunlight from the garden. I shut the door and I wait. There's a clock in the hall and I can hear its pendulum knock as I sit at the dining table and try to keep my nerves in check.

At last the door opens and Zoe is smiling.

'John, it's good news. We've decided to accept you. When can you move in?'

A week later I stand outside the house with my holdall and ring the bell. The door opens slowly and a dark, silent man emerges from the shadows, crooks his finger and leads me through the gloomy hallway to the office. The door is open and I can see a young, slightly built staff member with a full beard seated at the desk.

'Thanks, Edward. See you later.'

The bearded man speaks with an Australian accent. It sounds reassuring somehow, like meeting a surfer from Bondi Beach, wholesome and warm as sunshine.

The dark, silent man – Edward, obviously – walks off and I'm alone with the Australian.

'Hi, my name's Dan Cassady. I'm the warden here. Sit down, John, I've got some papers for you to look at.'

I put down my holdall and sit facing him. He hands me the papers, three sets of them: House Rules, Tenancy Agreement, GP Registration. He gives me a pen and our eyes meet. His are hazel and steady. He's sizing me up. I wonder what my file says, what my social worker from Friern has written about me.

'Please read these, John, and sign. Here are your keys.'

He hands me a Yale and a Chubb on a keyring.

'See the doctor on Monday. Jed will be your Befriender. He'll show you the ropes, help you get settled in.'

He looks thoughtfully at me.

'We make a point of not encouraging sexual relationships in the House. I'll get Jed to show you to your room, John.'

I'm tempted to say I don't need any encouragement but I sign the papers quickly and hand back the pen. He stands up and walks out of the office. I pick up my holdall and follow him into the hallway. One of the residents, blond, about twenty-five, is applying linseed oil with a rag to the oak panelling.

'Show John to his room, Jed. He's in with Paul.'

Jed lays his rag next to the bottle of linseed oil on a sideboard in the hallway. He says hello in a West Country burr, and leads me through the dining room and along to a room at the corner of the house on the ground floor.

'The house is divided into the 25 side,' he says, 'and the 27 side. It used to be a doctor's house, funnily enough. But now the lunatics have taken over the asylum. You're here. I'll see you later.'

He leaves me outside a room tucked in a corner of what must be the 25 side. I thank him and knock on the door. Jed goes off to his linseeding and I wait for the door to open.

'Yes?' comes a voice from inside the room.

'My name's John,' I say. 'I'm sharing with you.'

'Come in.'

I open the door. The room is large, with three beds and a washbasin, and a tall window that lets in the light from the garden. Paul is standing by his bedside cabinet. He's the one who asked me if I was ready to make the necessary commitment to the House. I can see that he doesn't really like me. It must feel as if I'm invading his space, a space he's reluctant to surrender. I walk in and stand a few feet from the door.

'Lucky to catch me,' he says. 'We're coming to the end of Work Group. I should be sweeping the stairs on 27 side. I've just nipped back for my tablets.'

'Great to be here,' I say. 'Who's in the other bed?'

'No one yet,' he says. 'Although we've just seen a bloke called Richard. He'll be joining us just as soon as they sort out his discharge.'

'Is it all right if I take this one?' I ask, walking over to the bed under the window.

'Fine,' he says. 'Work Group should be finishing soon. Why don't you leave your holdall and come and join us for a cup of tea? The staff will all be there. Did Dan tell you who your counsellor is going to be?'

'A woman called Liz?'

'Liz? She's good, Liz. I'm sure you'll get on just fine. She's very committed.'

I can see that commitment means a lot to Paul. I have my own commitments. In my holdall I have four exercise books and a foolscap folder full of poems. My life is in those exercise books and that folder. How do I explain that to a stranger? How do I tell anyone that as long as I write poems I know I'll be all right?

Anyone with any sense would say I was mad.

Jed's from somewhere in Somerset, about my own age, kindly in the way country people can be, with a kind of hayseed laziness his medication makes worse. We sit at the dining table before dinner-time and over cups of tea he tells me about the structure of the House, how life is lived here.

'There's Work Group every morning Monday to Friday for two hours. We all get a task, and basically it's about tidying up the place and keeping it clean. You have to look after your own room, but sharing with Paul that shouldn't be a problem. He's very tidy by nature.'

I'd noticed. Paul seems intent on removing all forensic evidence of human habitation from the room. His approach to

tidiness is almost military. I put it down to him being a math-
ematician. He'd studied at Nottingham before his breakdown.

'Have you guys seen Sarah?'

Dan Cassady walks into the dining room, a large marble-
backed book under his arm.

'No, Dan,' says Jed. 'Is she up in her room?'

'Just on my way,' says Dan.

Jed waits for him to leave the room before carrying on. I can
hear Dan bounding up the stairs and calling Sarah's name.

'Everyone takes turns cooking,' says Jed, 'and we do that in
threes. It sounds like a big job, cooking for twenty people, but
between three it's OK. Then on Monday evenings there's the
Monday Night Meeting. That's got a Business Session for the
first hour, where rents and prospective residents get discussed,
and Progress Reports are made. You're expected to make a
Progress Report after a month, then every three months until
it's time for you to leave. I'm making my Three-Month Report
this Monday, so you'll see how they're done.'

This sounds a little scary. I hadn't thought about making
'progress'. And I'm not sure what it means. Just staying out of
hospital would be good. I take a sip of tea and nod sagely as Jed
pauses to roll himself a cigarette. All I want to do at Grovelands
House is to wait out my time and not have to think too much
about the future. Writing the odd poem would be good as well.
I hadn't bargained for progress. And what happens if people
think I haven't been making any? Jed sparks up his rollie and
carries on.

'The second half of the Monday Night Meeting is a general
House Therapy Session. That goes on for about an hour as well.
Then there are the Small Group Meetings, and they happen
on Wednesday evenings once a week. They're therapy sessions
as well, only in small groups, where you can get more work
done. Project Group meetings are on Thursday afternoons,

and they're about learning practical skills like how to change a light bulb—'

'What if the light bulb doesn't want to change?' I joke, dead-pan. It sounds like an awful lot of meetings.

'Eh?' says Jed, looking confused as wreaths of smoke drift round him. Either he's a bit slow on the uptake, or he's lost his sense of humour.

'Never mind,' I say. 'Do you want to just carry on?'

He takes another drag on his roll-up and looks at me evenly through the smoke. I think he senses my scepticism about everything, my plan to take the line of least resistance. Slowly, a little mistrustfully, he finishes by telling me that there are one-to-one counselling sessions once a week, and that if you get a job you only have to come to the Monday Night Meeting and the counselling sessions. Miss two meetings without good reason and you're out. Finally, Jed reminds me of the two big House Rules: No Sex and No Violence.

Dan Cassady comes back into the dining room.

'You guys getting on OK?'

'Fine, thanks, Dan,' says Jed.

Dan looks at me again, that steady, even look. I hold his gaze, waiting for him to speak.

'I hope you make it, John,' he says at last, and walks out of the room.

'Give yourself six months, then move on and get your life sorted.'

John Knight looks very concerned as he says this. He's come to visit me with Ian Berry. Ian's another friend from schooldays, a graphic designer, modest, talented, with eyes like Winker Watson's in the *Dandy* and a broad grin. I'm on the sick, and John's temping for the council. Gone are the days when we'd all get together and mess about doing funny voices into Ian's cassette recorder. Back then we were the Three Musketeers – now it feels like we've been stood down. We're in a park near the House, sitting on a bench as the afternoon fades into early evening.

John's words send a chill straight through me. *Six months?* It's going to take me a lot longer than that.

'I'll see how I feel,' I say to John. John did really well at school. He got two As and a B in his A levels. He could go to university if he wants. For me those doors are all shut. I look away into the distance, as much to evade John's plan for me as to take in the view.

A line of poetry comes into my mind. Something about the trees at this time of year. Dusk is starting to fall as we leave the park. I walk with John and Ian to the station and see them off. By the time I've got to my room the poem is fully formed.

I write out the lines in my notebook.

And I wait for the next one to come.

There are four floors in the House. Downstairs the 25 side consists of the office, the bedroom I share with Paul, and the TV room. On the 27 side there's the dining room, kitchen and utility room, and the large living room where everyone interviewed me. The Monday Night Meeting takes place here. Upstairs on the first and second floors are the rest of the bedrooms and a couple of bathrooms. At the very top of the House in an attic tucked under the eaves is the staff flat.

The House's two sides mirror the vertical split that exists in Grovelands House. For the staff have a definite Them and Us attitude. They take no part in the domestic chores, the cooking, cleaning or gardening. And that attic flat of theirs sums up the relationships in the House, making it less of a commune and more of a mirror of society. For all of their nonsense about 'I'm OK, you're OK', the staff are in control. They call the shots. They're top of the heap.

The House lies on a quiet street near the fringes of Epping Forest in Hilltop Grange, not far from where I grew up and where my friends from school are. But in other ways it's light years from them. It's like a laid-back version of the vicarage, with therapy instead of middle-class family life holding it together. There's a vaguely hippy atmosphere in the air: quite a few of the residents were sixties people in their time. And the staff – the ones I've met so far, like Dan and Zoe – have some of this leftover hippyness in their clothes and their talk as well. Dan's always in lumberjack shirts and Levi's, like a self-sufficient backwoodsman, and Zoe pretty much dresses the same. And we are all 'guys', even the women, a word that sounds fine in Dan's Australian accent, but jars when anyone else says it.

I remember the graffiti from the Bridge House: Never Trust A Hippy.

'First call, eight thirty!'

I wake with a jolt, then close my eyes again. My mother and I are in Quiglough in a pool of clear water. Sunlight skims off the ripples like a shower of silver thrown into its depths. She is smiling at me, as if I'm all she's ever wanted. I am seven years old, on holiday in Monaghan. The warmth and the light are golden, timeless.

'Second call, you two: quarter to nine.'

The hammering on the door stops and I hear the foot-steps moving off, the wake-up call repeated, loud banging on another door across the landing.

'Come on, sleepyheads: time to be up and doing!'

The scene in my dream starts to fade. I want to stay there, to feel again the warm water on my skin, the sunshine freckling me, to see the light glinting off the ripples in the small pool where I bathed as a boy on holiday. Most of all I want to be with my mother. But the knocking is getting louder, the images are fraying and there's an urgency to the calls that won't let me sink back into my memories. I rise and dress. Paul's bed is empty, and there's a sudden bleakness to the room.

Seated around the large dining table, spooning muesli and drinking tea, the rest of the House are rushing breakfast before Work Group begins. I walk through to the kitchen and see from the clock on the wall that I have five minutes to get something to eat. Boxes of cereal stand on the kitchen worktops and I pour some cornflakes into a bowl, splash on a bit of milk, sprinkle it all with sugar, then hurry out to join them.

I sit next to a thickset man in horn-rimmed specs, open-necked white shirt and dark trousers. He's furiously stuffing muesli into his mouth, cheeks puffed out with it, racing to finish. There's something obsessive about the way he's eating, as if he's in a panic about getting enough into him. Then I see that it's Edward, the man who'd shown me into the office on the day I arrived.

'Hello,' I say.

He grunts by way of reply, his mouth still full of oats and nuts and raisins, a few flakes and pearls of milk trapped in his moustache.

Dan Cassady appears in the doorway, the large marble-backed book in his hand. He calls for attention in his drawling version of laid-back authority and addresses us all.

'OK, you guys, listen up. Planning Group time. Can we go through to the lounge and sort out who's doing what?'

We all stand, the chairs raking out from under us, making a noise like thunderous applause. I follow everyone into the lounge and head for an empty armchair by the far wall.

'Hello.'

It's the woman with the lined face and the lank hair. She eases herself into the seat beside me.

'Settling in?'

'Yes, I think so.'

'I'm Sarah. I'm with Paul.'

She smiles at me, and I think of what Dan Cassady said to me about discouraging sexual relationships in the House. Sarah's also about four inches taller than Paul, and I think about that too.

She lights a roll-up, her hand splaying out in an odd reflex as she smokes the burning thatch of tobacco hanging from the cigarette paper. I recognize the gesture: it's one I've seen in Claybury and Friern, a tic caused by medication. It reminds me that the wards aren't as far away as I thought, and for a moment I'm back in the queue, lining up outside the patients' canteen in Friern.

'OK,' says Dan. I snap out of my reverie, Maxie Reilly and Malcolm, Joe and Julia all dissolved into the past. Dan opens the large marble-backed book and the room comes to order. 'Bridget and Jed are foremen this week,' Dan is saying, 'so please give them your co-operation. They'll be checking your work so be nice to them. Now – who'd like to do the kitchen?'

A pale woman wearing blue plastic glasses quickly puts up her hand.

'Can I?'

'And me?' asks Edward,

'Off you go, guys,' says Dan.

They set off together and he calls out the next chore on his list.

'Laundry room?'

'I'll do it,' says Paul.

'Away you go, fella.'

Paul gets up and sets off for the laundry room.

'Stairs 25 side?'

This isn't a popular choice. Best avoided, judging by the reaction in the room.

'We'll give that one to Winston, then. Care to join him, John?'

Winston is still getting up by the look of it. He is nowhere to be seen.

'Well, if it's all right with you—' I start to say.

'Good. That's settled then. Winston and John to do the stairs side.'

'If it's OK with you, Dan,' I repeat, louder this time, making a stand. 'I'd liked to be excused the stairs.'

The room falls silent.

'Why's that, John?' asks Dan, giving me the Look again.

'I have a bit of an allergy to house dust, Dan. I only have to get near it and my eyes start streaming, I sneeze all over the place, and I find it hard to breathe properly.'

Dan is suspicious. He isn't going to give in that easy.

'I am willing to have a go at the garden though.'

'OK, John,' Dan drawls. 'But I'd like you to see Dr Miller about this allergy. We've got nothing about it in your file. Zoe can make an appointment for you.'

'Thanks, Dan.'

'Off you go,' he says, his eyes steady on me as I stand. I walk out through the French windows into the garden, taking in the scene. Behind me I can hear Dan going through his litany of chores as sunshine falls on the lawn like warm gold.

A window above shoots up.

'Hey man, what sort of rasclat business going on?'

Winston. He's naked to the waist, his skinny black body looming down from one floor up, dreadlocks tangled and matted behind him.

'They're doing Planning Group,' I say.

'I ain't doing no frigging chores, man. Meet me at the café, blood. I got some bread. I'll treat you. Better than rasclat muesli!'

Before I can say anything, Winston trundles down the window and disappears back inside.

Sarah, smiling and insouciant, steps through the French windows and takes me by the arm.

'Hello,' she says. 'I've come to help you.'

'Oh?'

'Yes, there are always two on the garden.'

There are?

Sarah seems very friendly, the kind of friendly that can only get me into trouble.

'I can't stay long,' I say quickly. 'You heard what Dan said. I've got to see the doctor.'

'You can go after Work Group.'

'I really think—'

'Oh, come on,' she drawls, squeezing into me, 'you're not afraid of me, are you?'

How had she guessed? And I'm afraid of Paul too – he's got it in for me, I can tell. He thinks I'm not committed. He may be right. I decide to appeal to her better nature.

'Afraid? Not at all,' I say. 'It's just that the surgery has got to be better than mowing the lawn.'

'Good idea,' she says. 'Why don't I come with you and show you the way?'

'Er, yes, why not?'

'Wait here and I'll square it with Zoe. She won't mind.'

She smiles at me and steps back through the French windows. I pick up a stone and throw it at the window where Winston had loomed down at me a minute before. It rattles the pane and up it shoots again.

'Hey man, what are you doing?'

'It's Sarah,' I say. 'She wants to come with me.'

'She'll eat you for breakfast,' he says. He grins at me in the sunlight, gives a great gust of giggles and the window comes down again.

'Zoe says that's all right. Shall we go?'

I turn just as Sarah is taking me by the elbow. She propels me round the side of the house and across the short gravel drive.

'What would you say to breakfast at the café?' I ask her. 'You know, a proper breakfast?'

'What a good idea! Come on then.'

Where is Winston? Paul? The Cavalry?

I'm feeling really nervous now.

We walk over the last of the gravel, me scuffing it as loudly as I can, a growl for help. The street is quiet, cars parked either side, milk still on the odd doorstep.

'Hello, you two. Off for a stroll?'

It's one of the Pollys. There are two of them, both in their thirties, and they share a room. The other Polly is always knitting, and makes shapeless jumpers which she wears herself. This one was a teacher but couldn't take it any more and has come here. She's wearing a purple blouse as glossy as her dark hair, and jeans.

'We're just popping out,' says Sarah. 'Where've you been, Polly?'

'Seeing Dr Miller.'

'Oh? Anything serious?'

'Just renewing my sick certificate.'

'I see,' says Sarah.

I sense Sarah and Polly don't get on. Before awkwardness descends, I hear footsteps behind me.

'Hey man, wait up!'

It's Winston. Thank God! I thought for a moment it might be Paul.

Just as we're about to say goodbye to Polly a voice says, 'Going somewhere, you guys?'

Dan Cassady soft-shoes up behind us.

'Just coming back from the doctor's,' says Polly.

'And we were just going,' says Sarah.

'Have you finished your chores?' asks Dan.

'Sorry, Dan,' I say. 'I had a very bad sneezing fit in the garden. Sarah thought it best to take me straight to surgery.'

'I did ask Zoe,' says Sarah.

'Zoe's too soft,' Dan growls. 'What about you, Winston?'

'I've got to see my social worker,' says Winston.

'This is just not good enough, guys,' says Dan. 'John – you go to the doctor. You'll find his surgery just beyond the level crossing. The rest of you – back to the House.'

'But Dan!' chorus Sarah and Winston.

'No buts! We can sort this out in the office.'

I set off in the direction of the surgery. The café is on the way. It's been a hectic morning, and I'm glad to be away from the House. The poem I started in the park is in my back pocket. I should be able to finish it over a fry-up. The delicious thrill of the mitcher runs through me, and I quicken my step to the caff.

'How's it coming along?'

Edward and Pamela look at me. I can see straight away that there is something going on between them. Or, at least, struggling to get going on between them. It's my first time on the cooking rota and they've given me the dessert to do.

'The *boeuf à l'orange* is fine,' says Pamela. 'Why don't you just attend to your pudding?'

Boeuf à l'orange avec gooseberry ...

I get on with making the crème caramel, a simple business of whisking together milk and powder from a packet. The whisk whirrs and rattles against the bottom of the Pyrex bowl like a Gattling gun.

'Have a taste, Edward,' she says, spoonfeeding him from her big pot of stew.

'Mmm!' he mmms.

I whirr and rattle, rattle and whirr.

'Will it be ready soon?' Jed walks into the kitchen, rubbing his hands together. Keen, I think. Dinner isn't until six and it's only five.

'Not long now,' says Pamela. 'How's the crème caramel coming along, John?'

I rattle and whirr, whirr and rattle, concentrating on the Pyrex bowl as if transfixed by it. I mumble an answer, and rattle and whirr some more.

'It's looking good,' says Pamela. 'Keep going.'

Jed grins, and I grin back. Edward looks at him, smug from Pamela's spoiling. The way to a man's heart. Is through another man's jealousy. I rattle and whirr, whirr and rattle. Why isn't the mixture thickening?

'Run along, Jed,' says Pamela.

'Can't I have a taste?'

'I'll be serving it up soon. You can have all the taste you want then.'

Jed looks a little crestfallen, but withdraws, leaving the kitchen to us. I look at the Pyrex bowl. The more I work the whisk, the more watery the mixture becomes. Surely it isn't supposed to go like this?

'Do you fancy a drink after supper?' Edward asks Pamela.

'I have to wash up,' she says.

'Perhaps John could do it?'

On my own? All these pots and pans?

'Oh, John,' says Pamela, 'would you mind?'

Yes, I bloody well would!

Rattle rattle. Whirr whirr.

'And we'll do it for you another night.'

Oh bloody hell!

'Please?'

'Come on, John,' says Edward. 'There's only a few vessels. I want to take Pamela out to the Essex Arms.'

'OK,' I say. As I rattle I imagine shooting the pair of them with a Gattling gun.

'That looks fine, John,' says Pamela. 'Pop it in the fridge, will you? An hour should do it.'

I stop rattling, stop whirring.

'Did I hear you say you were going out later?'

Jed stands in the doorway, looking hopeful.

'Look, mate,' says Edward, 'I'm taking Pamela out. On my own. Got it?'

Jed looks like a balloon that's had all the air punched out of it.

'So get along and find someone else to amuse yourself with.'

I put the bowl in the fridge. I'm sure Jed rattles and whirrs as he turns and goes into the dining room. Edward has wound him up tight. As he's my Befriender I think for a moment that I should say something to him. But perhaps that wouldn't be politic. This place is full of alliances I haven't worked out yet. I have to make sure people don't take against me. It would be easy to be out on my ear. I don't want everything ending up like it did with Jamie when we shared the garden flat in Hampstead.

I think about my poem. I still haven't worked it all out yet. This is what took up most of the other morning in the café.

Perhaps I'll be able to sort it out by the time we serve up.

'We have a new person coming to the House – her name's Becky Ward and she needs a Befriender. Any takers?'

I've been at the House now a month. The gentle rhythms of meetings and counselling sessions, of Work Group and the cooking rota, have soothed my fears about being back on the wards or out on the streets. Everyone seems a little depressed, even me, but the low level of expectation in the House makes it an easy place to get by. I think I've even worked out who's with who, and who's not with anyone. And I think I've won most people over. But I've still got a way to go. I've stopped taking baths and my feet are literally black with dirt. I wear sandals, exposing the blackness as if it was a badge of honour. The poems have stopped as well, and I still haven't sorted out the one about the trees in the park. I put it down to all the therapy. The grit is being polished smooth, leaving me nothing to make poems out of.

'I'll be her Befriender,' I say.

Dan gives me that look again, that steady, weighing-me-up look, then says, 'Fine, John.'

I remember Becky coming for her interview. She's from Bermondsey, a couple of years younger than me, with bobbed blonde hair and blue eyes, a cheeky smile and a nice figure. She left home at sixteen to move into a bedsit in Camberwell and work in a shoe shop. But she lost her job when the manager tried it on and she got more and more depressed. She spent six weeks in her room before she went into the Maudsley. She's a sweet girl, about as different from the Sarahs and Pollys and Pamelas as you can get, a cheeky sparrow amongst elegant swans.

The Monday Night Meeting rolls on, and I make a crucial decision: tonight I'm going to have a bath and wash those feet.

'Do you want to go to the pub?'

I'm in the middle of cooking. Becky's standing beside me in the kitchen, and I'm keeping her amused with tales of my schooldays and what we used to get up to. I chop the peppers, a vegetable I've never eaten until I came to Grovelands House, and throw the green slices into the pot of bolognese.

'I don't drink,' says Becky.

'I'll buy you some pork scratchings and you can watch me,' I say, grinning.

'Pork scratchings?' she says. 'You must be joking! I wouldn't feed them to a dog!'

'I didn't know you like dogs,' I say. 'There's a nice one I see quite a bit down the pub, drinking beer from a bowl.'

'Why doesn't he use a glass like everyone else?' she says, smiling at me. 'Now why would I want to go to the pub?'

'To get me out of washing-up? Edward and Pamela owe me – I did it for them before you came here. Look on it as what you owe me for being your Befriender.'

'All right,' says Becky. 'Fair enough. But I'm not drinking alcohol. And no pork scratchings!'

That night I kiss Becky. We sleep together, and the world turns in a new direction. The past suddenly seems very far behind. And the future – as long as we're in the House – has been postponed.

But not for long.

VII

Grovelands House, 1981

'What do you want to work on, John?'

Liz, my counsellor, is sitting opposite me in the small Quiet Room that lies in the middle of 25 and 27 side. We've been meeting once a week now for six months, and I still haven't made any of the 'progress' – therapeutic, practical, moral – the House demands I make.

I have the only child's air of self-containment, which grates in a community founded on self-revelation. What looks like aloofness on my part is actually a desire just to be left alone so that I can get on with writing poems. And now that I've figured out that all the therapy is stopping them coming, I take less part in the groups than when I started out, or send them up as subtly as I can. Because it's obvious to me now that the staff are hypocrites. They don't do any chores and they think there's something wrong with us. There's nothing wrong with me – I'm emphatic about that. I'm OK.

Liz seems weary of these sessions. She's in her early thirties, and wears denim dungarees, as if to emphasize that she's a feminist. She sports a range of badges on the bib of them: 'A Woman's Right To Choose', 'Pornography Degrades Women', 'Keep Your Rosaries Off My Ovaries'. She's been on demos and marches, and she's very protective of Becky.

I say nothing. The sun shines in through the window, an early promise of summer. Dust is illuminated in a long sloping ray of light, particles dancing in a suddenly visible universe. I am entranced.

This winds Liz right up.

She's annoyed with me because I won't go to Perivale, where Sebastian goes every morning, all the way across London, east to west. Sebastian is in his early twenties, a heavy metal freak who plays three-chord guitar to his Motörhead albums every night when he gets back. Liz has persuaded him to go to a centre in Perivale to make garden furniture, part of a back-to-work scheme for the unemployed and the long-term sick. It's not exactly the Marquee. It's not even the Bridge House. I'm amazed he's agreed to it. Because there's no way I'm going there. Which riles Liz no end.

She shifts in her chair.

'John, I want to confront you on your passivity. You don't seem willing to take any responsibility for yourself. You won't go to Perivale, you won't make plans for your future, and your relationship with Becky is not the kind we approve of in the House.'

'It's the kind Sarah and Paul have and you don't give them a hard time.'

'Focus on what I'm saying, John. You're not acknowledging what I'm saying.'

'No, Liz, you're not acknowledging what I'm saying. If there is a rule, then it has to apply to all of us. Otherwise it's not fair. Are you saying that I can't be in love with Becky?'

'You think this is about sex, John, and your right to have it. It's not: it's about exclusive relationships. They're a distraction in this House.'

'But not for Sarah and Paul?'

'They're not letting their relationship distract them. They're working on themselves. You're not.'

'That's because I don't have anything to work on. It's only you lot who say that there's something wrong with me.'

'It's not about wrong or right, John. It's a question of growth. You're just not growing here. You're stagnating.'

Liz talks a whole new language to me. I have to 'work on myself'. I have to 'grow'. I have to 'take responsibility' for myself. It's like she's talking in riddles, in a code I can't crack. Why can't she let me be?

It is all becoming clearer to me. It seems to me that in the House 'therapy' is a way of putting us down, and that this all comes from the fact that we've been mad, crazy, cracked. R.D. Laing, Liz's old mentor at the Philadelphia Association, says that the only response to an insane world is insanity. But Liz doesn't see it like this. She talks to me like she's talking to a feckless layabout. I don't like Liz and I don't like the way Grovelands House treats us, talks about us, patronizes us.

The sun goes behind a cloud and the ray disappears.

All the dancing particles of dust fade back into the gloom.

Becky's in the bath on 27 side. She's naked, lying full-length without head or toe touching either end of it. She smiles at me and I smile back. She turns like a dolphin swimming in a tank. I reach down and very gently wash her back with the sponge.

Robbie is in the TV room, leaning on his mop. He's tall and Scottish, with long dark hair and a smile that's part wolf, part leer. He came here from Friern a month ago, and we've become good friends. Becky has come into the TV room from doing the linseeding in the hall and I've come in from sweeping the stairs 27 side.

'They're a right bunch of comedians in this place,' says Robbie, mimicking Becky's Cockney accent. He sounds like Dudley Moore in the Pete and Dud sketches from *Not Only . . . But Also*. She's grinning, and I join in.

'Yeah, a right bunch of comedians,' I say. 'It's like a house full of funsters, all madly cracking gags and doing routines the whole time.'

'Yeah,' says Robbie, 'just like Butlins with Redcoats all over the place and not a holidaymaker to be seen. I can't take much more, I can tell you. All this laughter is making me ill.'

We start giggling. Becky's right: the House is a right bunch of comedians. Pamela walks in with the red foreman's book.

'Good to see you all enjoying yourselves,' she says primly. 'But could you please do a little more work? There's quarter of an hour to go, and you need to make sure everything is spick and span.'

We all wait for her to move on. As soon as she's left the room, we burst out laughing.

Walthamstow Market is the longest street market in the country. It reminds me of Friern, where they have the longest corridor in north-west Europe. Except that the corridor is a long whitewashed tunnel, with a honeycombed vaulted ceiling hanging low and heavy as you walk its length from Halliwick House all the way to reception and the main entrance.

I think of it as Becky and I get off the bus at the Granada Cinema. She wants to buy some clothes and I've said I'll go and get them with her. I mean to surprise her and buy them as presents. I have £150 in the Post Office, untouched benefit which accumulated over the six months I'd been in Friern, and now I'm going to give Becky a bit of spoiling.

We walk down Hoe Street and turn into the market. It's about noon, and already the place is bustling. Stalls full of t-shirts, bras, girdles, knickers, tights, bales of cloth, jars of pickled onions, beetroot, gherkins, tins of baked beans, pilchards, tuna, salmon, toys, radios, books, annuals, records, posters, sarsaparilla, fresh fruit and veg line either side of the street and crowds of shoppers weave in and out to get a look at a bargain, to nose and snoop, to pause, to move on, to clog the way and then to part again. The buying and selling sends up a huge buzz, stall-holders barking their wares like old music-hall comedians.

A blond man aged about thirty in a sheepskin coat with gold sovereigns on his fingers shouts the odds from behind his greengrocer's stall. 'Half a pound of bananas! Lovely ripe bananas! Half a pound for two dollars! That's fifty pence in new money, or ten shillings if you're taking it out of your mattress. We all know what you keep in your mattress, don't we, darling? No, not what you're thinking, sir: that's right, love – enough ten-shilling notes to buy Leyton Orient! Don't you think you should sort it out? Here, come and have a feel of this lovely banana of mine! You're not allergic to them, are you? Please yourself, missus! Get your bananas! Lovely ripe bananas! Half a pound – only fifty pence!'

We wander down the road, the crowds carrying us towards Wood Street, which lies about a mile away at the far end. I really don't want to spend half the afternoon dawdling in the market. I fancy getting a Wimpy and chips and perhaps going to the pictures.

'What are you after, Becky?' I ask her.

'I want to get some pants,' she says.

'What – knickers?' I say, grinning.

'No, you dipstick – trousers, but drainpipes, not crappy parallels like you're wearing.'

'If I wore drainpipes I'd have no room for anything,' I say.

She grins herself and takes my arm. We walk along and I can smell onions frying and burgers sizzling on a hotplate some- where beyond the knots of people we're caught up in. We're in the middle of the road, in a big scrum, and I guide us away from the hurly burly towards a gap between two stalls. My mouth waters and I think of that Wimpy.

But Becky has other plans.

'Look! There!' she says.

A pair of grey pants with a white piped seam down the middle of each leg hangs from a wire hanger on the stall in front of us. They're not great but Becky likes them. She asks the stall-holder to let her have a closer look. He takes them down and she gets them off the hanger and hands it to me. She puts the pants up against her waist and strikes a few poses.

'What do you think?' she says.

I don't think much of them but I want that Wimpy and I want to be away from the crowds and the market, the buffeting and the noise, the barkers and their wares, the bustle.

'They look great,' I say. 'Tell you what – I'll buy them for you.'

Becky frowns. 'But what if they've got a nicer pair further down the market?'

'I thought you liked those?'

'I do – but we might get them cheaper somewhere else.'

'They're only three quid,' I say. 'Three quid isn't going to break the bank.'

'Can't we see if they have a better pair further down, though?'

I give in and we start walking past stall after stall, checking out the odd clothes shop on the pavements either side, and eventually we come to the very end of the market. It takes ages.

None of the stalls or shops has what Becky is looking for.

'Shall we go back and get those ones we saw first?' says Becky.

My face is crimson by the time we buy the grey pants. We

go back to the House, Becky clutching a plastic bag in her tight little fist, the grey pants inside.

I boil all the way home on the bus.

'Hello. Can I take this one?'

A skinny, long-haired youth, about my age, pushes the door open and comes into the bedroom. I'm lying on my bed, reading the paper.

'Hello, Richard. Yes, take the one in the middle. You made it then?'

Richard's been waiting to come to the House ever since I arrived. Paul told me he'd be coming as soon as his discharge was sorted out. And now he's here. I know how it feels, the waiting. He grins a rueful grin, and puts his holdall on the empty bed between Paul's and mine.

'I thought they'd never let me out of Shenley. God, the days didn't half drag! It took ages! But I'm here now.'

He jumps as high as he can in the air and windmills his arm around an imaginary guitar.

'And I'm ready to rock and roll!'

The House is split into two factions. There are those who don't question the ethos of the House, who accept the values promoted by the staff, like Polly Fairbairn. Polly's strongest ally is Bridget, a stout London-Irish woman in her late twenties who calls Dan Cassady 'Danny Boy'. Bridget gets a lot out of the groups.

I've started to lose faith in them, to see them as counterproductive. Some people are running out of issues to 'work on', and have started manufacturing emotional crises as a way of getting attention. They're becoming hooked on therapy, which doesn't look healthy to me.

Sarah and Paul generally line up with this side of the house, although Sarah's more subversive by nature. She tells me one day that she used to be a heroin addict in Notting Hill in the late sixties and early seventies, and shows me the track marks down her arms where she injected herself. She tells me that in order to pay for her smack she used to turn tricks.

'But if they made me come, I wouldn't charge them.'

Sarah still has an anarchic streak but Paul is trying to tame her. They're like a married couple, always together, always a pair. Then there's Edward and Pamela who also line up with Polly and Bridget. They're not as vocal though as these others but they all accept the whole philosophy of 'working on yourself', 'growth', and 'taking responsibility'. I think some of their other allies, like Jed for instance, just want a quiet life.

But then there are a lot of us who don't want a quiet life, who are angry with the staff, and with some of the other residents, especially Polly and Bridget, for sucking up to them. The split is largely down class lines. The working-class residents – Winston, Becky, Robbie, Richard, me – are younger and more rebellious, but there are real problems with the staff, the way they see us and treat us.

Take 'therapy'. The whole approach to therapy in the House is based on the idea that you're the only person in the world who is going to sort your problems out. Since Sarah said at my interview that I'd had a tough time, no one's ever brought up my past, or what's happened to me. It's as if the day I entered Grovelands House I stepped away from who I was and towards what I have to become. There is something wrong with me – this is the message of the House. But if I work on myself, I can put this right. But I don't see it like this. Whatever went wrong in my life has nothing to do with me. Social workers, do-gooders, doctors: these are the people to blame.

My foster-parents have written to the House. They found out where I am, and the letter was passed on to me. Dan

Cassady asks me what I am going to do about replying. But I know I won't be seeing them again. Apart from that, my past doesn't intrude on Grovelands House.

I start to see that for some residents thinking about themselves is no problem at all. They're used to passing exams, forging careers, making sure that their progress through life centres on them and their success. So 'working on yourself', 'taking responsibility for yourself', 'growing', suits the way they've been brought up. The language I find so strange has been part of their thinking from an early age. I've been taught to love my neighbour as myself, to always think of others before me, to see 'success' in worldly terms as something suspect. 'Give up everything you have and follow me.' That cuts deep.

My parents wanted me to have a better life than they had. But having the kind of life they wanted in this place means being a selfish self-centred arsehole. Or at least, in the emotionally charged atmosphere of the House, that's how it seems.

I thought that by coming here I might get care and support, a space to work out who I was and who I could become. I thought I wanted to have the advantages middle-class people have always had, that these would help me, that having the trappings of comfort and prosperity would allow me to heal. That once I was writing and feeling better I could think about where I was going. But I'm not writing at all now. And I just feel angry.

I start to see that 'progress' is complicated.

'I played centre half for the Army,' says Robbie. We're in the pub, and he's walking round the pool table, potting shot after shot, beating the locals with dead-eyed, casual accuracy. I'm sitting next to Becky, eating a packet of cheese and onion and drinking lager. Cerys, who has spent most of the autumn and winter quiet, depressed and dowdy, is now Robbie's girlfriend. It's as if a light has gone on in her – from being a mousy wallflower, she's suddenly perky and punky and pretty. She's in tight jeans and a black leather jacket, her blonde hair has pink streaks in it, and Robbie's wearing a sleeveless green lambswool pullover, blue checked button-down shirt and jeans. His sheepskin jacket hangs off the back of his chair next to Cerys as he strolls around potting all the stripes. Outside it's raining but inside the pub it's boozy and warm.

'I was training to be a Red Cap, a military policeman. Only I didn't fancy the job, didn't fancy it at all. I just wanted to show my old dear I could amount to something. So as soon as I got the cap and the badge and my first posting, I found this directory of army bases. I looked up the place they were sending me and found one that sounded just like it. So I went there instead. I did that about four times till they discharged me.'

Robbie pots a stripe and walks languidly around the table to line up his next shot.

'Playing centre half was fun though. My motto was 'They shall not pass'. After I'd tackled them, a lot of them couldn't.'

He pots the black and says, 'Who's next, gentlemen?'

Robbie's been a heroin addict as well, although you'd never think it to look at him. He's the picture of a tall, lean, strapping Jock. He's originally from Edinburgh, and I remember him in Friern, having a drink in the Turrets, where we used to go towards the end of our section. He told me that one night him and two mates had all OD'd. They ended up in the Royal Free. His two pals died, and Robbie's heart stopped twice. He made it. I think he's haunted by what happened, by the fact that he supplied them with fatal doses of smack, that he lived and they died. But here in Grovelands House he seems to be doing OK.

'Robbie, I'm concerned about you.'

It's the Monday Night Meeting and we're all in the big lounge, round the walls on the lumpy armchairs and sofas.

Dan is giving Robbie the same level-eyed look he's given me. Only he's matching the Look with the kind of tone that means trouble is brewing.

'Oh?' says Robbie. 'What are you concerned about, Dan?'

There is a pause.

Virtually everyone in the House knows what Dan is concerned about. Robbie and Cerys have spent the past month going down to the pub nearly every lunchtime and coming back so drunk they have to help one another along the road.

'I'm concerned that you're abusing the House. That you're dragging Cerys down with you. And that you don't seem to give a fuck.'

There is a lot of swearing in these meetings. People are 'shit-scared'. They are 'pissed off'. And they are told to 'get their fucking shit together'. It heightens the drama of the meetings, but this is different. Dan's never laid into anyone like he's laying into Robbie.

'Do you think I should go then, Dan?' asks Robbie mildly.

Dan doesn't have much room to back down. The one weapon the staff have for keeping us in line – eviction – doesn't bother Robbie. He's already talked about moving on, even though he's only been here a matter of months. Robbie has a completely cavalier attitude to the House, to the ethos, the meetings. I'm not totally sold on it all either, like a lot of us, but Robbie just doesn't care. He's like our spokesman, the rebels' general, the Leader of the Pack. Robbie's been a Red Cap, played centre half for the Army, he has a heart that's stopped twice. Robbie's lived to tell the tale and no one is going to boss him about.

'Yes, Robbie, I think you should go,' drawls Dan.

'Fine,' says Robbie. 'I'll make a few calls in the morning,

pack my bags and be on my way. I've got a friend or two who'll put me up.'

Dan and Robbie's eyes meet across the room. Everyone is quiet. Then Dan looks down at his big marble-backed book, and tells us about the Open Day that's coming up. I look over at Robbie. He winks at me, and grins, and I grin back. But then I see Cerys. She looks shocked. I can't figure out if it's because Robbie's going, or if it's because he's going without a fight.

Either way, the whole House is shaken.

'The trouble with that bloody place is the staff.'

Cerys takes a drag on her fag, a red smoulder glowing down the tip of it. She lets out some of the grey-blue wisps, not blowing, just letting them out, making a dragon's mouth as she does so. The filtered smoke drifts up to the rafters of the Essex Arms, and mingles with smoke from the other daytime drinkers' fags. I've never really heard Cerys talk at any length before and I sit quietly as she opens up.

'They're fascinated by the likes of us, fascinated by madness, by derangement, because we've been there, we've seen heaven and hell, joy and despair. It means we've got dimensions they've never even dreamed of.'

She takes another languorous drag.

'We absolutely fascinate them. The groups – therapy – working on yourself. It's all just crap. They're not trying to help us. No. They want what we've got, but without going through what we've been through. The doors of perception have been wrenched from our hinges. We've seen what no one else has. But they're scared by the thought of that. They want to stay in control, they're too afraid to ever let go, of status, power, comfort. They're turned on by the idea of madness, but they just sink back into their conventional roles, their straight "careers", their schtick. And do you know who's the worst? Dan Cassady. Because he's the one with the power. He wants to be the Good Guy, Mr Laid-back, Mr Cool. But he'll be the first to kick any one of us out if we don't play by his rules. He's the one upholding the status quo, making sure we 'progress'. But progress to what? To everything we're running a mile from, for Christ's sake! Everything that's screwed us up in the first place: crap jobs, a society that's afraid of us, squalid accommodation. He's fascinated, obsessed. But where he sees sickness, I see health. And where he sees insanity, I see wisdom. Dan Cassady is exactly what is wrong with the world. I'd like to open his doors, to just smash them all down.'

Cerys finishes speaking, takes another drag, her face lost in wreaths of smoke. For a moment we are all silent. Robbie's farewell drink is turning into a wake.

'You're right,' he says. 'Who wants their Big Deal? A lousy council flat and a job to match. Keep your nose clean and we'll sort you a life that's not worth living. They're a right bunch of comedians.'

Becky smiles at Robbie.

'A right bunch of bleeding comedians,' she echoes.

'Let's have another drink,' I say. I've had quite a few already but it's not every day someone like Robbie says goodbye. I'll have as many as my giro can buy.

'What are you having?'

'Triple vodka and lime with a Pils chaser,' says Cerys.

'Same for me,' says Robbie. 'I'll be needing a few stiffeners. To help me pot these balls. Just call me Fast Eddie.'

We laugh and I go to the bar.

I look over at Robbie and Cerys. She's looking straight ahead, wreathed in wisps of smoke, short spiky blonde hair, eyes glassier than the bottles she's drinking out of. Robbie's up and playing a last game of pool. The pub is starting to sway.

I pay the barman, walk over to our table and place the drinks on its runny surface.

'The doors!' I say and hoist my pint. That boiling feeling rises in me again, the feeling I had when Becky dragged me all the way down the length of Walthamstow Market. But there's another surge rising up in me as well. Before I can kick-start the Revolution, I'm suddenly fascinated by the bulb of my glass. The whole room is reflected in it, spinning round and round in its translucent curves. I put it down on the table and bend over to take a closer look. As I tilt towards the glass a great giddiness whirls in my stomach. An awful roaring storms at my flung-open, wrenched-off doors.

I fall forward on to the table and pass out.

Robbie moves in with a woman he's met through Polly, the one who knits the shapeless jumpers and shares a room with Polly Fairbairn. He comes back to the House to see Cerys, but he's not the same. He talks to Dan Cassady about Vietnam, about the Army, about having a death wish. Dan is too bemused to know how to respond. I'm shocked, and don't know what to say myself. Because this is what happens if you're not 'committed'. You get chucked out. You end up back where you started.

Or somewhere that's even worse.

'I can't handle this place,' says Richard. 'I'm going back to my mum.'

He darts forward, opening the door of our room quickly. I'm shocked. Robbie's been gone a fortnight, and now Richard wants out as well. Since Robbie left, things haven't been the same. One half of the House think he should have been given another chance. The other half that Dan was right to let him go.

Richard comes back and tells me that he's had a word with

Dan, that he's given in his notice and will be away from all the aggro by the weekend. He says he can feel it building and just wants to go quickly before it all kicks off.

The divisions in the House grow deeper.

Becky and I have come to have a drink with Richard. It's Friday night, and he's leaving in the morning, grinning his rueful grin and flirting with Becky. Becky is enjoying the attention, and she knows she's making me jealous.

'Why don't you like me smoking?' she says to me.

'Because it's bad for you,' I say.

'Well, drinking's bad for you,' she says, 'but I never have a go at you.'

'Drinking's different,' I say.

'How is it different?'

She's raising her voice now, and I'm starting to get wound up.

'Because drink won't give you cancer!'

'Oh, yes, it will,' she says. 'Won't it, Richard?'

Richard holds his hands up. 'I'm staying out of this one,' he says, still grinning.

'So you won't buy me any fags?' she says to me.

'No, I bloody won't!' I say.

By now I'm seething.

Suddenly she lets fly, wallop! right in my face. I'm stung. I can feel my cheek reddening where she's slapped me; anger raging now.

'Right,' I say. 'Please yourselves.'

I stand up and walk out, a terrific roaring in my ears as I stomp every yard of the road back up to the House.

'Seen Becky and Richard?' I ask Edward. He's sitting on his own in the dining room, smoking a cigarette. It's past closing time and they're still not back. I'm hoping they've come in by the side door and that I've missed them.

'Wasn't she with you?' asks Edward.

'We were all out together,' I say. 'You've not seen them then?'

'No,' says Edward. 'Have they eloped?'

'Very funny,' I say. I walk out of the dining room towards my room. I can hear voices from inside. I open the door and there's Richard lying in his bed. He smiles his rueful grin at me. The bed looks odd though. He's just got the sheet over him, and there's a lumpy shape where his legs should be.

I come over and sit on the edge of his bed. On an impulse I pull off the sheet. There is Becky, naked, grinning, sheepish.

I walk out of the room, the roaring back in my ears, my heart in bits.

Cerys comes into the Monday Night Meeting pale and red-eyed.

She sits next to me.

'What's up, Cerys?' I say.

'It's Robbie, John,' she sobs quietly. 'He's dead. An overdose.'

That night in the meeting Paul accuses Cerys, Becky and me of colluding in Robbie's death. He says that if we hadn't gone down the pub with him so much, hadn't allowed ourselves to be sucked into his spiral of self-destruction, hadn't aided and abetted him, hadn't challenged the ethos of the House, he'd still be here now. We just did not show enough commitment.

Perhaps Paul is right. Perhaps it's an easy equation to work out: Pub + Robbie × Heroin = Death. But I think he's forgetting one crucial operation in this tidy little formula. Two dead friends, a father he never knew, the rejection of the whole House.

Because no one spoke up for Robbie, no one questioned the sense in him going.

He just looked so much stronger than the rest of us.

Like he was taking responsibility.

And now Robbie's gone.

VIII

St Mungo's, 1982

The building is on Agar Street, just off the Strand. There are two pillars either side of the entrance and steps leading up to the doors. It was a hospital once, I've been told, a large London hospital, but now it's a hostel for the homeless. It's starting to crumble, any grandeur it may have once had gradually flaking away, like Miss Havisham's wedding cake, flake by flake, crack by crack, knock by knock, the white stucco fading to smudged London grey. For all I know, Miss Havisham is waiting for me inside.

St Mungo's is the only building along the street, and it takes up the whole block. The sight of it, and the few men standing on the steps and hanging around on the pavement in their overcoats and jackets, smoking and eyeing me steadily as I walk towards them, makes me nervous.

I take a deep breath and mount the steps.

Inside it's very gloomy, as if light were scarce here, but I can see that there's a long counter which must be reception on my right and a large stairway further back leading up to the old hospital wards. I go up to the counter.

'Do you have any beds, please?'

A man with long hair, aged about thirty-five, looks at me, sizing me up.

'What's your story, then?'

Thinking carefully, I tell him.

*

The digs are poky. I share a room with Steve, a tall Mancunian, in a cramped terraced house in Walthamstow. An Irish family owns it, and the son, Arthur, looks after the property. When I come back from the shops, Steve's in the lounge, watching the telly.

'Hello, mate. Do you want a brew?' he says.

'No thanks, Steve,' I say. I've been chucked out of Grovelands House. Becky and I couldn't stop rowing. About Richard, about being together, about the weather – it didn't take much to set us off. Dan Cassady gave us an ultimatum: one of us had to go. It's good of Steve to take me in. But I'm not in a good way. I think of Robbie, of what Paul said, 'You could have prevented his death. But instead you chose to collude with him.' Sometimes I think he may be right. Robbie had so much to live for. He was tall, handsome, funny. I've been to confession, the first time in a year, St George's, Shernhall Street, not far from the digs. A very nice Irish priest. I think I'm being punished for my sins, that God doesn't approve of the way I treated my mother, of the way I've treated Becky, of the part I played in Robbie's death. But I've read something in a book, and it makes me think. 'There is no sin in love.' I loved my mother, I loved Robbie, and I think I love Becky, but sometimes I burn with jealousy and anger. The Church says that if I repent I'll be forgiven. And I do repent, but should I repent of love? But was it love when I broke up my mother and me, when I slept with Becky, when I got drunk with Robbie and Cerys?

'You all right, mate?' says Steve.

The room we share has four TVs in it. Steve repairs TVs. He knows how to fix them. But who's going to fix what I've done? Who's ever going to put things right? What act of contrition, of redemption, of reconciliation, would ever make things up to my mother, to Robbie's mother, to God?

'I'm OK, Steve. I think I need a lie down.'

'Yeah ... OK, John. Don't forget about your B1 and your B1C, will you, mate?'

I haven't sorted out my claim at the dole office. But it's the last thing I want to think about.

Robbie, leaning on his broom. Potting all the stripes. Laughing at his troubles.

'A right bunch of comedians.'

'See you, Steve,' I say, and I go to the room. My heart is big and hard and sore in my chest. It's the kind of sore that feels like it might never go away.

I take out all my notebooks and the folder of poems I'd written in Friern. What's the point of poetry? One by one I rip all the exercise books, all the poems, to shreds.

Arthur comes into the room. He wants his rent. But I don't have it. Why should I care about rent? All I can think about is Robbie, what I should have done, how I should have helped him. I couldn't even go to his funeral.

My mother's funeral, Robbie's.

I go round in a daze.

What good have I been to anyone?

Bradwell-on-Sea is about sixty miles away from Walthamstow. I went there once on a school trip, to an ecumenical community called Othona, run by a young vicar and his wife. I was happy there. I looked after a liquid-eyed Jersey cow, mucked out her cow shed, talked to her, told her how lovely she was. She had the highest milk yield that weekend. She rubbed her neck against my thigh when I came to say goodbye to her on the Sunday. But now Daisy is gone, slaughtered, eaten, and there are only German boys at Othona, the few Nissen huts near the ancient chapel full of them. The young vicar and his wife are away. I've walked the sixty miles for nothing.

The bleakness of Bradwell, just inland from the Essex coast, is hard to bear. The chapel is empty and cold, as if God has forsaken it. I set out to walk the sixty miles back. But the police find me on the long, hard, grey road. They drive me all the way to Walthamstow where John Knight comes to meet me in his new car. Everyone has been worried about me. And Steve is livid. What was I playing at? Didn't I think about anyone else? Next time, tell someone.

But there won't be a next time.

Arthur's had enough.

I'm out.

I walk the long grey roads of London, Leyton High Road, Whitechapel Road, Bishopsgate, the dense rush-hour streets of the City, trudge along Lower Thames Street, Upper Thames Street, until I come at last to the Embankment.

It's about nine o'clock when I arrive. The river is lit up, the fairy lights of the South Bank twinkling across the water. I walk through the station to the Villiers Street side. On my left are the shadowy shapes of people sleeping under the railway bridge on cold hard ground, some of them in cardboard boxes. It's got to be better than the derelict buildings I've tried to sleep in, the odd park bench, even one night the grounds of Whipps Cross. There are others here, others who are sleeping out, and I feel too weary to go any further. Where is there to go?

I wander over and take my place at the end of the huddled sleepers. There must be at least thirty of them. The upright world of late night revellers continuing on their way home, dashing through the station to catch the last trains, turns without us. I'm part now of a different world. My comrades have fallen as low as you can go.

I shiver a bit and some of the people sleeping out start talking to each other, about handouts, characters they know, where there might be work in the morning. It goes quiet for a while and then the vans come. First a soup van, then a little later a van giving out hot vegetarian stew, then a van looking for people to go off with them. I'm not sure about this last lot so I stay where I am. But they give me a couple of blankets and I thank them.

The vans are at least a distraction. I try to sleep under the blankets, but it's no good. I'm in a grey state, worried about the people lying on the hard ground a few feet away, afraid they might attack me, too cold to drift off, happy just to get a rest until daylight starts everything up again.

At 6 a.m. I rise and walk over to the Tube entrance. As I look up Villiers Street from the station, I see that it's still lit from the night before, or maybe it's just lighting up for the commuters coming in to the West End. It's a prospect of neon and bustle and pale cold morning light and though I'm there watching it all, taking it all in, I'm aware that I'm not part of it any more, that I'm beyond the commuters and the shop owners and the office workers.

I'm homeless.

It's a big feeling, being homeless. I'm free, free from responsibility, from B1s and B1Cs, from routine and convention, from my past and my problems, free of my memories.

But I'm not.

I'm not free at all.

I go to the Samaritans one Sunday afternoon, as much for company as for anything else. I've got just enough sense to realize that I can't last sleeping out on the Embankment. They tell me about St Mungo's and give me the address. I set off hoping I won't have to spend another night out under the stars.

But I don't really care any more.

The stars can have me if St Mungo's won't. The stars and the heavens above.

*

The man on reception looks at me.

'A likely story,' he says. 'We've had them all here. Tell you what I'm going to do. I'll book you in for tonight, then in the morning you come down and see us and we'll sort you out for Scarborough Fair. You're in Bed 105. Breakfast is at 7.30 a.m., and you report to reception at 8 a.m. You got that?'

I nod.

'Well, what are you waiting for? Bed 105 is up there.'

He points to the large stairway and I set off to find where I'll be sleeping tonight.

The stairs are inlaid with white mosaic tiles, each about a quarter of an inch square. It must have been a magnificent staircase in its time, during the Blitz, perhaps, or the fifties, but now there's dirt between each tiny tile, and as I mount the steps, gripping the balustrade, I'm aware also of a smell, a smell of mank and decay.

I reach the first floor. There's a narrow landing shrouded in gloom ahead of me and to my right is a large ward like a dormitory, lit by a bare electric bulb, with just the door frame where the doors once were, now open to whoever might want to see inside. There are two rows of hospital beds facing each other against the long walls of the ward, walls that were white once but are now stained a dull sludge. There are men standing, men lying on the beds, some talking, a few turned to look at me.

'I'm looking for Bed 105,' I say.

'In there, son,' says a tough-looking Scotsman in his forties. He's closest to the entrance, lying on his bed reading a paper. Beside each bed is a locker. There's no privacy at all.

I walk back a short way along the gloomy landing to another ward. This one has a blanket pinned up across its entrance. The numbers of the beds – 100–106 – have been scrawled in marker pen on the wall beside the blanket. I pull it back and say, 'I'm looking for Bed 105.'

The room is very different from the larger ward. There's a red light throwing a ruby glow over everything, and the ward is much smaller, with only six beds. As my eyes get used to the colour, I can see that there are three men in the room. Two are ferreting around in their lockers, one nearest the entrance on my right, one opposite him on my left. The other man is lying on top of his bed. He raises his head and takes a look at me.

'Here you are, son,' he says in a Scouse accent. He throws out his left arm as if to introduce a turn at the Palladium and not Bed 105. He's a small, spry man, with white hair and a face with more lines than the London Underground. I see that he's got a bottle of cheap ruby wine, and that he's a bit tipsy. The other two men look up from what they're doing to check me out. The man on the right of the blanket is black, tall, athletic-looking, and he nods as I enter the ward. The other man is white, forty-ish, in a cheap black leather car coat. He scowls as I pass him, and I walk towards the empty bed and sit down.

'Have you been skippering, Captain?'

I turn to the man with the Scouse accent. He's small, about five feet two. The ruby wine is like a large baby's bottle in his little gnarled hands.

'Skippering?'

'Yeah – you know: sleeping in a derry?'

He takes a swig from the bottle and screws the top back on to it.

I guess that 'derry' means a derelict building.

'I was,' I say. 'But I'm here now, thank God.'

'Thank the Blessed Lord,' he says, slurring the words, his eyes full of moonshine. 'And the Blessed St James. And are you off to Scarborough Fair?'

'I am,' I say. 'They want me to go there in the morning. What is Scarborough Fair?'

'It's the Brew, Captain, the Bank Manager, the Old King Cole.'

'What?'

I'm completely mystified.

'He means the dole,' says the black man. 'Scarborough Fair is the dole office for people who are NFA.'

'Parsley, sage, rosemary and thyme,' sings the little Scouser on the bed.

I'm still confused.

'NFA – No Fixed Abode,' says the black man. 'You might have a roof over your head, but the law still classes you as homeless.'

'The law is an ass,' snarls a tall, gaunt figure who appears at the entrance to the ward in an overcoat belted with string, leaning on a walking stick as he comes in. His hair is grey and long and greasy, and he's wearing glasses. There's a sticking plaster holding the frame together, and he could be any age from fifty to seventy-five.

'Our Irish friend will be in shortly,' he growls. 'And if he fucking tries any more funny business with me, he'll get my stick across his head!'

'Steady as she goes, Captain,' says the little man. 'No need for a punch-up. Remember the Good Book, and the words of the Lord: If your enemy smites you upon the cheek, turn the other cheek.'

'And what do you do if he smites you upon the nose? Turn the other fucking nose?'

His magnified eyes fall on me.

'You're new, aren't you?' he says. 'I bet you that bastard on reception wanted your whole fucking life story before he let you in?'

I think of the man on reception. It seems a bit odd, getting a roof over your head by telling someone a story. I nod to the man, and he scowls. He comes over and stands by his bed, and lays his walking stick at the far end of it. The black man takes out a wash bag from his locker and leaves the ward.

'My name is Robert Haines,' says the tall, gaunt man. 'You may have heard of me? I did some television adverts in the fifties and trod the boards in rep?'

I look blank.

'Never mind. I can see that it was before your time. And have you met Joey?'

'I've just piped him aboard, Captain.'

'Joey was in the Merchant Navy, you know.'

'Oh, aye, Captain. I was only the galley boy, like, but I did sail the Seven Seas.'

'Welcome, anyway. But watch out for the Irishman. He's a conniving bastard who would steal your eyes and sell them for drink.'

Robert Haines lies on his bed, and the ward starts to settle down. I notice that he's said nothing about the man in the leather car coat, or the black man who popped out with his wash bag. I guess that he's wary of them both, that his aggression is a show to protect himself.

The sheets are clean and cool as I get into them. I'm dead beat and fall asleep before the Irishman, whoever he is, gets back. There's a long day ahead of me and I sleep soundly for the first time in a week.

I can smell the porridge as I come down the stairs. Men already in overcoats are coming up them and edge past me as I make my way to breakfast in the basement of St Mungo's. I come to the bottom of the stairs and follow the smell. There's a corridor with three metal food trolleys ahead, all lined up in a row, loaded with bowls and cups and saucers and slop basins full of leftovers, grey lumpy-looking splodges of porridge, slices of white bread and marge, tinned tomatoes, the odd bit of gristle. A serving hatch set into the wall just beyond the trolleys is still open and a balding, white-haired man with rolled-up shirt sleeves is bustling about, a tea towel slung over his shoulder, a tinny radio playing as he puts away a stack of plates in a steel sideboard.

'Excuse me,' I say.

He slides the doors of the steel sideboard to and turns round.

'And what do you want?' he says.

'Is there any chance of some breakfast?' I say.

'No chance at all,' he says, standing up. 'Breakfast is finished.'

'Oh,' I say.

We look at each for a moment, then I walk off.

'Who do you think you are?' he shouts after me. 'Prince Fucking Charming?'

I go back upstairs to reception. His taunt follows me up to the ground floor, like bats released from some dark cellar below. There's a different man on this morning, a dark-haired wiry Scot with a pencil-thin moustache.

'I'm new,' I say. 'I came in last night.'

He reaches under the counter and pulls out a brown envelope.

'Take this to Scarborough Street,' he says. 'The nearest Tube's Aldgate East.'

'How do I get there?' I say.

'How did you get here?'

'I walked,' I say.

'You'd better start now then, son,' he says. 'We'll keep your bed for you till six o'clock. If you're not back by then we'll have to give it to someone else.'

'Parsley, sage, rosemary and thyme.'

I look around. It's Joey, wearing a flat tweed cap and a thin navy blue raincoat.

'Off to Scarborough Fair, lad?'

'Yes,' I say.

'Try going via St Martin-in-the-Fields,' he says. 'If you ask them nicely, they might give you a bus ticket that'll take you all the way there.'

I thank him for the tip and follow his directions to St Martin-in-the-Fields' Social Services Unit. It's beside the church, down some steps in front of the vicarage. There's a queue when I arrive, about fifteen of us, all men, all waiting for the door ahead to open. We don't have long. After about ten minutes a young man with a light ginger beard and Dr Martens lets us in.

Most of the men know what they're doing. They all head off to a room where there are easy chairs and a set of bookshelves with board games and books, and some pictures hanging on the wall. I must look a bit confused because the man with the light ginger beard and Dr Martens comes up to me and asks if I'm new here. I tell him that I am, and that I need a bus ticket to Scarborough Street.

'Come into the office,' he says. 'My name's Tom. What's yours?'

I tell him as he leads me down a short hallway to an office at the end. We sit either side of his desk and he asks me some questions and fills out a form.

'We're here if you need us,' he says. He gives me a brown bus ticket, very different to the tickets on London Transport, and I say goodbye. I cross back over to the Strand and wait for a bus. Although the clock is ticking down to six o'clock it's only about half past nine, and I know I can easily make it back to St Mungo's before they give my bed away. I feel a sense of freedom – I'm not dashing off to work like the rest of London, and I'm not doing some job I can't stand. But underneath it all, there's anxiety.

Just what am I going to do?

A Number 15 bus pulls up and I hop on. I go upstairs and try not to think about that missed breakfast as I gaze out of the window. Watery spring sunlight falls on London, illuminating the plane trees and the roads full of traffic, the grimy grey buildings, the glitter of shops and arcades, the signs and the lights and the zebra crossings, the churches and the pubs, the statues of statesmen and soldiers, the small parks and railings and blocks of mansion flats, and soon we are leaving behind the West End, the Aldwych, Fleet Street and St Paul's, and meaner streets lie ahead.

Aldgate East looms up through the window and I run downstairs and jump off the bus.

The Supplementary Benefit Office looks like it might be any other light industrial unit in the heart of the East End. Inside they could be making saris or shirts or leather jackets. The small building could have passed from Jewish owners to Asian newcomers. It could be a hive of industry and purpose.

When I walk inside it's none of that. Small crews of drinkers, sherry bottles in hand, are getting steamed and the air is a thick fog of roll-up smoke. The leering threat of violence hangs in the air as well, like thunder building. There are about a hundred men altogether, rough and scruffy, some of them stewed already, and I join a queue near the door. The line of men edges towards a bolted-down stool and a reinforced glass screen, one of about five against the wall on my right. I don't want any hassle so I keep my head down, not meeting anyone's eye, just wanting to get it over with and away again. There's a blonde woman in her thirties behind the screen and she's interviewing the man at the front of the queue. I look around.

'Hey, you! Yes, you, sonny! Have you got anything for me?'

He's Scottish, part of a gang passing around the red biddy, in a grey overcoat opened at the waist, fat and bald, but with his mates as bold as he likes. Before I can say anything he comes over and his hands go quickly through my pockets.

'You haven't a bean,' he says. 'And I thought you were an eccentric millionaire come to give us all a fiver!'

His mates laugh and he walks back over to them. The queue moves forward and I turn my back on him and his drinking buddies. What can I do? There are five of them. But now I'm on edge.

The queue moves forward again and another man takes the place of the one before him on the stool. My stomach starts to gnaw at me, hunger and fear butterflying around my insides. We lurch forward slowly, each man getting about ten minutes. At last my turn comes. The blonde woman takes the letter from St Mungo's and asks me if I've ever thought of trying Arlington House.

'A lot of our gentlemen like it there,' she says.

That word – gentlemen – is a mark of tender courtesy in this grim bunker of a place. I thank her for the suggestion, but tell her that I'll stick with where I am. She asks me to wait, that my name will be called when a giro has been made out for me. I thank her and pass back out into the crowd of men.

My stomach is still gnawing away at me. The hunger is making me giddy but I reckon I shouldn't have too long to wait. I look at the clock by the payout window. It's eleven o'clock.

Plenty of time.

*

I still haven't been called. It's four o'clock now and I'm getting really wound up. If they don't sort me out soon I won't have time to cash my giro, get something to eat – I'm starving now – and make my way back to St Mungo's by six.

There are about fifteen of us left in the office. Each of us is wired. Some patrol up and down, burning off their nervous energy by walking from wall to wall and back again. Some are sitting down on the stools in front of the glass screens, waiting it out. Some, like me, just stand around near the clock, watching the long hand sweep the seconds away until our names are called.

At last my turn comes. It's 4.30 p.m., and I sign for the giro and hurry off to the Post Office in Aldgate to cash it. There's not much of a queue and I don't have to wait long, but by the time I get my money it's 4.50 p.m. There's a bakery over the way and I cut across the busy road and step inside. They sell chocolate éclairs, and I buy four of them. I make my way to the bus stop just as a Number 15 is pulling in and pay for a ticket back to the Strand. I run upstairs with my box of éclairs and settle myself in the front seat on the right. One by one I eat them, a feast of choux pastry, sticky chocolate and fresh cream. They are glorious and I devour every last sweet flaky crumb.

'You made it then?'

The Scotsman with the pencil-thin moustache is still on reception.

'Just about,' I say.

It's 5.45 p.m. Another fifteen minutes and I'd be sleeping out again.

'All right,' he says. 'Let's book you in then.'

I hand over my rent for a week, and sign the register.

'You've another new boy in beside you,' he says. 'You might want to watch out for him. He's a big lad.'

'Thanks,' I say. I go up to the ward and pull back the curtain. A fat burly man with a small moustache and a flat cap is standing by his bed. He's taking some clothes out of a holdall and putting them into his locker. His bed is right at the end of the ward, opposite mine.

'Hello,' I say.

He turns round and squints at me through narrow eyes.

'Hello, la'. Name's Chopper. If I look hard it's because I am. Used to be a bouncer. I'm still partial to chucking the odd muppet off the nearest wall, just to see if they rebound.'

He's big, another Scouser, about thirty-five, but he's too fat to be that hard. Still, it's been a long day and I just want to take it easy.

'There's nobody with too much bounce in here,' I say. 'I think it's what they put in the tea.'

Chopper snorts, a grin spreading across his fat face.

'Are you not getting it regular then, la'?'

'It's a long story,' I say. 'What about you? You looking for work down here?'

The curtain over the door opens and a young girl stands in the doorway.

'Good evening, gentlemen,' she says. She has a Kerry accent, and is aged about twenty, I reckon, with green eyes and blonde hair. She's the first woman I've seen in the place. 'Don't forget – we change the sheets tonight. You'll find fresh ones in the basement. My name's Siobhan, by the way, Siobhan Ferry.'

'I'm Dr Livingstone and this is Stanley,' says Chopper. 'We were lost in darkest Africa and seem to have taken a wrong turning. Perhaps you can point us in the right direction?'

Siobhan smiles.

'You'll find all you need in the basement, lads. Take it easy, now.'

She ducks back out through the curtains.

'Not my type,' says Chopper when she's out of earshot. 'But you might be in with a chance, la'.'

'I've got a girlfriend,' I say.

I go over to my bed and strip the sheets before he can ask me any awkward questions. Now that I've got some money I can phone Becky from the call box round the corner. I'll tell her I'm safe and ask her how she's doing.

And perhaps she'll tell me she's doing OK.

I've never been in this part of London before. The houses look very grand, long streets and squares of white stucco-fronted townhouses. They even have steps going up to the doors, and pillars. I turn into a quiet square and come to a large villa. I take a deep breath, mount the steps, and ring the bell.

The door opens. Becky stands in the hallway, light spilling out on to the darkening street. She looks a bit worried, but lets me in.

'This way,' she says. She takes me along to the kitchen, just off the hallway.

'Do you want a cup of tea?' she says.

'Yes, please.'

We look at each other, then fall into each other's arms. For a moment, everything's just as it's always been. When we stand apart again, though, there's sadness between us.

Sadness and guilt.

The Chailey Community House in Ealing is Becky's new home. I go to see her every weekend. She's already been in a big London hostel herself, Regent Towers in the East End. That's where they put her before her social worker found her this place.

There's a man called Des in the House and he doesn't like

me. One night I find out why. Becky keeps a diary of sorts on scraps of paper. Some are on her bedside cabinet and while she goes to the loo I take a quick peek at them. One catches my eye. *Slept with Des*, it says.

I'm hurt but I can't blame her. After all, he's doing piece-work, bringing in a few bob. But who am I to Becky?

I'm just someone whose life is spiralling downwards.

'You're going to do me a favour, la'.'

'Oh, yes?' I say. 'And what's that?'

It's Sunday morning and I've just come back from Ealing. Chopper is lying in the bed opposite me. He's turned bright yellow, his squinty eyes and fat belly making him look like a sick Buddha. There's a bucket by his bed, the smell of vomit hanging in the air.

'You're covering for me at the Caprice.'

'I am?'

'Yes, la'.'

'I don't know about that—' I start to say.

'You are, you know. Because if you don't, when I get better, I'm going to batter you to bits.'

I think about it for a moment. I could do with the money. I could take Becky out at least. And working at the Caprice will save me some aggro.

'OK,' I say. 'But what's up with you?'

I'm worrying that what he's got is infectious.

'Hepatitis. I caught it off the tart whose piss I drank on Friday night. Any more questions?'

Le Caprice lies at the back of the Ritz. The shifts I have to work run from 10 a.m. to 3 p.m. and from 6 p.m. to finish. It's up the road from St Mungo's, about a mile or so away on Regent Street. The Head Chef is called Jules Debord, an amiable

Frenchman in his mid-thirties. I'm on the pot wash, which means I get to do all the saucepans and the heavier vessels used in the kitchen.

There's another lad who does the plate wash, which is a lot easier, as they all go into a machine, a big industrial dishwasher, the Hobart. He stacks them on blue plastic trays which he slides into the guts of it. As it slooshes away he stands around and I think of what it must be like to have his job. It's about 8 p.m., and service is starting to go into overdrive as the covers for dinner arrive and the orders come in.

'You see this fork?'

The Maître d' stands in front of me and holds up a fork inches from my face.

'Well, I need all of them, like yesterday.'

He throws the fork down on the drainer by my sinks – there are two of them, side by side – and marches off. There's a load of cutlery all jammed into a blue plastic rack on the drainer, which is piled up with pots and pans, and I stop what I'm doing – scouring out a large saucepan – and grab a handful of forks from the rack. I dunk them in the hot soapy water and wash all of the food off. My water turns gooey but I get them all done quickly, and then rinse and dry them with paper from the dispenser, ripping great curls out of it as I polish the cutlery till it all gleams. I head off to find the Maître d' and give him his forks. He's talking to Jules.

'Excuse me,' I say. He turns round and looks at me as if I stink. He tells me to place the cutlery in a large sideboard beyond the pass and walks off.

As I trudge back to my station, a tall blond Belgian commis chef comes over and drops a pot into my water. He turns on the hot tap and lets it run. The commis hasn't said a thing to me and I don't know if he wants me to leave the tap running or not. So I plunge my hands down into the hot water of the other sink and grab a green wiry scourer from its greasy depths. I start scrubbing one of the pots I've left soaking.

The tap runs and runs but the commis says nothing. I look over at him a few times, but the pots are flying in like mortar shells landing in my dugout and I have to clear them before I'm sunk by incoming. It's the hardest work I've ever done, hot, steamy, fast, knackering. There's one perk, though – I put the pot Jules has used to make *sauce champignoise* to one side on the drainer. During quick breaks in the slog of potscrubbing I scoop out the sauce with my bare hand and lick it, like Pooh Bear with a honeypot. It's delicious, light and creamy, with hints of white wine and a delicate mushroom taste.

I get my head down and work like crazy scrubbing and scouring. There's heat and noise everywhere, as grills and pans suddenly ignite, pots and pans clatter on the hotplates, and a kind of controlled panic breaks out in the kitchen. Jules is shouting and waiters are flying in and out, kicking the two little half-doors that lead from the grills to the floor of the restaurant. I watch one practically sprint through the half-doors, plates in both hands.

For a split second I can see out on to the floor of the restaurant. I look straight into the eyes of a chanteuse whose record is in the Top Ten. She looks straight back into mine. The half-doors flap shut again and the moment is gone.

'It's not bad money, but they stopped some of my pay at the end of the week.'

I'm in a phone box on Regent Street. I'm calling Cerys. She's left Grovelands House and moved into a flat in Catford with Winston. I want to go and see them, to get away from the West End for a bit.

'Oh, because I ran out of hot water one night. A stupid Belgian commis left the tap running and at the end of the evening there wasn't enough hot water to get all of the pots done. But I still got them done the next day. No, I don't think it's fair either. Anyway, I'm out of there now. Becky? Becky's ... fine.'

Chopper is lying on his bed. He's still a bit yellow but he's been back at Le Caprice for about a week.

'That bastard Jimmy Douglas is going to get a pasting from me,' he says. Jimmy Douglas is the son of Johnny Douglas, who manages the hostel. He's a Scotsman in his late forties or early fifties and Jimmy's in his twenties.

'What's up, Chopper?' I say.

'Never you mind, la',' he says. 'Never you mind.'

I'm in the big TV room. The news is on and there are about twenty of us watching it. Mrs Thatcher has ordered the Task Force to set sail for the Falklands. We watch the fleet set off, the crowds along the quayside waving at their sweethearts, their sons, their husbands, their fathers.

'Can't see them winning, can you, Captain?'

Joey is sitting in front of me, an old seadog with the scent of salt spray still in his nostrils. He's talking to a man I've seen at breakfast, sandy hair, stocky, Scottish, wearing a neat grey suit.

'Who's that, Joey? The Argentinians, or this lot?' he says.

'The Argentinians, Captain. They'll be smashed to smithereens.'

'That'll make a nice change, Joey,' says the man.

'A change, Captain?'

'From smashing everyone else who gets in her way.'

The door to St Martin-in-the-Fields' Social Services Unit opens and the early evening crowd all move forward. There are about ten of us and I'm first in the queue. I've come for a pork pie, a cup of coffee, and a bus ticket. Between the soup kitchen in the Crypt on Sunday morning, the Folk Club on

Sunday nights, the Day Centre during the week and the hand-outs every weekday evening, I've become a bit of a fixture. I'm one of their youngest clients, one of their regulars. Two sisters about my own age, Moira and Isla Macpherson, have taken a special shine to me. They dole out the soup on Sunday morning before singing in the choir and running the Folk Club in the evening. I feel like they've adopted me as a kind of mascot. They call me 'John the Poet', and I read them my poems in the Marquis of Granby and sing the odd song at the Folk Club. It says a lot about them that they treat me like they'd treat anyone else. They make me feel like I'm one of the gang. I might live in the Big House, as they call it in St Mungo's, but I never feel like there's a huge distance between the Macpherson sisters and me. If I didn't have the scene at St Martin-in-the-Fields and Becky at weekends, I'd probably crack up.

I go into the office, the same office where I first saw Tom. There's a thin man I've seen round the church before, with ginger hair and a ginger beard.

'What can I do for you?' he asks.

'My giro's run out,' I say. 'I was wondering if I could get a pork pie and a cup of coffee, and possibly a bus ticket?'

He opens a file, then looks up at me.

'Don't you think you've had enough from us, John? Don't you think it's time you tried to make a go of it on your own?'

It's the Knockback. It comes to everyone. It's an occupational hazard, like indigestion for shiftworkers, or hepatitis for tarts.

I walk out of the office and back to St Mungo's, hoping Joey might be around.

'Look lively, Captain – she's coming.'

Joey parts the curtain and slips quickly into the ward. Before I can move, Siobhan is standing there.

'There's a casual going at the Charing Cross Hotel,' she says. 'Six to midnight. Do either of you lads fancy it?'

There's only Joey and me in the ward, and Joey isn't keen. I'm not that fussed either.

'Ah, no,' says Joey. 'Thanks all the same, like. Only I get very bad rheumatism off the steam, and I was off to Tooley Street tonight anyhow.'

'What about you, John?' Siobhan turns to me.

'Can't,' I say, looking sheepish.

'Why not?' she says.

'I'm going to Tooley Street with Joey.'

Siobhan flushes.

'So you'd sooner go to some old handout for your supper than get out and work for it?'

'That's about the size of it, Siobhan,' I say, reddening myself. 'Ever slaved away in a hot busy kitchen?'

Siobhan looks at me, then turns on her heel and disappears back through the curtain.

Darkness is falling as we cross Waterloo Bridge. A cold breeze comes off the river, and the lights of the South Bank ooze into the water like burst baubles.

'I'm starving,' I say. I haven't eaten anything except breakfast for the past two days.

'Nearly there, lad,' says Joey.

'Do you think there'll be a lot at it?' I ask.

'Oh, aye, Captain,' says Joey. 'You can't do much better than Tooley Street.'

We turn a corner and I see a long shadowy queue of men lining up before the railings of a church. As we get closer a figure at the end of the line turns and nods to Joey.

'Aye aye, Captain,' says Joey. 'How've you been?'

'Not bad,' says the silhouetted man. 'Who's the boy?'

'He's new, Captain,' says Joey. 'Just showing him the ropes.'

The man gives me the same nod he gave Joey. Up ahead, the chain holding the gates together rattles as it snakes through the rails and the queue marches forward.

'Brethren, we have all sinned. But tonight I want to preach to you the gospel of God's love. Because God loves each and every one of you very much and He wants you to return to Him. He wants to forgive you your sins. He wants you to start afresh. To give up your old ways. Oh, there will be those amongst you who will scoff. Who will try to belittle what I'm telling you. Who will sneer. But when you leave here tonight, I want you to think about what I've said, about what God is offering. The chance to lead a better life. Because you cannot do it on your own. You need God's grace.'

We're sat near the back of the draughty church hall next to the man who nodded to us. Rows of overcoated men sit on chairs with a narrow aisle up the middle of their ranks. A fat man in a grey suit stands at the head of us all, brandishing a Bible. Everyone listens in silence. A smell of cooking wafts across the hall.

'I want you to consider in your hearts what I've been saying here tonight. I want you to take away with you God's message of love and forgiveness. I want you to come to Him in all your worthlessness and despair and ask Him humbly to take your burdens from your shoulders. 'Come to me all you who are heavily laden and I shall give you rest.' That is the Lord's promise. That is what He will do for you.'

I catch the fat man's eye and quickly look away. The smell of food is making my mouth water.

'We will all now stand and sing hymn number 132 in your hymn books.'

We all stand up and take out the hymn books from recesses in the back of the chairs. I turn to look at Joey. He sings the hymn all the way through, not bothering to look at his book, which he holds upside down. Everyone sings loudly. When we finish there is a hush in my ears as the sound of fifty men singing gives way to sudden silence.

'Right,' says the fat man. 'Lift the hatch.'

A bolt shoots back and a hatch in the wall behind the fat man flies up, rattling as it goes. The men all rise from their seats and make for the front. They crowd round the hatch, collect their meals, and walk away, eating in silence. Our turn comes.

A white-haired lady in a yellow nylon overall stands behind the aluminium counter framed in the hatch's tight square. Paper plates of sausage roll, mash and beans lie before us. Joey picks his up and asks for a knife and fork. The white-haired lady frowns as she gives him the plastic cutlery, and does the same with me when it's my turn. Some of the men have already finished their plates now and return to the hatch as we move off with ours. The white-haired lady pours out tea from a metal tea urn into blue plastic mugs, and the men thank her as she fills them up.

'Well, Captain,' says Joey. 'What do you think of it? Not bad, eh?'

We stand together by the far wall eating, and I can see that Joey's gnarled face is seeking approval, reassurance from me.

'No, Joey,' I say between mouthfuls. 'Not bad at all.'

We finish up, chuck our plates and cutlery in a black plastic dustbin by the hatch, and collect our mugs of tea. We go over and sit on a pair of chairs to drink them down. The tea's hot and sweet and takes the taste of the packet mash away.

'Hello, I haven't seen you here before. Are you new?'

I turn round to see the fat man in the grey suit standing over me. I nod between swigs from my mug, wishing I hadn't caught his eye earlier.

'Perhaps you'd like to come to tea tomorrow at the vicarage?'

I hesitate.

'Oh, the lad would like that very much, Captain, very much indeed.'

He looks at Joey, then at me, and I can see he's trying to figure the pair of us out.

'Come at four,' he says. 'Here's something to read until then.'

He hands me a leaflet which looks like the Highway Code. It's got a green motorway sign on it and is called 'Journey Into Life'.

'Thank you,' I say, taking the leaflet.

'Until tomorrow,' he says, and walks away to talk to the white-haired lady behind the serving hatch.

'You're in there,' says Joey. 'Tea with the vicar! You could be meeting the Archbishop of Canterbury next! Come on, lad. We'd best be going.'

On the way back to St Mungo's I say nothing to Joey about the vicarage I stayed in before I was fostered. I'm thinking instead about whether there might be another casual in the morning. Because I need to see Cerys and Winston. I need to get out of St Mungo's, away from the West End, from handouts and hotel kitchens and weekends where I'm having to play cat and mouse with Des and wondering if Becky and I can ever make a real go of it. Unemployment has risen to 3 million. The out of work and the homeless are everywhere. Where is the England I was brought up in? Something is happening to the country and no one seems to know how to stop it.

The darkness deepens as we come to St Mungo's and I

wonder if Joey has a bottle in his pocket. I hope he has and that I can forget for a while where I am, and who I am, and what I'm doing here at all. I want to get drunk and sleep and never wake up.

IX

New Cross, Spring 1983

'I can't really cope there any more.'

The young housing worker looks at me. I'm sat across yet another desk, asking someone I've never met before to help me sort my life out. The Patchwork offices are in Islington, a short bus ride on the Number 38 from St Mungo's.

'Just a minute,' she says. She gets up and leaves the room. While she's gone I look at what she's been writing about me on the application form lying on her desk. *Severely depressed*. I hear her footsteps coming and I turn the form back the way it was.

'I think there might be something for you,' she says. 'South of the river. Could you move in this weekend?'

I'd been in St Mungo's six months. I started to get seriously depressed, as if I'd fallen into a big black hole. If I looked ahead, there was only darkness. If I looked behind, darkness. I lay in my bed for three days. I didn't care any more. The world could turn without me. I thought about pills, and where I could get enough to do away with myself. I had ended up in this hell as a punishment. Where were Becky and I going? Nowhere. I was dragging her down with me, down into a squalid world of halfway houses, hostels, homelessness. I'd not known what to do when my father lay dying. I'd ruined my mother's life, and I hadn't been able to save Robbie. Christ! What was I born for at all? In the depths of it all, as all of their faces revolved in my mind, laughing, crying, pleading, looking at me with reproach in their eyes, with sorrow and sadness, I thought of a way to end it all.

There were two routes out of the Big House. One was Patchwork, a housing association that had properties all over London. The other was a hostel St Mungo's ran out near Olympia, with an ex-policeman in charge. It housed young men like myself. I hated the thought of being sent to a place that needed an ex-policeman to run it. But St Mungo's wouldn't even consider me for Patchwork. They wanted to send me to the hostel instead. As soon as a vacancy came up, I'd be off.

I'd been a fool. I'd adapted too easily to life in St Mungo's instead of looking beyond it. The weekly trips to Scarborough Street, the giros that never lasted me four days let alone seven, the casuals in hotels and restaurants, the handouts and the soup vans down by the Embankment, the Crypt of St Martin-in-the-Fields, the Day Centre, even the Folk Club and the trips to Becky – I'd sunk so low my horizons were subterranean. And what lay ahead? I bet that policeman believed in cold showers and short sharp shocks. I'd had enough shocks to last.

After three days I got out of my bed and went to the Patchwork offices myself. Soon after, I left the West End one warm Saturday in a van driven by Siobhan Ferry.

I was off to New Cross.

'It's nice here.'

Becky stands in the kitchen, wearing jeans and a cotton granddad shirt, its narrow blue and white stripes reminding me a little of a nurse's uniform. The house in Casella Road is a tall Victorian villa, on three floors, and I have a small room overlooking the garden on the top floor. I share the place with Nick and his French girlfriend. Nick is tall and well built, with dark hair and eyes so blue they could be neon. He has a Beetle Convertible and is always playing with his Zippo lighter. She's as lanky as a model, wispy in cotton dresses, with long blonde hair and a scatter of freckles across the bridge of her dinky nose. I call her Fifi and I have a nickname for him as well. I call him Mr Atlas but not to his face.

'We could ask if Patchwork would let you stay with me? That's if you wanted to?'

'Do you think they would?' asks Becky.

'I don't see why not. Nick and Fifi are together. And besides, I think you need a place like this.'

Becky smiles and puts her arms around me. We go upstairs and for a while forget everything as the afternoon melts into evening, and evening into night.

Patchwork must have had licences on at least thirty properties in New Cross. The houses were all more or less like the one I lived in, large old properties that needed occupying. The housing association had negotiated five-year licences on the houses with the council, and into this white working-class area of south London, near the old Millwall football ground and not too far from the docks – or 'Docklands' as it was becoming – moved a lot of hippy single mothers, a few second-generation West Indians, some young men on probation, the odd refugee from straightsville, and three very nice girls round the corner who actually earned a living.

In fact, everyone seemed to live round the corner, and we were a little close-knit village in a neighbourhood of plasterers, builders, dockers and their families. They didn't like us. I say 'us', but I was closer in some ways to the locals than I was to the likes of Big Doug. I'd grown up with them, or at least with people like them. So I had a foot in both camps.

Which is not the best place for them.

'She will bring the whole house down.'

The Patchwork housing worker is sitting in the living room with Nick and Fifi on one sofa, Becky and me on the other. Becky's been staying for the weekend, our roles reversed. Now it's me who's putting her up, offering her a break from the new hostel she's in, Brownlow House, run by the Charles Community. But it's Monday lunchtime and Fifi has called a meeting to discuss Becky.

'What do you mean, the whole house?' says Becky. 'There's only you and him and John here. And John doesn't mind me being in the house. He likes me being here.'

Fifi looks at Becky like she's some kind of savage who's just threatened to eat her.

'But you can't stay here,' says Fifi. 'You are not a tenant, and you are not welcome here.'

I sense that Fifi thinks Becky will be a threat to her and Nick, that Nick might stray. Or perhaps she senses that the balance of power would shift in the house if there were two couples living under the same roof. She doesn't want anyone else in her *ménage*.

'Well, couldn't Becky become a tenant?' I say.

Everyone looks at the housing worker.

'John, you should have said when you applied that you had a girlfriend. Then we could have considered a joint application. I'm afraid we just can't consider Becky moving in with you.'

I'm shocked. And Becky is shocked too. I thought the laid-back hippy atmosphere of Patchwork would mean they'd be willing to accept Becky, not necessarily here – just wherever they had room for us. It looks like they're keener to keep Nick and Fifi happy than to help us out.

'OK,' says Becky, standing up abruptly. 'Don't worry about me. I'm off. And I won't be back. You can stick your stripped floorboards and your Persian rugs up your poncy arses. That's if they'll go up there. I bet you're all too mean to shit.'

She storms out.

'You see what I mean?' says Fifi.

I glare at her before getting up and running after Becky.

'I think there's someone you should meet.'

Big Doug stands at the front door. I've got to know him in the same way everyone else has got to know him – by seeing him on the street. Big Doug is a huge hippy with a forty-inch waist, long black hair and a Norfolk accent, aged about thirty-five. Today he's dressed in loon pants that have lost their lustre, a Hawaiian shirt the size of a small tent, and tan brogues he has hand-made because his feet are so large. Like the rest of us he's on the dole, but he's too much of an old hand to make do on the few quid the government gives him. So he ducks and dives, totting old furniture or ripping cast-iron fireplaces out of derelict buildings and selling them for scrap, or peddling small lumps of dope to the Patchwork stoners.

His size and his presence make him a hate figure to the locals. They reckon we're all soap-dodgers and no-hopers. At least, that's what the landlady of the Royal Archer, the pub at the end of my road, says. Big Doug doesn't disappoint. He's the most visible, most instantly recognizable Patchwork tenant in the neighbourhood. He sometimes makes me think of my mother's saying: 'Where there's dirt, there's comfort.'

'Come on,' he says. 'Let's go and see Keith.'

I shut the door and fall into step beside him. A few turn-ings and we come into Nettleton Road. Big Doug goes up to a small house with pebbledashed walls and some junk in the small front yard: the frame of a rusty old pushchair, a telly with a busted screen, its shattered insides lying on the ground, a couple of raggedy baseball boots. The wind rises and I turn up my collar.

He rings the bell and a tall lad about my own age stands framed in the doorway. He's wearing jeans and a jumper like the ones Nick Heyward, the lead singer in Haircut 100, wears. He looks smart, lean, clean-cut, the first decently dressed man I've seen in New Cross who isn't a local. He's like a young Roger Moore.

'Hello, Doug,' he drawls. He's got a country burr, and smiles widely at Big Doug.

'Hello, Keith. This is John. I was thinking that you two look like a pair of likely lads, so I thought I'd best introduce you. I've got to shoot now – have to see a dog about his man.'

He grins and walks off. The wind blows around the door as Keith watches Big Doug disappear down the road.

'He's like Del Boy on acid, him,' he says. 'Do you fancy a cup of tea?'

I follow Keith inside. The house is smaller than mine, only two storeys high. There's white woodchip wallpaper in the hall, a makeshift air about the living room. A sofa covered in some blue artificial fabric and a television are all it contains.

'How do you like it?' asks Keith.

'White with two sugars, please.'

He goes into the kitchen and comes back with two mugs of tea.

'The first time I saw New Cross I thought, "What a dump." And I've got to spend a bloody year here.'

He settles himself on one arm of the sofa and I sit on the other, our feet resting on the cushions in the middle.

'How come?' I ask.

'Because I'm on probation. I have to see my probation officer once a week. It's what comes of being a burglar.'

'Oh,' I say. 'You do a lot of burgling?'

'I have done,' he says, 'but I've only been caught the once. In Bristol. That's where I come from. I got a year in Exeter for nicking a grand in cash and some jewellery from this big house I'd staked out.'

'Exeter?' I say. 'What was it like?'

'It was all right as long as you didn't take any shit. I did my time, but I did lose it once. Had a fight with a sweaty and got put in solitary. Mind you, he ended up in the hospital.'

'What's a sweaty?' I ask. It sounds like someone with really bad BO.

'A sweaty?' says Keith. 'And I thought you were a Londoner! You sound like one.'

I still look blank.

'A sweaty is a sweaty sock – Jock. You know – from Scotland. They can be a bit too fond of aggro, the sweaties.'

I remember Chopper in St Mungo's. It turned out his beef with Jimmy Douglas kicked off after some backhanded compliments he'd made about Jimmy's girlfriend. They were so backhanded Jimmy took exception to them. There was a bit of noising up, a bit of pushing and shoving, but I guess honours were even. So Jimmy Douglas got a team together – sweaties, as Keith calls them – and they set about Chopper one night in the ward. I was in the big TV room and even from there, with the sound blaring out, I could hear the rumble.

When it was all over I walked in on him. Chopper didn't look too badly hurt but he was shaken up.

The next day he moved out. It was one of those dismal incidents that started to bring me down, that made me want to get out of St Mungo's as fast as I could.

'What about you?' says Keith.

I offer to make the next brew and as the late morning winds into the early afternoon, I tell him.

'Becky? Can I come and see you? Tomorrow? OK. I'll be there about nine.'

I put the receiver down and push the door of the phone box open. At least, after all we've been through, Becky and I are still together. There's a light breeze blowing and I think of her in Grovelands House, the times she used to sing the Isley Brothers hit, 'Summer Breeze', to me. I sing the song all the way back to Casella Road, to the big house and the stairs. I climb to the top floor, to the room that's empty without her.

New Cross Road is busy, as busy as only Friday nights can be, cars flying past, buses lumbering along, lorries rumbling away to dump their loads somewhere far from New Cross, down the Old Kent Road and past the Elephant and Castle, across Tower Bridge and into the heart of London and beyond. There are couples hurrying along to cuddles on the sofa and a quiet night in, shoppers dragging their bags home, drunks skanking along smashed out of their brains even though it's only half past seven.

The burnt-out house – number 439 – where thirteen young black people were killed in a house fire, is just across the way. I shudder whenever I think about it. It's the black community's Bloody Sunday. 'No blacks, no Irish.' I think of the signs that went up in lodging houses in the fifties. They can't put those signs up any more. But they can lob petrol bombs into house parties. The black community reckon the house was deliberately firebombed but no one has ever been brought to justice. Someone must know something but no one's telling.

As I get near the bus stop, I see that there's a little gang stood just ahead of me, four of them, lolling about outside the chip shop.

'Here, John, where's the russell?'

It's one of the local lads. I've no idea what he's on about.

'The russell?'

'Yeah, you know, the russell: Russell Harty – party.'

'I was hoping you'd tell me,' I say.

They all laugh and I laugh too although I'm never completely relaxed around the local lads, especially this lot.

'Do us a favour, John?' he says, the friendly grin suddenly gone from his face.

'What's that?' I say.

'If you see Big Doug tell him we're going to kill him.'

The pub is loud and noisy and full. It's well on the way to the kind of raucous crescendo you only get on Saturday nights, when there's only a long lie-in ahead.

'Do you fancy another?' I say to Becky.

'Not really,' she says. 'We'd better be going. There's a curfew at the hostel.'

We stand up and leave. The night is cold and starry, and Becky links my arm as we head off for Brownlow House. Eventually we arrive at her place, another large house, this one tattier than the last, and she turns to look at me.

'Thanks,' she says.

'Is that it?' I ask. 'Aren't you going to ask me in?'

'I can't,' she says. 'I'll get into trouble.'

'It's never stopped you before,' I say.

'Yeah, well, it's different here.'

In a flash I see why.

'You've got someone else, haven't you?'

'So what if I have? It's no business of yours who I see!'

'It bloody well is!'

The row has been simmering all evening. Becky's been off with me, indifferent and cool, and I've been wondering if she's trying to pick a fight like she did the night I found her with Richard. I rip right into her, spit out all the hurt she's caused me, all the hurt we've caused each other, any love gone in a blazing rage. She shouts back at me, calls me a tramp, a nutter, a waster till the door opens behind her and she tries to dash inside. I grab her shirt by the sleeve as she disappears across the threshold and bangs the door shut behind her. I hold a piece of her sleeve, but she's gone and I'm alone on the doorstep.

That's it. That's the last time I'll put up with her. The last time I'll have her mess me about. I tell myself it's over all the way back to New Cross. I've been weak, a fool, an idiot. I climb the stairs to my room, tired and wrung out. The mattress is cold when I get under the covers and I curl up into a ball. There's a very faint smell of her in the bed, a scent of jasmine and summer breezes and cooking coming through a window. I think of Sunday and how I'm going to get through it and some time towards a very grey dawn I finally fall asleep.

Labour are losing the General Election. Neil Kinnock looks crushed on TV. His speech is short, unscripted.

'I warn you not to be ordinary. I warn you not to be young. I warn you not to fall ill. I warn you not to get old.'

In his face, his eyes, heartbreak.

I've been coming along to the workshops for about a month now. We meet every Tuesday evening, in a room at Goldsmiths, about nine of us. We all turn up with copies of our work and read them out to each other. Then we discuss them and go to the pub for a drink afterwards.

Blake Morrison used to take the workshop, but he's gone now and a poet called Paul Brown takes them instead. But

Blake Morrison is returning to visit the workshop tonight. It's quite exciting, the prospect of meeting a famous poet. He's just published a study of the Movement, and edited *The Penguin Book of Contemporary British Poetry*. I've read both from cover to cover.

There's an Iraqi poet I like who comes to the workshop, a middle-aged refugee who has published thirteen collections. He reads us all an unfinished poem remembering his journey into exile through the colours of the rainbow, the green of his passport, the red of the blood on the streets of Baghdad, the blue of the sky as he flew to freedom and safety.

His poem – even in its unfinished state – is very good. I'm struck by the depth of his experience, by his ability to describe simply and effectively the shifts that have happened in his life. He makes all of our work seem parochial, trivial by comparison. We've not had to deal with a regime set on crushing large elements of the population.

We finish and Blake Morrison arrives.

He's welcomed warmly by Paul and we all troop off with them to the Goldsmiths Tavern. On the way I manage to talk to Blake. I tell him that I've read his books. He's gracious and patient and in the streetlit darkness glows a little brighter. We arrive at the pub and everyone throngs the bar, a coterie forming around him.

'Look,' says my Iraqi friend, pointing at the scrum. 'Blake's 7!'

I laugh. There's something very English about a small crowd getting worked up over a poet.

It all seems a world away from Baghdad.

The shopkeeper is watching me. I'm walking up and down the crammed aisles of his small corner shop, looking suspicious. When I first came to New Cross I was kitted out like an impoverished mod. I had a smart navy blue overcoat I'd found one night on the steps of St Martin's vicarage, some shiny blue drainpipe trousers, and a pair of brown shoes with broad insteps and pointy toes. Now I'm like a hippy. I wear a dark blue Indian collarless shirt with trellises of yellow flowers printed on the front, mole-skin trousers, and a pair of girl's sandals. My hair is still short, but I've turned into one of the soap-dodgers the locals loathe on sight. No wonder the shopkeeper has his beady eye on me.

Keith, by contrast, is as smart as Paul Weller. He's wearing his Crombie, his Levi's, his Fred Perry shirt, and looks clean, neat and honest.

I go to the counter with my copy of the *Beano*. It's the cheapest thing in the shop that I actually want. Keith is behind me and he pays for a Mars Bar.

We meet outside, a little further down the road.

'Did you get it?' I ask.

'Of course I did,' he says with a broad grin.

He opens his coat and sticks his hand down his jeans. From his crotch he pulls out the shrink-wrapped steak he's nicked from the cooler cabinet.

'I can't keep doing this,' he says.

'Why not?' I ask.

'Because one day my goolies are going to freeze and drop right off.'

We both laugh. We're a good team. We might only be allowed enough to survive on but we're resourceful. At least with Keith I'm not schlepping off to some handout when my giro's all gone. And steak is a lot better than the brown rice, tuna fish and peas I usually live on.

Even if it has been down Keith's crotch.

Freaky Frankie's house is around the corner. It's the place a lot of us go to in the afternoons. We sit around, propped up against the walls of the living room, passing spliffs and talking. I'm there the day it all kicks off.

'I had one old lady, she took care of me when I came out of Wandsworth.'

Freaky Frankie, young, slight, hairy, a 'freak', as he calls himself, is rolling a joint. One's already on the go, and it's up the far end of the room, working its way back to him. There are about fifteen of us, sprawled around on beanbags and cushions, sweet hashish smoke thickening the air in the room.

'I was in the Paras,' says Peter. I hardly know him. He's small and slight with a red Van Dyke beard and a drawling way of talking. 'Used to jump out of aircraft at 10,000 feet.'

'You were never in the Paras,' says Sterling, laughing. Sterling is mixed race, far more 'street' than any of the hippies and drifters sitting in Freaky Frankie's front room.

'I was. But I bought myself out. Not because I couldn't handle it.'

Peter takes a huge drag on the spliff he's been holding for slightly too long.

'No, it was because they were on to me. I had a stash I scored after the Falklands. One day I got back to barracks and it was gone. Either it had been stolen or was going to turn up as evidence at my Court Martial. Luckily, my old man had enough money to get me out.'

He passes the spliff and Sterling laughs again.

'Peter, you are the biggest bullshitter I've ever met!'

'My old lady, she used to bring me breakfast in bed, and the papers. Mind you, I had to give her what she wanted.'

Now Freaky Frankie is off. This is what we do all day, rapping and bullshitting and headfucking. Headfucking is playing with someone's mind. It's like a version of every therapy session I've ever been in, from Claybury to Grovelands

House. Except that it's snide and arsey and stupid. Why everyone has to bullshit and headfuck I'm not sure. Perhaps it's because you should Never Trust A Hippy. Perhaps it's because the room is full of men. As much as it passes the time, it's nasty as well.

'What about that shop in Deptford?' says Sterling. 'Have you seen it? The one with the basketball shirts, the Walkmans in the windows, the skateboards and helmets, the elbow and knee pads, and the great big baseball boots? I call it 'The Packaged Nigger Shop'.'

Everyone laughs.

'As if being black meant that all you wanted to do was skate-board around wired for sound! Imagine what it would be like if all the ethnic tribes of London started getting the Packaged Nigger treatment. If your lot, John, had Packaged Paddy shops. Green, white and gold tam o' shanters, shamrocks on your roller skates, Celtic shirts and Guinness shades, and a pig to go under your arm.'

There's more laughter, and then a knock at the door.

Freaky Frankie goes to see who it is. The buzz of chat and heads mellowing stops for a moment, all ears cocked for who's at the door.

'Why did you grass me?' shouts Freaky Frankie. He's in the hallway and we don't know who he's ranting at. But the 'freak', the gentle, dope-smoking hippy is gone and in his place there's a south London boy who sounds like he's about to hurt someone.

The atmosphere in the room grows icy. I'm down from the ceiling now, the lush hashish feeling cut through with adrena-line. What is going on? Who's at the door? And what's going to happen next?

Freaky Frankie drags in a young Asian, taller than him, but limp in his ferocious grip.

'This bastard,' says Freaky Frankie, 'has split on me to Patchwork. They reckon I'm running some kind of drug den here and have given me notice. You cunt!' he shouts and lamps his housemate in the face, as hard as he can. The Asian lad is startled, shocked, too afraid to fight back. There are fifteen of us, and he must reckon that we all want to give him a kicking as much as Freaky Frankie does.

But I don't. None of us does. It's Peter who gets up first.

'This is too heavy for me,' he says. 'I've got to go.'

He walks out and slowly everyone else gets up. Sterling hands the joint to Freaky Frankie on the way out.

'Thanks for all the spliffs,' says Sterling. 'I hope you find a new place soon.'

Out on the street I meet the local lad and his mates. He's holding a machete.

'Seen Big Doug, John?'

'No,' I say, eyeing up the broad blade in his hand. 'I think he's gone away for a bit.'

'Gone away? Where?'

'This farm Patchwork have got. Somewhere out in the sticks.'

'Well, let's hope he doesn't come back,' he says. 'Because he's going to get this when he does.'

He walks off with his mates.

Sterling comes up behind me.

'Looks like they mean business,' he says. 'I wonder what that big idiot has done to upset them?'

'It would have to be something more than soap-dodging,' I say.

Sterling grins.

'Yeah,' he says. 'He must have sold them something dodgy. They're just like the hard nuts I grew up with in Peckham. A good job they haven't got it in for us. Otherwise we'd be dog meat. See you later.'

I say goodbye and head off to Nettleton Road. On my way I wonder what my Iraqi friend would make of all this.

Perhaps Baghdad isn't so very far away after all.

X

New Cross, Autumn 1983

It's been four months since I've seen Becky. Outside my window snow is falling on the trees and into the back garden. I miss her. As each day passes I miss her more and more. There's a big icy hole in my life and there's nothing I can do to ever fill it up again.

It gets deeper and deeper and my heart sinks slowly into it.

Becky turning, turning like a dolphin in a tank . . .

The bus to Catford takes about half an hour. Cerys and Winston are living together in a flat on Brownhill Road. It's a long, leafy avenue that sits back from the bustle of Catford High Street, away from McDonald's and Woolworths and Kentucky Fried Chicken, from the litter and the exhaust fumes, the big red boxy buses and the traffic. It's quiet and peaceful now in the middle of the afternoon and as I walk up the long road I wonder how they've been getting on.

I ring the bell of a modest terrace house towards the end of the road and Cerys comes down and opens the door.

'Hello, John,' she says. 'Come in.'

She smiles at me and I follow her up to the first floor. She hasn't changed much, still blonde and slim, in jeans and a grey silk blouse, but I sense that she's worried about something. Perhaps she misses Robbie and sees me as a reminder of him, the times we had together. The door to her flat is open and I walk in after her.

There's a fug of hashish smoke in the living room. Winston is sitting on a sofa with a blanket draped over it, smoking a joint, his eyes bloodshot, his mouth grinning as we catch sight of each other. His drawings are pinned to the walls, and there's a telly and a rug but not much else in the small room. It has the same makeshift air as Keith's place.

'Hello, John,' he drawls in his soft Jamaican lilt. 'Welcome to Catford.'

Cerys sits beside him but there's nowhere for me to sit.

'Let me get you a chair,' he says, and disappears into the bedroom.

'Everything all right?' I say to Cerys.

'Fine,' she says, 'except—'

Winston comes back in with a chair, a little dark collie dog following.

'This is Betsy,' says Winston. 'We got her from Battersea Dogs Home. Sit down, man, sit down.'

Winston places the chair about three feet in front of the settee. Betsy settles herself at the far end and I sit down on the chair. It feels a bit awkward, as I'm higher up than they are, but we soon get chatting about how we're all doing, and about Grovelands House.

'They said I was a schiznophrenic,' says Winston. The word comes out as if he's added a bit of syncopation to it, the skanking rhythm making it sound more foolish than it is already. 'I ain't no schiznophrenic.'

'What about that time in the garden when you thought Earth was being invaded by Venus?' asks Cerys. 'He thought I was one of them,' she says, turning to me.

'That was a joke,' says Winston.

'It didn't seem like it at the time,' she says.

I see now why Cerys was looking worried when I arrived, what she was trying to say when Winston was away getting the chair. He's been violent to her, and the violence has come from him lapsing into paranoia and psychosis. There's a silence between them that starts to become uncomfortable, a whiff of menace amidst the sweet sensimillia.

'What about Becky?' he asks, turning at last to me. He's smoked the joint down to the roach, and hands it across. I don't like the thought of trying to smoke a bit of cardboard torn from a Rizla packet so I pass. He turns to Cerys but she doesn't want it either.

'Give me that hashtray, darling.'

Cerys passes him the ashtray that's on the floor by her feet. It looks like they've had a few spliffs before I arrived. But they're not that stoned. Suddenly I start to get the creeping feeling some people get on dope – the Fear, a dread that comes from too much wacky baccy and the premonition that something bad's about to come down. It all happens in the space of three quick thumping heartbeats.

'Becky?' I say. 'I don't know, Winston. I haven't seen her for months. We had a fight and that was it.'

'She was sweet,' says Cerys. 'She came here the other weekend. Said you always had a great sense of humour.'

Cerys talks about Becky in the past tense. I start to feel lonesome for her. This, along with the vibe I'm getting from Winston, makes the walls and ceiling of the small flat feel like they're closing in on me.

'Why have you come here, John?' he says quietly.

'To see you both,' I say.

'Why you so interested in Cerys?'

His bloodshot eyes look straight into mine. The Fear is now on me like gunk dumped from the ceiling. It's green and sticky and messy and it's clinging all over to me.

'I'm not as interested as you think, Winston,' I say softly.

He suddenly stands up.

'You couldn't keep Becky so now you come here looking for Cerys. I'm going to get a knife and cut you, see what you made of!'

'OK, Winston,' I say. 'Do what you've got to do.'

He storms into the kitchen and rattles around in the cutlery drawer. He comes back into the living room with a big bread knife. Cerys gets up quickly.

'Winston!' she says. 'What's the matter with you?'

'I'm vexed, Cerys! I don't want him here, the way he look at you.'

I sit as still as I can, cool now that it's come. I figure Winston is sounding off, that he isn't going to cut me. Not that I'm going to antagonize him. But I'm not going to run either. I would never see Cerys again if I did. And she's all that's left of Grovelands House, of Becky, of Robbie.

'There's nothing between John and me, Winston. Why don't you calm down? I'll roll you another spliff and we can all get stoned and have a chat about everything.'

Winston is staring at me now. Betsy is watching us all from beside the settee, her head resting between her paws, her ears down, fear in her eyes.

I say nothing. I just return Winston's gaze, determined not to look away.

'I don't want no spliff, Cerys. Not with him here.'

Cerys looks at me but I'm still saying nothing. As long as Winston has the knife in his hand I have to stay cool. With the odds in his favour, I figure Cerys is going to have to talk him down. I'm only going to wind him up even tighter.

'What about if John goes on his way then, Winston? I can see him off downstairs and then we can have that spliff when he's gone?'

Winston is still staring.

'Get him out of here,' he says at last.

I stand and leave the flat, Cerys behind me as we come out on to the landing. We make our way to the front door in silence.

'Why do you stay with him?' I ask her at the bottom of the stairs.

'He's all I've got,' she says.

I think of Becky, about how I feel without her, and think how things might have been if Robbie was still alive.

'Goodbye, Cerys,' I say.

She kisses me on the cheek. From the flat Winston calls her and she turns quickly and dashes back up to him, taking the stairs two at a time.

Keith's girlfriend has come back from Greece. She's tall like Keith, dark-haired, with model good looks, sensuous lips, and the same Bristol burr. She looks as thrilled as he is to be in New Cross. It must seem a long way from Greek skies, Greek beaches, Greek tavernas.

'Keep an eye on her, John,' says Keith. 'I've got lots on at the moment.'

It's coming up to Christmas and money is tight. Keith is shoplifting duvets so that he'll have enough readies to see him through till the New Year. I've got no idea how he manages to nick duvets from the Oxford Street stores where he dodges security every day. The duvets all come in large boxes and must be the biggest items he could walk out of the shop with. You can't exactly hide them down the front of your keks. But Keith is like a magician. He could steal the hair off your head and you wouldn't even notice you were going bald.

'I really admire Keith,' says Susie, his girlfriend. We're in his bedroom, amongst the knick-knacks he's picked up on previous expeditions: a match that's about two feet long and two inches square with a torch in the big black head of it, a nice new duvet with a pale blue cover, a couple of James Dean and Marlon Brando posters on the wall, and a red bulb.

'If you or I go out to work, we're risking nothing,' she says. 'When Keith goes out he risks his liberty.'

'What about when Big Doug goes out?' I say. 'He's risking life and limb.'

'But he's only got himself to blame, John. He shouldn't have messed around with the locals.'

It's been getting worse. The other day a brick came through the window of the big house on the corner. It missed a toddler's head by inches. It turns out that the beef with Big Doug is over turf. He sold some Black Leb to two local girls. The lad with the machete is dealing himself. He doesn't need any competition, especially from the likes of Big Doug.

We wait for Keith to get back, not knowing if he's been caught or not. As much as Susie admires him, I also get the feeling she'd like Keith to find a more settled way of life. But the times themselves are unsettled. If it's bad on the streets of New Cross, it's even worse elsewhere. I think about what Neil Kinnock said.

'I warn you not to be ordinary. I warn you not to be young. I warn you not to fall ill. I warn you not to get old.'

That covers just about everybody I know. I remember what Keith told me about the time he was first arrested and sent to Exeter. He'd been doing an accountancy course and was sitting the exam. Two policemen marched into the examination hall. They had a word with one of his lecturers and came down the long aisle to Keith's desk. He was taken away, and never got to finish the paper.

But he did finish his studies. At Exeter, the finest criminal college in England according to Keith.

'I'm good with figures, John,' says Keith. 'Just a shame I never got a chance to prove it.'

Underneath all his Jack the Lad attitude I sense that Keith is bitter about Exeter. Not about the sentence. That's part of the code: 'Don't do the crime if you can't do the time.' No, he's bitter about being robbed of the chance of making it in the straight world. Who's the bigger thief, he seems to say, me – or the courts that took my future? And now there are no jobs even if he could get one. I see why he takes pride in being such a good thief. He sees himself as Robin Hood, stealing from the rich department stores and selling cut-price to punters on the dole. He goes down to Bristol every weekend and flogs the duvets to his mates.

Christmas will be a bit cosier in Bristol this year.

Or at least it will be if Keith isn't caught.

Sammy Leadbetter is at the door. His time as a community service volunteer at St Mungo's is up so like me he's come to New Cross. I ask him to come in and we go up to my room.

There's no furniture, apart from a mattress on the floor and a few books lined up against the wall beneath the window. Sammy and I sit on the duvet Siobhan Ferry gave me, and he tells me how it's going.

'You know that house just up the road? The one with the brothers in it.'

There's a Patchwork licenced house about halfway down Casella Road. A young black family – Mum, Dad, young baby – live there. The dad likes me. When we get together we talk about books and philosophy, although I'm a little out of my depth when it comes to philosophy. I think he's a student at Goldsmiths. She once cooked corned beef hash when I was round there – corned beef, onions, half a tin of tomatoes, mashed potatoes. Delicious ...

'I know the house, Sammy.'

'You won't believe this,' he says. 'They told me I wasn't black enough to live with them.'

'What do you mean, not black enough?'

Sammy's the blackest man I know. His skin is like ebony, jet black, blacker than anyone else's in New Cross.

'I think it's political,' says Sammy. 'I'm just not right-on enough for these cats.'

'So what are you going to do?' I ask. Sammy's trying to get in somewhere, somewhere in this little village of misfits and drifters.

'There's nothing else I can do, John. I'm going to have to make a terrible compromise.'

'What's that, then, Sammy?'

'I'm going to have to live with you white folks all over again.'

Cerys has a cat now as well as Betsy. I've come to see her on a day when Winston's away visiting his mother.

'Oh, I meant to tell you,' says Cerys. 'The cat had kittens. Would you like one?'

That afternoon I bring a little ginger kitten home with me. Nick and Fifi are away on holiday in France. He's asked me to keep an eye on his Beetle Convertible. I think he's hoping someone steals it, so that he can claim on the insurance. He deals dope and I get the feeling he's having money problems.

I should have asked them about Scamp, the little kitten I've brought from Catford, but I have a feeling they won't mind.

The Patchwork House in Kings Langley is a large cottage on two floors. Sammy's wangled a place there and seems content away from the simmering tensions, the poverty and drugs of New Cross. He meets me at the station and we walk the half-mile or so back to the house. The other people Sammy's sharing with are a hippyish couple and their baby, and Mick, a young dark-haired man in velvet loons, cotton granddad shirt, bare feet.

We cross the threshold into another world. There's a music stand in the centre of the living room, which looks like it's been knocked through to make a bigger space, French windows giving out on to a large garden, and the Hippy Dad is practising a piece by Bach for the viola. A smell of cooking is wafting from the kitchen, and we tiptoe past Sammy's housemate to check out what's for dinner.

'Hello,' says Hippy Mum. She's standing over the stove, stirring a pot full of something delicious. 'I've made a nice vegetable stew and rice. I bet you're both hungry. Come and tell me all about New Cross. How's Big Doug? How are the locals treating you? Still hostile? It's such a shame.'

She's homely and down-to-earth, small and round and rosy, and seems at home by the cooker, an Aga like the range my aunt cooks on in Ireland. There's a large table in the middle of the kitchen, set for us all, two church pews either side of it, as if we were about to sit down to break bread together in some rural American sect.

Hippy Dad drifts in from the living room and we all settle ourselves into the pews.

'Where's Skylark?' asks Hippy Dad.

'She's asleep,' says Hippy Mum.

'Did you feed her?'

'Yes. She's down now. She doesn't take long. She's got her father's belly. Guzzles and snorts like a pig at a trough.'

Sammy and I exchange glances, or at least, I try to exchange a glance. But Sammy isn't looking my way. His eyes are downcast. I could swear he's blushing.

The local pub has a scattering of hippies in it, and Sammy and I nod to a few of them.

'That's Archie,' says Sammy, pointing out a blond, long-haired, ginger-bearded man in a blue and white checked lumberjacket. He's standing at the bar collecting his pint, and smiles at us, holding up his glass. We're sat at the back of the saloon, its beams and horse brasses as far from the Goldsmiths Tavern's sticky carpet and faded Victorian fixtures as the shires are from the metropolis.

'Evening, Sam,' says Archie in a thick Glaswegian accent. He's come over to our table and is standing over us. 'Got to be careful out there tonight. Lots of bad karma in the air. We were rolling along in Jim's motor, minding our own, when this fucking Panda car pulls up in front of us. Pig and a Passenger Pig get out. Wanted to breathalyze us. Lucky they can't test for drugs. They gave us a right nasty look getting back in their Pigmobile. I'm telling you, when it comes to the polis, I'm strictly kosher. I'm not Jewish myself, but I have passed the physical. Who's your friend?'

Sammy introduces me, and Archie drifts off again to join his pals.

'He reminds me of all those Scotties in St Mungo's,' says Sammy. 'But along with the och aye you get a bit more Third Eye with Archie.'

I leave Kings Langley at Sunday lunchtime. It's a very different experience from New Cross. I'm looking forward to getting back though. The weekend with Sammy has done me the world of good.

'What is that smell?'

Fifi's back. I haven't house-trained Scamp, and while I've been away he's piddled and shat all over the house. It's been great to have him for company, but no one's told me how to get him to do his business in the garden. I asked Keith and Susie to look after him while I was gone, but they've been called down to Bristol. One of Keith's punters has been arrested for receiving stolen goods – those duvets. So Scamp has been left alone with some catfood and water. Nick and Fifi's furniture has come off worst. It doesn't take her long to discover what he's done. Nick and Fifi get the Patchwork housing worker round again. I'm out, notice to quit, with immediate effect.

'But where can I go?' I ask the housing worker.

'Freaky Frankie's got a squat,' she says. 'Why don't you go there?'

'What are you doing in New Cross if you don't want to do drugs?'

The squat is just around the corner from Casella Road. We're in Freaky Frankie's room upstairs. He's looped stripy curtains from the ceiling and they hang down in flowing billows, running like patterned waves above us. There's a bank of TVs up one wall, a mattress on the floor, and his junkie's works below the window. The whole effect is trippy and scuzzy and squalid.

'Who says I have to take drugs to live here?'

I look at them both, Freaky Frankie and Prash, an Asian skaghead who has come round to score some heroin from him. They're giving me a hard time. But I hate heroin. It killed Robbie.

'It's not about living *here*,' says Prash. 'It's about being able to experiment, to try out new experiences.'

'I don't want to experiment,' I say.

'But you don't know what you're missing!' says Freaky Frankie. He's getting impatient with me. 'Look!'

He picks up the long thin piece of black rubber tubing that's part of his works, shoves up the sleeve of his shirt and wraps the tubing tightly round his arm, just below the bicep.

Prash bends over and picks up the blackened spoon. He puts his lighter under it till the black stuff in the bowl starts to bubble. Then he lays down the spoon on the bare floorboards below the window and reaches for the needle.

'Watch this,' says Freaky Frankie.

Prash slides the needle into the liquefied heroin. He draws up the dark brew into the chamber of the syringe and carries it over to Freaky Frankie. Freaky Frankie pulls the black tubing tighter round his arm and taps a vein with the first two fingers of his left hand. Prash slides the needle into the raised vein and slowly squeezes the plunger of the syringe. The heroin courses into Freaky Frankie's bloodstream and he shuts his eyes in heavy-lidded orgasmic ecstasy. Still in his trance, he stumbles to the window and shoves up the lower half of it.

A great gush splashes into the garden below.

Soon they're both gouched out, and I get some relief from them.

I can't stay here.

But where else is there?

PART III

Where Are We Going?

XI

Banstead, 1984

'Do you want to use the glubs?'

Maria hands me a pair of yellow Marigolds. Her Filipina accent mangles the word, but somehow makes it fit the floppy rubber gloves even better than standard English.

'No thanks,' I say.

The sink is full of plates and cutlery from lunchtime. I like Maria. She's the cleaner on our ward. And I have so much energy that doing the dishes isn't a chore – it's a release. I steam into the large sink full of plates and wash them all in a frenzy. Maria takes handfuls of them off the drainer and dries them, stacking them on a trolley when they're done.

Washing and wiping: it's a little domestic ceremony that almost humanizes this place.

Banstead is the third psychiatric hospital that has sectioned me. It lies somewhere out in Surrey, which might as well be a foreign country. I've never been here, never had reason. But there's something very familiar about Banstead. I suppose after four admissions to three different hospitals – Claybury, Friern and now Banstead, all under section – there should be. But the difference this time is that I'm an old hand. I know the rituals, the routines, the customs of this place.

Take the ward. It's smaller than O2, bigger than Oak Ward, but it has the same kind of layout. A men's dorm at one end, a women's dorm at the other. A dining area linking these, like O2, with a TV lounge off this corridor just before the men's dorm, and a nurse's office halfway along. There's a little kitchen, and washrooms and bathrooms, and a smell of industrial cleaning agents.

But there are big differences too. I think back to the notes I wrote up the second time I was in Claybury, the field survey I made as a budding student of sociology. All of my observations about hierarchy and class amongst the staff still apply. With the patients, though, it's a different matter. There's no one like Miriam or Julian or Jimmy or Catherine. It's as if they've been banished. In Banstead everyone is like me – part of a harsher society than the one I grew up in.

I'm walking along a country road. I've jumped a train from New Cross and now I'm somewhere out in the countryside. It's the height of summer, the sun warm on my reddening neck, fresh hedgerow smells of grass and dew and wildflowers on the breeze, the odd butterfly floating across my path as I walk along.

New Cross seems a long way away. Here there are no drugs, no squats, no Freaky Frankies. The harsh streets and traffic might be on another planet. And the complexities of relationships – of Keith and Susie, and me in the middle – can't put any strain on the day. I'm free, the same feeling I had when I was first on the streets round the West End, but now with a kind of rural vastness no city could ever match.

A police car pulls up.

'Are you looking for a few days in the country?'

I'm wondering if anyone spotted me at the station.

'I wouldn't mind,' I say.

'Hop in,' says the policeman.

I get in the back. There are two of them, and they seem pleasant enough.

By the time we get to Banstead I've changed my mind.

———

'Wouldn't you like a nice hunk of bread, a bit of cheddar, and a cold bottle of brown ale to wash it all down?'

Jack was admitted this afternoon, in a high old state. He's in his forties, grey-haired and strong-looking, with sideburns and a Brylcreemed quiff. He looks like he might run the dodgems on a fairground, something of the Teddy Boy he once was lurking still in his middle-aged frame, the tough, gnarled knuckles, the tattooed muscular arms. Even though he's in regulation pyjamas and dressing gown he's got a Ted's style in his swagger and aggressive, restless strut. He's going to have to be careful.

'That'd be nice,' I say.

'Better than what they give us in here. When we get out I'll treat you to some real food.'

I decide to mind Jack, to make sure he comes through his section without them extending it or doing anything worse to him. He's had a row with his missus, Margaret, something to do with her fancying another bloke. I know the feeling. And while I boil with anger and frustration at being here, while I rage inside at the police picking me up and dumping me in this place, at least keeping Jack out of mischief gives me something to do.

———

'Can't you take her off my hands, John?'

Keith is sitting at the end of his bed. It's the New Year and Keith's duvets have all been sold down in Bristol. But he's come back to find a brown envelope waiting for him. Having Susie stay in his room has led to complaints. Keith's out.

'I don't think she fancies me, Keith.'

'Trouble is, John, I don't fancy her.'

He gets out a wrap of something, some tin foil and a lighter.

'Do you want a bit?'

'What is it?'

'Just a bit of skag. Fancy chasing the dragon, to see in the New Year?'

I hate heroin. There's so much of it now in New Cross. Even some of the girls are taking it.

'OK,' I say. I want to show Keith that I can try it once and leave it. Because it seems to be doing everyone in, turning them into zombies. It's like they've all just rolled over and accepted their fate. I'm not going to do that. And I don't want Keith to go that way either. But his drug-taking is turning him into someone I don't really know any more. He's grown more fatalistic, less angry, angles and edges all softened.

He unwraps the skag from its clingfilm and makes a little triangle of the tin foil. Then he ignites the lighter, lays a crumb of heroin in the middle of the tin foil and runs the flame under it. As soon as a few twists of smoke from the cooked skag rise from the silver triangle he runs his nose along it, catching it all in three quick snorts.

He leans back, his eyelids closed.

'Mmm,' he says. He opens his eyes again, and offers me a fresh piece of foil, the crumb of heroin in its clingfilm wrap, the lighter.

I repeat the ritual, loathing every moment.

Afterwards, my head feels like I've woken up with the makings of a hangover. It does nothing for me. I'll never take it again.

But it's everywhere, and everyone in New Cross is doing it.

I'm walking outside with a male student nurse. Banstead is nothing like as extensive as Claybury or Friern. There are the same kind of Victorian buildings looming over us, but fewer of them, and far fewer meadows and paths, fewer copses and hideaways where it's possible to escape from the gloom of the wards. I'm still not allowed out on my own, and once a day this nurse takes me out for an airing. Dusk is falling, and we make our way through a shadowy quadrangle, lights on in the upper storeys of the buildings, like a great liner sailing through the night to a strange new port.

'You want to ask for parole,' he says.

'Parole?'

It sounds like a prison word. I've never come across it in hospital before. It sounds sinister, nothing to do with care or nursing.

'Permission to take a walk on your own. That's what it means.'

No one's ever explained to me when I've been sectioned just what my rights are, what I can do and what I can't do, or who I can see about helping me. I realize this is the first time someone has ever given me advice like this.

I thank the nurse and we return to the ward.

Tomorrow I'll take a walk on my own.

The day after I'm going to escape.

<hr/>

Keith and Susie have moved into a council flat in Wapping. I think they've paid key money for it, from someone they've met in a pub. They have no other connection with Wapping. I see less of them, but in some ways this is OK. I was never going to take Susie off Keith's hands. Neither of us fancies the other and we only really have Keith in common. And now that she's pregnant the whole situation is completely different. I hear he's been asking after me. I'll go and see them, but I fancy a trip out to the country first, just to clear my head, to get a change of scene.

———

'What you doing here, John?'

Keith's country boy drawl is as welcome as a rainbow over England. Susie's not showing yet, but she's blooming. It's over three months now since she fell pregnant and she looks lovely. I think of Becky, and the last time I saw her, the row we had. And I wonder how she's doing, if she's making a better life for herself.

'Not much, Keith. Washing-up, mostly, the odd walk in the grounds. Any chance you can get me out of here?'

'No problem,' he says and grins.

I'm in hospital pyjamas and dressing gown, a pair of brown felt slippers on my feet. Doing a runner with Keith and Susie is going to be tricky. But I know I shouldn't be here. I was conned, those two policemen just getting their arrest record up, 'a few days in the country . . .' Hah! I hadn't bargained for this. And being with Keith and Susie has to be more fun than the wards, with their rounds of mealtimes, medication, moods.

'OK, Keith,' I say. 'Let's do it.'

We all stand and leave the ward. I'm surprised at how easy it is. There are other visitors around, and a few nurses keeping an eye on things, but Keith tells the charge nurse that he's just taking me down to the tea bar for a coffee, that he'll have me back in no time. He thanks the charge nurse for doing such a good job of looking after me and says goodbye. He's all charm and courtesy, respectably dressed in his Crombie and jeans, Susie looking beautiful and elegant in a full-length sheepskin coat, as we all move off together right under the noses of the staff.

As soon as we're out in the grounds, we all burst out laughing. Keith takes off his Haircut 100 jumper and gives it to me and we head off for the station.

But we're not going to Wapping. Keith and Susie leave me back at Freaky Frankie's. Freaky Frankie takes one look at me, and gives a chuckle.

'Welcome home,' he says.

The police are at the door. Freaky hisses at me to get rid of them. He says they're asking for me. I get up and pull on some clothes as quickly as I can. Half-dressed, my t-shirt on back to front, bleary-eyed, I stand in the doorway. There's a police car, a Rover 3500, in the road, and two policemen on the doorstep.

The Welsh male nurse from Banstead grins at me from the back of the car. In a couple of hours I'm back on the ward. I'm madder than ever. Not clinically mad, like I was in Claybury or Friern. I'm angry. Seething. Why the hell am I here? Even Freaky Frankie's shooting gallery of a squat is better than this place.

We're all just in time for dinner.

'Now,' says the Welsh nurse. 'Aren't you glad to be back? We've all missed you, you know.'

I feel like punching him in his fat, smug face. The patients are shuffling towards the tables in the dining area.

'You bastard,' I say. I've never ranted at anyone who's looked after me before. But I can't help myself. I shouldn't be here.

Before I can snarl at him some more, an old Polish boy, an airman who fought in the Battle of Britain, lets fly with a haymaker smack in my face. Three male nurses, including the Welsh one, jostle me away, and lead me off out of the ward.

'You need to cool down, boyo,' says the Welsh nurse. 'We've got a treat for you. Somewhere to take it easy, learn yourself a few manners.'

We're hurtling down the stairs now and along the corridor past the other wards on the way, sounds of rattling cutlery, plates and muted chatter, the smells of dinner, drifting down to me, all magnified by my pumping heart.

'You think you're Steve McQueen, don't you, eh? The Cooler King?' He's taunting me now 'OK. Let's see how you like it in here.'

We all stop.

Ahead of me is a door. It has a window in it, a few figures through the square frame lolling against the wall inside. Across the window are bars.

The Welsh nurse's two colleagues are either side of me, gripping my arms, as he presses a bell. A big black nurse, his eyes on me, comes to the door and rattles several locks before it opens.

'One for you, Clyde,' says the Welsh nurse. 'Look after him. We'll be back when he's calmed down.'

Clyde takes hold of me. He slams the door shut behind us with a bang and I walk into the Locked Ward.

I think of Sean, up in Broadmoor. One of the Kray Twins, Ronnie, is there. What is it like? Is it like this place, with locks on the doors, bars on all the windows, nurses so big they look like bouncers? I'm watchful, wary. Before, everyone I met in hospital was either depressed or disturbed. In here, they're supposed to be dangerous. That's why we're on the Locked Ward. But I'm not dangerous.

I'm just scared.

At the far end of the ward a black man of about forty-five, dressed in a sports jacket and dark grey slacks, is crouching over a table. Beside him is a ghetto-blaster and he's wearing earphones plugged into his sound machine. He's drawing, tracing and filling in the outlines of incredibly nubile women, which seem to be part of some kit. As he draws, he skanks his knees back and forward, the music throbbing, in a frenzy that's sinister and sexual. I watch him, fascinated by his energy.

He looks up, sees me staring at him.

'Sex, boy,' he says. 'It's a gift, a man's reward for the hurts this wicked world will inflict upon you. It has a magic to it, an energy, that nothing else has. That is why this society is dripping with sex. Because it is hurt to its core, and needs the soothing of sex, the magical potency of the carnal act.'

He speaks like a demented preacher, rolling the words off his tongue, a man who has become entranced by the delusional voodoo of his own mind. And yet he makes a mad kind of sense too. Peace, love and understanding have been smashed to pieces. The world that used to exist has been bewitched, changed for this one, cast by a curse. I'm twenty-five, in the Locked Ward of Banstead Hospital.

And all because a couple of coppers thought it would be funny to bring me here.

There's a TV in a small room off the main ward. The *Six O'Clock News* is on. There's footage of policemen attacking miners, charging them on horseback, lashing out with truncheons and batons. The striking miners scatter and one of them falls. The scene cuts to another line of miners charging down a small incline at mounted police. Truncheons and batons start flying, and then a maul of cracked heads and fists. The picture tilts as the cameraman is jostled. It's frenzied and bloody and brutal.

One of the nurses has left a paper on the chair beside me. I look at the headline: 'Thatcher Attacks "Enemy Within"'. I read the report and a quote catches my eye:

'We had to fight the enemy without in the Falklands. We

always have to be aware of the enemy within, which is much more difficult to fight and more dangerous to liberty.'

It's as if Mrs Thatcher thinks the whole country should be sectioned.

I leave the room and go for my medication.

XII

Liverpool Road, 1985

The windows of the café on Upper Street are covered in posters – Rock Against Racism, the Anti-Nazi League, Support the Miners. Keith and I wander in. There are long wooden tables in the middle of the room, young hippies sat round them either side eating vegetable gloop with spoons and forks. The walls are covered in more posters – Crass, Test Dept, New Model Army – and there's a corkboard by the stairs leading up to the first floor with scraps of paper and badges pinned to it. A few anarchists, all in black, lurk at the back of the room, plotting and planning. The café is full of dropouts and their dogs, mongrels that all have a good bit of lurcher in them, lean and long-jawed, brindled and brown and moth-eaten.

'Are you looking for a squat?'

He comes up to us out of the crowd of hippies sitting at the table. He's dressed in baggy flared jeans, an old light blue shirt, sleeves rolled up to the elbow, and a green crocheted tam o' shanter. His matted hair is stuffed into the tammie and he's got long sideburns. He's quite short, about five feet six, and he's grinning like he's just eaten a dry kilo of mushrooms. I wonder what they put in the vegetable gloop.

'Yeah,' says Keith. 'As a matter of fact we are.'

'Follow me,' he says, and we step back out on to Upper Street. He leads us across the busy road, past Highbury and

205

Islington Station, and we walk along to a corner where a small park adds an acre of green to the grey city.

'It's just along here,' he says. 'We've got the one next door, so you're more than welcome to it. Have you been busted then?'

'Yeah,' says Keith. 'We had a place on the Barnsbury Estate, but we got our Notice To Quit yesterday.'

We turn into a long tree-lined road. It's a lot quieter than Upper Street, with tall Victorian villas either side. They're all about five storeys high, with steps leading up to the front door. The trees and the quietness and the size of the houses are very different from the smashed-up flats of the Barnsbury Estate. I know this area a little, know its squares, its pubs with the benches and parasols outside, its canal further down. It feels like Old London, a place where you might see a hansom cab go by, a boy on a penny farthing, a man in a stovepipe hat strolling along the broad pavement. A sign above me on the wall of a house says 'Liverpool Road' and I wonder how the long tree-lined avenue got its name. We go another hundred yards or so until the young hippy stops.

'Here it is,' he says.

It's one of the five-storey houses, steps up to the front door, large windows looking out on the street, a flat roof at the top.

'Do you think you can get us in?' I ask Keith.

'No problem,' he says. 'Let's see what's through here.'

He goes down the small pathway at the side of the house to a door. One quick shove with his shoulder and it flies open. We follow his tall figure through the door and down the pathway into a large expanse of garden. French windows from the house give on to a small yard about eight feet square, and we stand here and look up at the back of the house, the enormous size of it. A patch of weeds, the wheels of an old pram sticking up out of them, lie behind us, and then a no-man's-land of rubble and junk beyond.

Keith takes a rolled-up tea cloth out of the inside pocket of his Crombie. He kneels down and unrolls the tea cloth on the hard concrete of the yard. There's a hammer and a chisel lying on the check pattern and he picks up the tools and the tea cloth and takes a step towards the French windows.

'Watch this,' he says. 'I won't make a sound.'

He places the tea cloth against the window, and holds the chisel up to it. He gives a whack from the hammer and the window pane breaks, but any sound of splintering glass is muffled by the cloth. He puts his hand in through the hole and reaches for the handle. The French window opens.

We're in.

I was discharged from Banstead and moved in with Keith. Susie had gone back to Bristol to have the baby and he found himself a squat off the Caledonian Road on the Barnsbury Estate, halfway between King's Cross and Islington. I couldn't go back to Freaky Frankie's. Freaky Frankie was in a worse state than I was, his heroin habit slowly destroying him. The social workers at Banstead were talking about 'resettling' me, but I said, 'No thanks'. I just wanted to get out of there as fast as I could. I didn't want to wait months while they found some hostel or group home where I'd have to start all over again. So when Keith said I could move in with him I kept my head down on the ward and counted the days until they let me out.

There were quite a few squats on the Barnsbury Estate, a series of mid-rise blocks full of hard-to-let council flats. They were home now to hippies, dropouts, drifters. But mostly the damp, dilapidated hard-to-lets were occupied by young, single, homeless people. Some even had jobs. We were there about three months, a good run, until the Notice To Quit came from the council. The day it dropped on the mat, Keith said, 'Well, John, it looks like this scene is over.'

This is what life is, I thought. A series of scenes, played out across a stage where the back-cloth and the flats, the props and the lighting rig, are all taken down and put up again in some other distant place, new performers quickly assembled, old parts recast, make-up and costumes changed to suit the bill. And now it's time to move on again.

To the next scene, and a new set of characters.

'There's a few Scottish blokes we met at the café. They're looking for a place too. I said they could come round and have a look.'

Frankie has popped in from next door. She lives with the young hippy who took us round and showed us the place. His name's Phil, and he helps run the squatted café in Upper Street. She's about nineteen, a year younger than him, short blonde hair, with an afghan coat and monkey boots.

'Fine,' I murmur.

What else can I say?

'When are they coming?'

'Some time this afternoon?'

I feel like putting up a notice in the window, like the 'No blacks, no Irish, no dogs' signs that greeted my parents in the fifties.

'No stoners, no junkies, no lurchers.'

But what would be the point?

Jerzy is a handyman. I know him from the squats on the Barnsbury Estate. He's changed the locks on the front door of the house and sorted me out a key. We're down in the basement. There are bars on the window, blue and white tiles on the floor, a few meters and pipes on the far wall. He's wiring the electricity, turning on the water.

'Now,' he says, when he's done it all. 'You'll have light, heating, and hot water.'

Light, heating, hot water.

And the Black Watch.

'Thanks, Jerzy,' I say.

They should be here any minute.

There are four of them.

'I'm Mickey.'

'I'm Angus.'

'I'm Alistair.'

'And I'm Andy.'

Mickey and Andy are wearing green mackintoshes, Angus and Alistair chef's checked trousers and white tops. They're all grinning, all made up to be here.

'Right,' says Frankie. 'Who wants a spliff?'

I've got the big room up on the first floor looking out on to the street. I drag a mattress from a skip down the road back to the squat and up the stairs. There's an old Persian carpet in the skip as well and I go back for it. The carpet and the mattress are all that's in the room, which looks big and bare. Frankie and Phil lend me a sleeping bag and I nab a couple of drawers from a small abandoned chest in one of the rooms downstairs. I place them turned up on their sides, facing towards the wall at the end of my mattress. There's an old grey phone, a curl of wire hanging out the back of it, in another room, and I lay this facing outward on the two upturned drawers.

It's not much, but it's home. At night, the storage radiator in my room comes on and I'm as cosy as toast by the morning.

Keith can't handle Scotsmen.

'I had too many run-ins with them in Exeter, John,' he drawls. 'Me and the sweaties don't get on. I reckon you'll be all right though, mate. You've got the way with you.'

Keith moves in with Jerzy, a place on City Road. I think about what he's said, about having the way with me. And I hope that Mickey, Angus, Alistair and Andy all think so as well.

There's a long wooden table in the kitchen. It stands in front of the French windows that look out on the back garden. Light streams into the room as we sit around the table and talk. The Scots lads have made a brew, and Frankie's got a spliff on the go.

'See, oop in Easterhoose it's nae gud feelin' aw dreichy aboot yersel'. Thassnae gud at all. Ye need tae haulf a bit o' get oop and gae aboot yae.'

Andy's accent is so thick I can hardly understand what he's saying. He's just down from Glasgow, from Easterhouse, a really tough estate. He sounds like he's threatening everyone, as if he's noising them up. Mickey tells me they were all in a pub the other night on Upper Street and were asked to leave. The landlord thought they were going to break up the place.

'But we were just talking about the weather!'

Frankie passes Mickey the spliff and he takes a long drag into his lungs. He's in his mid-twenties, the same as me, the same as Angus and Alistair. We're all a little older than Andy, a lad of nineteen, twenty.

'Doon here I ken we'll aw be braw, licht, laddies.'

Frankie starts laughing.

'What the hell are you saying, Andy? I can't understand a bloody word!'

Everyone is high, the dope and the sunny spring day putting us in a good mood. What the hell *is* Andy saying? We all crack up. Even the Scots lads, their accents softer after a year in London, think he's funny. But there's a glint in Andy's eyes, a glint of danger. Or perhaps it's a glint of attraction? I catch him looking at Frankie, grinning, eyes locked on hers. Phil shifts awkwardly in his seat. It's like there's static in the air.

There's a loud knock at the front door.

Everyone goes quiet.

'You expecting anyone?' says Mickey to me.

I shake my head.

Andy is out of his seat before anyone can stop him. We can hear him in the hallway.

'What dae yae wan'?' he shouts.

'This is the owner,' says a voice. 'I want to come in and inspect my property.'

We can hear Andy opening the front door.

'Oh, soo there's tae o' ye?'

'I have brought my associate,' says the voice. 'This is Terry, my junior partner.'

'Well, come in,' says Andy. 'There's not much tae see.'

We hear footsteps walking along the hall. Then another voice, harder, heavier, London.

'You think you're fucking tasty, don't you, you Jock cunt?'

'Why don't ye find out, Terry?' says Andy loudly. 'See this little blade o' mine? It'd make mincemeat o' ye and your big fat boss.'

There's silence, icy as a meat freezer.

'Ye'll turn on yeer heels now, gintlemen, and leave me to mah hoose. And next time ye come round here, make sure ye have the law. Otherwise I'll hae to defen' meself from trespassers like the pair of ye. Now git!'

We hear the scurry of feet, the door slamming shut.

Andy comes back to the kitchen.

'I dinnae think we'll see young Terry for a while. Or his boss!'

We all laugh.
This time the glint is in Frankie's eye.

Frankie gets us organized. She says she'll do all the shopping and cooking for six quid a week each. She goes down to Chapel Market with Phil, and comes back with bruised vegetables, dented cans, bags of lentils, packets of muesli, loaves of Hovis, and jars of piccalilli. She cooks a big vegetarian meal every evening, Phil chopping up the ingredients, and we eat muesli for breakfast, and piccalilli sandwiches for lunch.

For the first time in years thanks to Frankie and her kitty I have some spare cash. I see a pair of Levi's in Chapel Market and buy them out of my dole money. They're shrink to fit, and that night I sit with them in the bath until they've had a good soak, thinking about what they'll look like when they're the right size. I step out of the bath and walk sopping across the landing to my room. I take them off and leave them on the storage radiator to dry overnight, steam rising from the legs. I can't wait to get into them. I'm like a kid before Christmas. Eventually I fall asleep and dream of cowboys and saloon bars and glasses of rye whiskey, of Woody Guthrie and Jack Kerouac, of riding the trains like a hobo, of hitchhiking right across America, of being On the Road.

I wake up the next morning and run over to the radiator. The Levi's are dry and wrinkly and warm and I ease them up over my naked bum. They feel great, tight and snug. I pull them up some more and suddenly my cock is on fire. The fly buttons! They're all as hot as branding irons – the fly buttons are searing my dick!

I wrestle the Levi's down round my ankles and wriggle over to the tall window. I must look like I'm in a sack race. I stick my cock against the cooling panes and close my eyes in relief. Perhaps my member has been branded, perhaps Levi Strauss is burnt into my most private part! Christ! What am I going to do? I open my eyes to take a look. No, it's OK: it's just a bit red.

On the street opposite two old ladies in coats and headscarves stare up at me, open-mouthed. I give them a big wave and they hurry off.

I wonder if Woody Guthrie or Jack Kerouac ever burnt their cocks on their jeans?

There's a knock at the door.

'I'm just going to the market. Do you want anything?'

'No, thanks, Frankie.'

If she came in now, what would I say?

'Are you all right, John? You sound a bit odd?'

I bet I do.

'I'm fine thanks,' I say. 'I've just woken up.'

'OK,' she says. 'See you later.'

Her footsteps move off across the landing and I hear her going down the stairs and out the front door. It starts to rain, the air cooler now, milder. I wonder how long it will be before I can wear my new Levi's. I take them off and hurl them all the way across the room.

Fucking things!

'You'll like him,' says Phil. 'He's an actor. He came into the café this morning, looking for a place to crash. Why don't you pop down and say hello? He's in the basement.'

Phil grins at me.

'His name's Ken. He's a bit weird, but OK.'

'Come in!'

The basement has been transformed. The blue and white tiles are still down. But there's a naked mannequin in the left-hand corner of the room, a long black wig on her head, like a

213

figure in a dream. A mattress covered in a black duvet lies on the floor by the far wall opposite, and a coffee machine with hot black liquid bubbles away below the bars of the window. On a small card table in the middle of the room a couple of paperbacks lie open, face down, Rizlas, strands of tobacco and an open packet of Benson and Hedges beside them. It all looks like a British Pop Art collage of the early sixties, an assemblage as much as a place to live in.

'Hello,' says Ken. He's wearing a Prince of Wales check three-piece suit and white shirt open at the neck, black plim-solls and aviator sunglasses. He's six feet tall and looks like he's just got in from LA, apart from the plimsolls.

'Would you like a coffee? Vitamin pill? I've got B, C, E and K.'

He goes across to the coffee machine, takes a plastic cup from the window ledge, pours me a cup of the hot black liquid, talk-ing the whole time, and hands me the coffee.

'You must be John. Phil told me about you. I'm putting on a play at the Hen and Chickens about Maggie's police state. I can let you have a couple of tickets if you fancy coming.'

'OK,' I say. 'When's it on?'

'In a couple of months,' says Ken. 'We're workshopping the script at the moment. Then there's rehearsals. That's why I'm living on coffee and vitamin pills – all my dole money is going into the play. You sure you won't have a vitamin pill? My mother sends them. She worries about me.'

'No thanks,' I say. I finish my coffee and hand him the cup. Phil is right about Ken.

A bit weird but OK.

The Scots lads have bought a black and white TV from a junk shop on the Holloway Road. It sits on the long table in the kitchen. On the *Six O'Clock News* the miners are going back to work. The strike is over. We watch the scenes in silence. It feels like something in the country has died.

'Come on,' says Mickey. 'If we're to have a wake, let's have it in the pub. Come on!'

Down in the basement a phalanx of cardboard policemen stand against the back wall, row on row, ready to charge. Their uniforms are painted dark blue, outlined in black marker, and their pointy helmets all sport silver badges and black chin straps, frowns drawn on their brows, eyes narrowed, mouths grim, truncheons at the ready.

'What do you think?' says Ken. 'There are fifty of them. I call them the Corrugated Squad. It took me a week to do them all.'

Ken looks like he's lost weight, his clothes a bit looser than when I first met him. The show at the Hen and Chickens had only two policemen in the cast. I thought they looked a bit lost.

'Getting them all to Edinburgh is going to be tricky,' says Ken, 'but they'll steal the show.'

'Tricky?' I say. 'Because you might get hassle from the cops?'

Ken reckoned Special Branch had been in the audience at the Hen and Chickens. There were two men in raincoats in the front row. But I thought they might have been there because of Anita, Ken's bombshell girlfriend. She played Margaret Thatcher as a dominatrix, in a rubber suit and blue rinse. There was something furtive about the raincoats, but I didn't think it had anything to do with them being Special Branch.

'I'm not worried about the cops,' says Ken. 'It's the thought of getting the Corrugated Squad in the back of Anita's Mini. Vitamin pill?'

I look at Ken. If he gets any thinner he could join the Corrugated Squad himself.

'No thanks, Ken,' I say. 'I'm trying to give them up.'

I come out of the Royal Festival Hall and make my way over Hungerford Bridge. The Thames lies either side of me, light skidding off the river's silver-grey surface, the dull brown depths below full of silt and mystery. I come to Embankment Station, tourists and students, backpackers and day-trippers spilling out of the Tube, and walk briskly through to Villiers Street.

Summer is here, the day sunny and warm, and London is suddenly a prettier place. Around our way kids are playing out in the street, ice cream vans chiming, girls in skimpy tops and ra-ra skirts, boys in t-shirts and jeans, eyeing each other up, grinning as they go by, a different, lazier pace to the streets as the sun shines down on us. It's a good day to go out and explore old haunts.

I cross the Strand and go down Agar Street. St Mungo's is all boarded up now. I've heard rumours that they're going to turn it into a police station, and I wonder what's become of everyone, where they are now, what they're doing, Joey and Chopper and Robert. I walk through a warren of streets towards Soho, the sun lost amongst shadows, and then I'm out into Covent Garden, a busker in a burst of light entertaining a small crowd.

It's not long before I come to Soho Street. There's a vegetarian restaurant there, Govinda's, run by the Hare Krishnas, and a sign in the window catches my eye: 'Free Holiday in France. Stay at our Chateau in Provence'. There's a number, and I ring it from a phone box. They take my address and say they'll send details.

I dream about Provence, about green fields and sunlit rivers, medieval towns with narrow cobbled streets and light-filled squares, of cafés with awnings and tables on the pavements, of dawdling over my coffee and croissant each morning as I write in my notebook and look forward to the day. The grape-picking season will begin in about a month and I daydream about staying in a barn in the heart of France, living on bread and cheese and wine and getting in the harvest, of coming home tanned and hardened and with money in my pocket.

A week later a letter with a French stamp arrives. I tell everyone in the house to keep an eye on my room, that I'll be gone a couple of months. I see Keith and borrow his birth certificate and a letter with his new address. I go to the Post Office and use these to get a British Visitor's Passport over the counter. Another few days and I set off for my dream.

I've been in Arles Station for the past four hours. The Hare Krishnas said they'd meet me on arrival and now I'm really worried. I'm by the ticket windows, afraid to move away in case I miss my pick-up. Travellers come in and out of the station, the anonymous business of buying tickets and boarding trains going on without me. Everyone looks chic and confident and very French, full of *savoir faire* and Gallic indifference. I cut a forlorn figure in Levi's, a grey shirt with frayed collar, brown Dr Martens and a Harris tweed jacket, an old canvas rucksack lying at my feet. I have no return ticket, very little money, and now I'm stranded, with no idea what to do. As people calmly go off to catch their trains, I start to feel invisible.

'Are you John?'

I turn around. An American girl about my own age, in a white sari and headscarf, is smiling at me.

'I'm sorry I'm late – problems with my wheels. Come on – let's get out of here.'

She walks quickly out of the station. An orange camper van is parked by the forecourt and I follow behind her. She gets in and opens the door on my side and I climb up and dump my rucksack behind the seats. She tells me her name, and says, 'I'm a devotee.'

The camper van kicks into life and we take the main road out of Arles, tall trees lining the route, elegant white buildings and blocks of apartments either side of us as we roll along. She talks to me the whole time about the Bhagavad Gita, about Krishna and Arjuna on the field of battle, about all the little cow girls and cow boys, about how sweet they all are, about how much I'm going to love it at the chateau, until we've left the town behind us and are cruising down a long grey stretch of French motorway. I don't understand a word of what she's on about.

Suddenly she puts her foot on the accelerator and we zoom along the road, through the little hills that undulate away before us, lifting off over them like she's riding the wind. She talks all the time, a continuous babble I can barely follow or understand. All I can do is hold on.

We come to a turning off the motorway and she drives down a road bordered by billboards for a mile or so till we come to another turning. The camper van pulls into a long tree-lined drive and we roll along it, crunching and bumping on gravel till we come to an opening at the end. Up ahead a white chateau gradually comes into view, a huge building rising up before us, with turrets and balconies and shuttered windows. It's like something out of a fairy tale. Three orange-robed Hare Krishnas are standing at the bottom of steps leading up to a large wooden door built into the front of the chateau. She pulls the van up by the small flight of steps and the three Hare Krishnas smile as we get out.

'Welcome,' says the tallest. He joins his hands together and bows his head. 'Let us show you to your room.'

I flop down on the bed and stare at the ceiling. My room isn't in the chateau – it's in a small block in the grounds, behind the fairy-tale castle, a low-rise barracks of a building. There are about twenty rooms either side of a narrow hall, with showers and toilets at the far end. It's basic, but at least I have a roof over my head.

A gong sounds in the distance and suddenly there is bustle and movement. The early evening lull is broken as doors open into the corridor and voices echo down the hall.

'I don't think I can take any more of this vegetarian crap.'

'Me neither. My guts haven't been right since I got here. I'm shitting through the eye of a needle every time I go.'

I get off my bed and open the door. Two backs are disappearing down the hall.

'Been here long?' I say, coming alongside them.

They eye me up. One is tall, like Ken, all in black, his long, chestnut mane tied in a ponytail. The other is about my height, in white t-shirt and blue jeans, his dark hair cut short.

'Too long,' says t-shirt and jeans.

They tell me that they've been travelling round the Continent. They heard about this place in Spain, and have been here nearly a week. They don't intend to stay long. The tall one is called Martin, and his mate's name is Alfie.

'The food is utter crap,' says Alfie.

We're walking towards the castle, the sun starting to fade in the late evening light. Hare Krishnas in yellow robes and white robes, men and women, Europeans and Asian, are all walking towards a gap in the trees at the edge of the castle's grounds. We follow them through the gap where a sunlit meadow lies ahead of us. A large white tent stands in the middle of the meadow, and through the open flaps we can see people sat at long trestle tables eating.

'Yeah, utter crap,' says Martin. 'And there's never enough of it.'

There's a loud knock at the door. Outside, it's still dark, and I wonder where I am. I get out of bed and pull on my jeans. The stone floor is cold as my bare feet slap across its surface to the door. It's the American girl.

'You want to come over to the chateau? We need to sort out a few things. It won't take long.'

'What time is it?'

I'm still stiff from the journey, my eyes bleary with sleep.

'It's 5 a.m. We start early but you'll soon get used to it.'

I dress quickly, and come out into the corridor. I ask her to wait a few minutes while I brush my teeth and have a wash.

'Go right ahead,' she says. 'And if you need to use the meditation chamber, it's down there on the left.'

I'm ready in a matter of minutes and we walk over to the chateau in the pearly grey light of dawn. She leads me up the steps and through the large wooden door into a gloomy wood-panelled hallway. There's a white marble staircase at the end of the hall and we climb the stairs to a big room on the first floor. There are about ten Hare Krishnas and a few visitors in jeans and t-shirts sitting cross-legged on the floor as we stand in the doorway. They're all gazing at a statue of an old Asian man in saffron robes seated on a throne in front of the windows, which are lying open. Already it's getting warm, and a faint breeze stirs in the room.

We go in and sit with them. After a few moments, a tall American in saffron robes enters the room. He starts talking to us all about 'spiritual life', and then the entire room begins chanting the Hare Krishna mantra, a droning, repetitive litany: 'Hare Krishna Hare Krishna, Krishna Krishna Hare Hare, Hare Rama Hare Rama, Rama Rama Hare Hare.'

The meeting breaks up and we all troop over to the white tent in the meadow for breakfast. The American girl introduces me to a young devotee who does maintenance work around the grounds.

'How would you guys like to work together?'

I look at him across the long table. He has the same shaven head, the same yellow insignia painted between his eyebrows and down his nose, the same saffron robes, as the other male Hare Krishnas. What's different is his accent.

'Nae bother,' he says. 'Let's get to it.'

'I used to be like you,' says the Scots Hare Krishna. We're lugging logs into a wheelbarrow from a big pile in front of an outbuilding, somewhere well away from the chateau and the barracks and the white tent in the meadow. There's a red gravel track behind us, a big field in front, and an old rusting tractor by the side of the outbuilding.

'I was living in London,' he says, 'squatting in Vauxhall. I'd come down from Glasgow, thinking the streets were paved with gold. But I couldn't find any kind of job. Three million unemployed at the time – there was no work at all. So much for getting on your bike.'

He talks as we work in the sunshine, the French countryside green and golden all around us, the sun hot on my back.

'So I started drinking. There were a few Scots lads I knew in the squats and we all started getting tanked up. Weekends only, but you'll know yourself – your dole goes nowhere in the pub. So we decided to rob this social club. There were three of us – Mickey, Alistair and Angus.'

I nearly drop the log I'm carrying.

'Do you know them?' he says. 'Ach, they could be anyone. I'm sure London is full of squatters from Glasgow. That's not the point. Wait till you hear.'

He puts his log on the pile we've built up in the barrow and looks into my face. He wipes the back of his hand on his fore-head and I stop what I'm doing.

'There was 200 quid in the till. A tidy sum between us all. But instead of blowing it, Mickey said let's go into business.

Yeah – you can guess the business he had in mind. Soon we were supplying the whole of Vauxhall with wacky baccy. Mickey had a connection in Glasgow and we all went up the road with him for the Big Score. That's what he called it – one Big Score, lads, he'd say, and we'll all be right.

'And we were good at it. We turned our 200 quid into 400 quid in a fortnight. That's how much we were knocking out. We had it all – bongs, chillums, weights. And then one day it came home to me: I'm a drug dealer. People think hash isn't a drug, that having a joint is like having a cup of tea. But I knew better.

'That's when I found the Hare Krishna Movement. I was up in Oxford Street one day and they gave me a leaflet. I went along to the Temple. See, they knew I was looking for something, for a better way. I've been a devotee ever since. My life before becoming a devotee – that's my maya.'

I've come across the word before. It's an Eastern concept that means 'illusion'.

'Where I am now,' he says, 'I couldn't be happier.' He grabs hold of the wheelbarrow by the handles, and walks off with it down the red gravel track.

I watch him for a moment, then set off after him.

That evening in the white tent the American girl comes over to my table.

'Well?' she asks. 'How did you both get on?'

'Fine,' I say.

'I bet you had a lot in common.'

'Mostly maya,' I say.

She laughs.

'You're already talking like a devotee.'

Then she looks serious.

'You should think about it,' she says. 'Really.'

Before I can say anything, she smiles again, and walks off to join her friends at another table.

The knock on the door. Outside, it's still dark. The footsteps move away down the corridor. There's a knock on another door, then another.

'You must be joking!'

It's Alfie's voice.

'We're tourists here, OK? Leave us alone!'

I get up and pull on my Levi's and a t-shirt. Out in the corridor the young American girl is waiting for me.

'You coming over to the chateau?'

'OK,' I say.

'I'll see you over there.'

She smiles and walks away, out of the accommodation block and into the dark.

A door along the corridor opens and Alfie pops his head out.

'They've done a right number on you, haven't they?' he says. 'That's what this is all about, you plum. They're looking for recruits. If you show any interest in them, they won't let up. Do yourself a favour – tell them all to fuck off.'

He scowls at me and shuts his door.

Back in my room, I think about what's been happening. The Scots Hare Krishna had impressed me. Ever since I'd left Frank and Ivy I'd always lived with other people. I think I was looking for the sense of community I'd experienced in Claybury, and that this is why I ended up in Grovelands House, St Mungo's, Patchwork. All very different, but all places where I knew camaraderie, company, some measure of care.

I can see that the Hare Krishnas are a community as well. They offer camaraderie too. But it comes at a price, a price I'm not prepared to pay. Alfie's right. I can see that they've been softening me up since I got here. I make a decision – I've got to get away.

I gather my stuff, put on my Dr Martens, and slip on my jacket. I hitch my rucksack on to my shoulders and open the door. I go quickly down the corridor and out into the fresh morning air. Over the distant hills a huge red sun is beginning to rise. I walk towards the tree-lined drive, crunching the stony grey gravel underfoot as I head for the road and whatever lies beyond.

XIII

The Whittington, 1986

The Whittington stands on Highgate Hill, a complex of hospital buildings I look down on from the seventh floor of the Psyche Wing. They're sprawled across either side of the steep rise, low modern buildings scattered amongst the hospital's Victorian edifices, the car parks and bits of green that make up the grounds, traffic climbing in a slow ascent up the slope to Hampstead and beyond. I was born in this hospital, in St Mary's Wing across the road, nearly twenty-six years ago. I feel like I've come full circle.

The Psyche Wing looks very new, all straight lines and plate-glass windows, a tower block built of sand-coloured brick about ten storeys high on the right-hand side of Highgate Hill. There's a canteen on the ground floor and wards on all the rest. As I look down on the buses and the cars straining and stretching to climb the hill, I think back to how I got here.

On either side of the long grey ribbon of road lie fields of golden sunflowers. They stretch away before me, strange and alien, their long stems, tall as a man, swaying slightly, their great round heads looming up out of the endless fields. There are mile after mile of them. As I walk, they buzz in the clear blue summer air of France, a low monotonous drone rising up in the heat: *Hare Krishna Hare Krishna, Krishna Krishna Hare Hare, Hare Rama Hare*

Rama, Rama Rama Hare Hare. They are chanting in the mild breeze, and the sound of them echoes inside my head. They're a million periscopes and every one of them swivels round to follow me.

I walk on, the hot sun high in the sky. It must be noon – I've been walking now for at least six hours. I'm parched and sweating. I think I must be dehydrated. Perhaps I'm hallucinating – my brain feels as if it's being boiled in my skull. The sunflowers are like heatlamps, radiating energy, frying me as I walk. If I keep going, if I don't give in, if I can just put one foot in front of another and not stumble or fall, I might make it. But first I have to get past all of them, sinister and alien in the baking heat of August.

Over the noise from the fields I hear another sound, a low drone in the distance. I turn around and see a small white van coming towards me. I might not get another chance.

I step into the middle of the road and hold up my hands. The driver has no option – he slows down and stops about three yards in front of me. He sticks his head out of the window.

'*Monsieur?*' he says.

'*S'il vous plaît, monsieur,*' I say. '*Vers Arles?*'

He shrugs, and leans over to open the door. I get in, and he drives off, the sunflowers hissing now as we disappear into the French countryside.

❦

'I've been on the streets years, man.'

He sounds like his vocal chords have been sandpapered, deep and rough and raw. There are just the two of us in the small TV room. The television is on, but the sound is down low, and neither of us is watching it. They've taken my clothes away, and I wear hospital pyjamas and striped dressing gown. He's in pyjamas and dressing gown as well.

'My brains are fried,' he says. 'Too much heat from the streets. Too much glare. Too many fucking rays.'

His long dark hair is greasy and lank and his black beard is matted and streaked with strands of ginger. He fishes a tobacco tin from the pocket of his dressing gown, takes off the lid, and starts rolling a cigarette.

'It's getting worse, man.'

He takes a box of Swan Vestas from his other pocket and slips the tin back in his dressing gown. He lights the roll-up, taking an enormous drag that seems to burn half of it away. He looks at me through a haze of grey smoke.

'Do yourself a favour,' he says. 'Don't drink the water. It's fucking deadly.'

I look at the TV. The midday news has come on. Pickets are clashing with police outside Rupert Murdoch's new print works in Wapping. It's like the miners' strike all over again. There are the same scenes of truncheons flying and bloody heads, the same mayhem and brutality, the same vicious, violent riot.

He's seen me looking at the box, and now his glazed eyes are gazing into mine. He takes another long drag, and sucks the smoke deep into his lungs.

'There's your Revolution, man,' he says. 'Looks like the fucking pigs are winning. You want a smoke?'

He starts coughing as I rise out of my chair and go over to turn up the TV.

The driver stops the van.

'*Au revoir, monsieur*,' he says.

We've come to a crossroads in a flat, featureless landscape. The sunflowers are way behind us, but we're still in the middle of nowhere.

I open the door and get out, dragging my rucksack behind

me on to the grass verge. Ahead is the long grey road, a sign a hundred yards up in front. We've been travelling for about half an hour, hardly speaking, listening to the radio, trapped either side of the language barrier.

'*Au revoir*,' I say. '*Merci beaucoup, monsieur.*'

'*Bonne chance*,' he says, and slams the door shut. The van turns left and I watch it disappear into the distance. The sun is still beating down, and I hitch up the rucksack and walk towards the sign.

It says Arles is straight ahead, thirty-five kilometres. I try to work out what that is in miles. I think it might be about twenty. Perhaps I'll get another lift. I start walking, hopeful now, my thumb out just in case.

***

'You know where you are, don't you, man?'

He's called Mitch. I'm not sure if it's a nickname or short for something, but it suits him. He's still on about the rays, the heat, the glare, in that voice that sounds like it's been blowtorched. But I kind of understand him.

'This is where Dick Whittington heard the Bow bells and turned again. Remember? About him coming to the Smoke like some runaway and ending up Lord Mayor? Man, we must be on one powerful ley line up here. This is the city limits, right here where we're under heavy manners. This is where Old London runs out. So what do they fucking do? They put up a Psyche Wing. You ever thought about that? You ever thought about why they would want to put it right here? It's because all the psychic power is concentrated in this weird fucking zone. If you listen, man, if you're tuned in, you can hear the city speak. And you know what Old London is saying? It's saying, "You can run but you can't escape."'

***

Arles Station is busy with mid-morning travellers, all hurrying to catch their trains. I still have my ticket from Paris. It's my only hope of getting through the barrier. If I flash it at the ticket collector, I might just have a chance.

I've been in Arles since about eight o'clock last night. I had to walk all the way from where the white van stopped. I came to a little supermarket on the outskirts of town and managed to shop-lift some cheese and bread and a bottle of water. I took it all off to the park where I sat on a bench and wolfed it down. I hadn't eaten all day. Then I waited for darkness, and slept in the park until dawn came. I freshened up in a toilet near the station and now I'm here, steeling myself to walk quickly through the ticket barriers.

I take a big breath, and fall in behind a family who look like they're on holiday. The parents are in their late forties, casually dressed in tan slacks and pastel-coloured polo shirts, and the children – two blonde teenaged girls, like extras in a pop video, all pouts and sulks – wait while Papa shows the ticket inspector their *billets*. They're travelling light, just nylon rucksacks, and I figure they must be off for a day trip somewhere. As the youngest girl is about to pass under the gaze of the ticket inspector, I spot something and walk quickly forward.

'*Mam'selle*,' I say. I bend down and pick up her earring. She's dropped it on the floor. I hold it for her, and she smiles at me and takes it from my outstretched palm.

'*Merci, monsieur*,' she says.

I've got my ticket in my other hand, and, not taking my eyes off her, I flash it quickly at the ticket inspector.

'*C'est mon plaisir*,' I say, smiling brightly.

Papa has turned round to see what's going on, but Mama nudges him, and he moves forward. The whole party – Papa, Mama, the two girls – all follow. I whip the ticket away again, shoving it into the inside breast pocket of my jacket, my heart thumping, and walk quickly through the barrier after them.

As I come out on to the platform I turn away and stride towards the big board giving details of arrivals and departures. I can feel myself tense as I wait for the ticket inspector to come running after me and call out. But he doesn't. The moment has passed.

I've done it – I'm through. As I get to the departure board, I see that I have five minutes to wait for the train to Paris. I look down the track, and after a couple of minutes there it is in the distance coming towards me.

It grows larger and larger as it bears down on us, and then it's here, a long SNCF Express grinding to a halt. I can't afford to hang about. As the doors slide open I climb on board with all the other passengers, and walk down the aisle to an empty seat at the back of the carriage. I shove my rucksack up on to the luggage rack and soon the train is pulling out again.

The miles roll quickly by, away from the town of Arles, away from the park I slept in, from the long grey ribbon of road, from the baking-hot sun, from all the fields of sunflowers, from the chateau and the Hare Krishnas. I look out of the window. The rhythm of the train starts to lull me, and within moments I'm fast asleep.

They've moved me up to the seventh floor. The ward downstairs with Mitch doesn't have any windows. This ward up on the seventh floor has a great big window, and I spend time looking out of it, gazing down on Highgate Hill, on London laid out below me. I listen to the city, strain to hear Old London, but there are only the sounds of traffic droning away up the hill, the odd shout in the street, a helicopter clattering overhead. As hard as I try, I can't hear anything else.

The sunflowers are coming. There are millions of them, hissing and spitting as they advance towards me. I'm surrounded by them. They're looming over me. I shut my eyes, scream till my lungs burst. When I open my eyes again, a man with a lined face is saying, '*Monsieur?*'

It's the ticket collector, his SNCF uniform and peaked cap suddenly more frightening than any field of sunflowers.

'*Votre billet, monsieur.*'

The train is speeding through the French countryside, away from Arles and towards Paris. I should have hidden somewhere, in the toilets, or in the carriage at the very back of the train. Now it's too late. Suddenly I'm wide awake.

'*Pardonnez, monsieur,*' I say quickly. '*Je suis anglais. Toutes mes choses sont volées.*'

I hope he doesn't look up and see my rucksack tucked away in the luggage rack. He grins at me.

'*Vous avez gagné,*' he says. He winks, his official mask suddenly slipping to reveal the rogue beneath. He walks off, through the sliding doors into the next carriage and I let out a long, low sigh of relief.

In another hour the train pulls into Paris and I set off to find the British Embassy.

'I'm afraid we can't help you.'

I've been waiting for an hour to see him. The queue of people before me has all gone now and a queue just as long stretches away behind and down the stairs. He looks over my shoulder to see who's next.

'But if you get out to the motorway where the lorries go to Calais, perhaps you can hitch a lift there? This may be useful.'

He slides a photocopied map towards me under the perspex window.

'Next,' he says.

There's nothing I can do. I thought I might get repatriated, that the Embassy would help me. But they get people coming to them every day with stories like mine. I pick up my rucksack and trudge down the stairs and back out on to the streets of Paris.

The Gare du Nord is teeming with commuters. It's five o'clock and the rush hour is at its height. I reckon I have one chance. The train to Calais goes in two minutes But I haven't got a ticket for it. I run quickly up to the barrier and stop.

'You dropped your passport!'

On the platform beyond the barrier is a knot of girls. They're English – I've heard them speaking on the concourse. One of them turns round. As she does so, the ticket inspector comes towards me.

'*Monsieur,*' I say breathlessly. '*Ma soeur. Elle n'a pas son passeport. Permettez-vous?*'

I'm holding my British Visitor's Passport up for him to see. If he looks closely at it, he'll know it's mine, not my 'sister's'. But the train will be pulling out any moment now. If he doesn't let me through I won't get it to her and she'll have to miss her train.

'*Allez, monsieur,*' he says. '*Allez, allez!*'

I rush forward and catch up with the English girls.

'Did you mean me?' asks one of them, a pretty blonde aged about seventeen.

'I'm sorry,' I say. 'I thought you were someone else.'

The train is sighing and hissing as I climb aboard. People are leaning out of windows, making their last-minute farewells. Either I'm going to be arrested, or else this train is going to pull out. Have they alerted the driver? Is that why we're taking so long? A whistle blows, and suddenly we're moving.

'Is this seat taken?'

He's a short Frenchman with a broken nose and a suntan.

He's wearing jeans, a dark jumper and sunglasses. He carries a small bag in his hand and looks like a crook.

'No, there's no one sitting here,' I say. He eases himself in next to me. I figure if I get talking to him he'll make me look less suspicious.

As the train speeds towards Calais he tells me that he's from Marseilles, and that his business is 'import/export'. By now I think he's definitely a crook. He tells me that his name is Gérard and that he's off to London for a short break. No, he hasn't made a reservation at a hotel – do I know of any good places to stay? I tell him that he's welcome at my place, that I live in a big house in the middle of London with some really interesting people. There's a spare room and he'd be very welcome. By the time we get to Calais we're firm friends. As we're getting off, I realize that no one came round to collect the tickets. I thank Joan of Arc, the patron saint of France, for watching over me, and follow Gérard towards the waiting ferry.

⚓

'What are we going to do with you, Mr O'Donoghue?'

The hospital social worker is one of the old school. She has white hair and horn-rimmed spectacles, a neat twinset and pearls, and could well have been a Wren or a Land Girl during the war. She wears stout brown shoes and has a prim, military air about her. She's almost from another age.

I've been in the Whittington a month now. The days have passed like they always do in hospital – slowly.

'There's a couple of places I can think of,' she says. 'One is the SOS Hostel. It's quite near here and they do a good job. The other is a new project which Patchwork Housing Association are starting up.'

'Tell me about Patchwork,' I say, as casually as I can. 'They sound interesting.'

'It's a large house off the Holloway Road in Tufnell Park. Half the tenants in the house have a background in social work, and half are people who have got into the same kind of difficulties you have. Would you be interested in something like that?'

'Definitely,' I say.

'All right, Mr O'Donoghue. But you can't go on like this, you know. You have to try to make something of your life. Put all this behind you.'

I thank her and get up to leave.

'Oh, and Mr O'Donoghue?'

I stop at the door and turn round. She's peering at me over her horn rims.

'Yes?' I say.

'Don't let me down.'

'John – what are you doing here?'

Phil looks shocked to see me. I've finally made it all the way back to Liverpool Road from the south of France. No ticket, no money, no proper papers. But I've done it.

'France didn't work out, Phil. Can I come in, please? I'm shattered. This is Gérard, by the way. He's a friend. He'll be staying in my room for a few days.'

Phil lets us in.

'There have been a few changes, John,' he says. He stops in the hallway. 'There's someone in your room.'

I look at him.

'What? Who?'

'He's a Geordie called Alan. We all thought you were going to be gone for a couple of months. What happened about the grape-picking?'

'I got homesick,' I say. I wasn't expecting this. But I feel too exhausted to explain, to argue about the room, to make a fuss.

And besides, Phil is right. I did tell them all that I'd be gone for two months. And here I am, back inside a fortnight.

'This room here is free,' he says. He opens a door just along the hallway. Gérard and I look in. It's a lot smaller than the room I have upstairs, and even barer. There are just floorboards and a window that looks out on to the back garden.

'OK, Phil,' I say. 'But we'll need a couple of mattresses.'

'No problem,' he says. 'We've got a couple going spare next door. You can have those.'

Phil pauses a moment.

'A lot has happened since you went away, John. It's been quite a couple of weeks. We'll talk about it later. Perhaps Gérard would give me a hand with the mattresses?'

They go off down the hallway towards the kitchen. Exhausted, I drop my rucksack on to the floor and wait for them to come back.

I walk down the stairs to the kitchen. I'm still a bit sleepy but after a long night's rest it feels good to be back. I stand in the doorway and take in the scene. Two girls are gabbling away in Spanish on what looks like a payphone they've set up on the kitchen table. Behind them, Phil is crouched over the sink, washing up. A couple I haven't seen before, him tall and blond, her dark-haired, are standing a few feet to the right of Phil at the gas cooker, talking in low voices as they cook porridge in a big saucepan. Through the open French windows I can make out four people sitting around on chairs in the back yard, talking and smoking. Music – the Psychedelic Furs – is buzzing away from a ghetto-blaster set in the middle of them all. A cloud passes across the sun and suddenly the garden is as grey and derelict-looking as ever.

I hear footsteps on the stairs behind me and turn to see Frankie and Mickey coming down them side by side.

'Hello, Johnny Boy,' Mickey says. 'It's good to see you. So you went off to see the world? Well, now you're back the world is on your doorstep. Come on – I'll introduce you to everyone.'

Frankie and Mickey walk past me into the big kitchen and I follow. The Spanish girls are still gabbling away into the pay-phone. Outside, the smokers on the kitchen chairs are passing around a spliff. I wonder if one of them is Alan, the Geordie who's taken my room. As Frankie and Mickey walk towards the big table and sit beside the two Spanish girls Phil seems to flinch. There's a strange atmosphere suddenly, as if there's just been a row.

'*Adios!*' the Spanish girls say quickly and put the phone down. Phil carries on washing up, laying the pots he's done on the draining board to dry. The couple cooking porridge serve up and turn round. They take their bowls through the open French windows and stand facing each other in front of the smokers by the back wall of the house, eating their porridge.

'Phil, can you make a brew?' says Mickey.

I see what's happened. Frankie's no longer with Phil – she's with Mickey. Phil isn't the King of the Castle any more – Mickey is and he's lording it over his rival. Phil walks silently over to the kettle and puts it on the cooker. There's an uneasy silence for a moment, then Frankie breaks the ice.

'You haven't met Anouk and Paola, have you, John? They're from Madrid.'

The two Spanish girls smile and Frankie tells me about everyone else. The couple who are eating their porridge are Brian and Jennifer. They're from Sydney, and are just passing through. So are Anouk and Paola. And the smokers out in the garden. They're from all over: Canada, Israel, Wales, Tyneside.

'Couldn't you find anyone from these parts?' I ask. It's a joke, but like all jokes, there's a point behind it. Half of these people aren't homeless – they're just enjoying a free holiday.

'That's so racist!' says Frankie.

'What are you talking about?' I say.

'Is that what they said to you when you were in France? France for the French? You fascist!'

'My point is—' I start to say, but Frankie is shouting me down.

'Why don't you fuck off, John? If you don't like it here, piss off!'

Dazed, I look into Mickey's eyes.

'Frankie's got a point,' he says.

The kettle has boiled while we've been talking. Phil has made five cups of tea. One each for Frankie and Mickey, one each for Anouk and Paola, one for himself.

Nothing for me.

I get up and walk out of the house, slamming the door as hard as I can behind me.

'Are you all right?'

Mass is over and the early morning congregation is dispersing. St Mellitus' on Tollington Park Road is only a couple of miles from the squat, near Archway. I've been walking around in circles ever since I left it, all through the night, trying to figure out what to do. But I haven't got a clue.

I look up. A young man is bent over me as I sit on a pew at the back of the church, dazed, stupefied.

'Not really,' I say.

He's Irish, a little older than me, skinny, with a bit of a beard.

'Well, I'm not going to pass by on the other side,' he says. 'Come on, I know what to do.'

I get up and walk with him towards the big wooden doors. We stop and bless ourselves at the holy water font and come out on to the steps of the church. Some of the parishioners, old dears going off for their shopping, look round at us as I stand at the top of the steps and take in the scene. I must look rough – one of them frowns at me before hurrying on her way.

'Take no notice,' says the skinny Irishman.

'Thanks,' I say.

He asks me what happened, why I seem so out of it. I tell him, and as we come to the Holloway Road he says that it's his Christian duty to help me, that he's taking me to the hospital, that his name is Michael, that I'll be fine in no time.

I'm too exhausted to argue. The Psyche Wing looms into view as we walk up the hill and away from the streets and the teeming life of the city behind us.

It's been sorted. I've been accepted by the Patchwork House in Tufnell Park and today I'm moving in. As I come out on to Highgate Hill, I look back up to the seventh floor, to the big window I used to look out of when I was on the ward. There's a figure standing framed in the large pane of glass, which catches the light as I look up and dazzles me, making my eyes squint. The figure gazes down on the traffic below, exactly as I used to. I can't be sure, but I think he has a beard, long hair, a roll-up on the go.

'Good luck, Mitch,' I murmur, and set off back down the road, turning again towards the city and yet another move.

XIV

Fairmead Road, Spring 1987

Fairmead Road is a quiet street tucked away in a residential neighbourhood off the Holloway Road. It lies 500 yards from the din and bustle of Holloway, which could be in another borough, another district altogether, for here all is calm, leafy, suburban. This is N7 not N19, and that subtle distinction seems to make all the difference. It's almost like the difference between north and south of the river.

I've settled in quickly to life in the House. It's a large solid Victorian villa, done out by Patchwork in Habitat and Heal's. It has none of the makeshift feel of the houses in New Cross: this place is designer. The kitchen is at the back of the open-plan dining area on the ground floor, towards the rear garden. It's a large kitchen with all the latest equipment, including a Miele washing machine and drier tucked into a small utility room by the back door. The kitchen units are all sleek pine, and the cooker is a big gas outfit. There's a fridge-freezer and a dishwasher, ceramic sink units, and pale green linoleum on the floor. The table in the dining area is sleek pine as well, big enough to fit eight chairs comfortably, a vase of flowers and a full bowl of fruit always on display in the middle of it. The whole look is light, airy, stylish.

The large living room, with its high ceilings, windows and cornices, has space for two sofas and three armchairs, all from Habitat, a Sony TV with remote control, and a large coffee table from Heal's. Sometimes there's a copy of the *Face* lying around, but these are Patrick's and he doesn't leave them lying around long. The rumour is that he irons them after he's read them.

Patrick's a social worker, a gay man in his thirties with long black hair, a lopsided smile, and a generally laid-back attitude. There are two other gay men: Gregory, who was into drugs but is now studying at North London Poly; and Albert, a black fashion designer. Then there's Cassie, another ex-drug user, dark-haired and reserved, but about to start up her own business on the Enterprise Allowance Scheme, and Tiffany, who graduated from Camberwell Art College and has been a set designer in the West End. She's been clean for a year, and has a boyfriend, Toby, who works in the City. Rachel lives under the eaves, in a large attic that's almost self-contained. She works for the Chailey Community, the House in Ealing, another strange coincidence about Fairmead Road. It's like being back at Grovelands House, except that the look here is more yuppie than hippy. It's as if the two houses are emblems of the country's rollercoaster ride these last few years, from the dull and dowdy shabby chic of Grovelands House in the early eighties to this designer look in the late eighties. Boom and bust, bust and boom – it's been a mad decade.

'During the war I was billeted down in Wales. Hot stuff, those Taff birds.'

I'm in the grounds of Bethnal Green Hospital with George O'Shaughnessy. It's a geriatric hospital now, but once it was a general hospital. There are wards, corridors, a large courtyard outside. It's a smaller version of the Victorian asylums I know so well, right down to the same red bricks of Claybury, the same dark Gothic buildings.

The Community Programme has been brought in to get unemployment down and I've been given a job, my first regular job since I was at the Royal Free eight years ago, working in

Bethnal Green three days a week. The Bow bells are only about a mile or so up the road, but Bethnal Green is now a world away from jellied eels, pie and mash, and chicken soup. There are now more curry houses than fish and chip shops, and saris and pashminas have turned the long drabness of Commercial Road into a bazaar, a souk, a casbah. The London I grew up in is changing right in front of me.

George sits in his wheelchair, the mild spring sunlight on his old gnarled face. He wears pyjamas and a dressing gown, dark blue glasses, and speaks in a gruff Cockney voice, the voice of an old docker, which is what he was for fifty years.

'They liked it regular, those Taff birds. Which was just as well, because so did I.'

George laughs and lights up his panatella. He likes a cigar, and chatting up the nurses on the ward. The Community Programme is funding a project to bring art to the hospital. A whole army of apprentices work away under the direction of Mervyn, himself a mild-mannered Welshman, a Taff as George calls him, in a big studio specially set up in one of the disused wards. Large square canvases from the studio hang down the length of the corridors, bright studies of Pearly Kings, market stall-holders, pie and mash shops. They seem like they're almost from another time, like costermongers, crossing sweepers, and stars of the music hall. Mervyn's artists also get the patients to do some painting on the wards, but George O'Shaughnessy will have none of it.

'Like being back at bleeding school,' he says. 'Nah. I ain't doing it.'

I've never even whitewashed a wall, but Mervyn has taken me on. He says I might be good with the patients, which is why I get to spend so much time with George.

I lie on my futon and pull my sleeping bag up over my head. It's the middle of the afternoon, and the Dread has come. The feeling that Fairmead Road will all end in disaster, that this scene will go the way of all the rest. Everywhere I've been, every decent place I've ever had, every job, they've all ended the same way. Frank and Ivy, the flat in Hampstead, Grovelands House. I've managed to cock up every time.

It's because I'm not right, because there's this darkness inside me, inside my mind. It's waiting for me, waiting to surface. I've tried to fight it, to tell myself that I have had so many knocks I was bound to flip. But I know I'm kidding myself.

I'm mad.

And there's nothing I can do to stop it.

'My daughter, she won't come and see me.'

I'm out in the courtyard of the hospital with George. A few of the workers from the studio have built a pergola just outside the ward and I sit on a chair beside George as he looks into the distance through his dark glasses.

'Why's that, George?' I ask softly.

'I'm an embarrassment to her, son. She lives in Harold Wood. It's a right trek to Bethnal Green. And what's she going to see when she gets here? An old man on the way out, that's what.'

I think George might be blind, that he wears dark glasses to hide his sightless eyes. Sometimes when he looks at me it's as if I'm being X-rayed by him, as if his real eyes are looking right through me. He turns round now, the dark blue lenses catching a glint of sunlight, my face reflected twice in the twin curves of George's shades. He slowly takes off his glasses and rubs his bony knuckles into cloudy grey eyes.

'She'll never come,' he cries, 'never!'

His deep sobs echo round the courtyard, the sound of an old heart breaking.

*

The Half Moon is a large pub on the Holloway Road, not far from the House. I need a drink, a stiff one. From the top deck of the bus I can see the pub as we snake through the traffic. George's words have been haunting me all day. They're exactly the same words my mother said about me before she died, that I'd never come, never. My heart is raw. I get off the bus and walk the few yards from the stop to the Half Moon. Inside it's quiet, the Friday night crowds still on their way home or having their dinner. I order a whiskey and a pint of Guinness, and take the drinks over to a table near the door. I just need a steadier, one to set me right again, to ease the pain in my chest.

I look up from the glasses in front of me and see a young woman walking up and down, as if she's looking for someone. I catch her eye, a worried, anxious eye. She's smartly dressed in a grey leather jacket, a black skirt and boots, a floppy-brimmed black hat on her head. She's plump and pretty and not too tall.

She passes back in front of me again.

'Looking for someone?' I say.

She stops walking up and down and stands right in front of me.

'Yes,' she says. Her accent is Irish, somewhere from the west. 'But he's stood me up. God, I need a drink!'

'I know the feeling,' I say. 'What are you having?'

She asks for a pint of Guinness and I tell her to take a seat while I go and get it. I order one for her and another for myself and get a look at her from the bar. She takes her hat off, and shakes out a tumble of red hair, settling it over her shoulders. She seems a little more relaxed and catches my eye, grinning as if we're both in on some joke. I grin back, glad of her company, glad that she's Irish, that she's from home. I bring over the drinks and settle myself in beside her.

'Cheers,' she says, holding up her glass.

'Cheers,' I say, clinking mine against hers.

'My name's Theresa,' she says, 'Theresa Bradbury.'

'Bradbury?' I say. 'That's a very Irish name.'

'My lot came over with Cromwell,' she says.

'That's odd,' I say.

'What?' she says.

'Well, you look more like a Cavalier than a Roundhead.'

She grins again, dimples in her cheeks, mischief in her eyes. At closing time we totter up the road and round the corner to my place.

And she tells me who stood her up and why.

On Monday the City of London Festival is running a poetry competition. It's taking place in the Cheshire Cheese pub on Fleet Street, where W.B. Yeats founded the Rhymers' Club. The advert says entrants should bring along a poem and read it out to the judge, Alan Brownjohn, and the rest of the audience. I go along in my lunch hour from Bethnal Green, a poem in my pocket, hoping I can get back to the hospital before I strain Mervyn's patience.

Downstairs at the Cheshire Cheese, in the gloomy vault where the poets have come to read, I take a seat at the back, a pint in one hand, a pork pie in the other, as a middle-aged lady reads out her poem. There's a smattering of applause and then another reader is called up. I keep an eye on the clock. I've told them upstairs that I've brought something along but if I'm not on soon I'll have to get back to work. More applause and suddenly my name is called. In the dim, winey light I make my way up to the front and pull out a piece of paper from my back pocket.

I read the poem and make my apologies, leaving quickly and sprinting for the Tube, making it back to the hospital only just in time. George is not on the ward, but one of the nurses tells me not to worry, he's gone to the Whitechapel for some routine tests and will be back in a week. I count the days, forgetting all about the Cheshire Cheese, Alan Brownjohn, and the City of London Festival.

All I can think about is George.

I call her Braddie. She has a Roundhead hardness her ancestors – 'Cromwell's lot' – would be proud of, as well as something of the emigrant's awkwardness. She came to the Half Moon to meet her boyfriend, Mick. Braddie lent him some money when he was in a fix. She's a bit mysterious about exactly what kind of trouble he was in, but he stood her up, disappeared, and now she reckons her money has gone with him. All told he has a hundred pounds in his pocket, and her curse on him to the grave.

'He was only a scut, anyway,' she says, taking a sup of her pint. We're in a pub near Homerton Hospital, where she's training to be a midwife. It's a short bus ride away from Bethnal Green, and over a few pints she tells me where she's from – Limerick – about the diaries she's been keeping since she was twelve, her love of writers and writing, the scene she left in Dublin before she came over for the nursing.

'You should come up and see my etchings,' I say.

'You etch?'

'I used to,' I say, 'until the doctor gave me something for it.'

She gives me an old-fashioned look.

'I mean my poems,' I say. 'I've been writing since I was fourteen.'

'Any by heart?' she says.

I think about a poem I wrote for my mother. When I was a child she taught me a card game, Twenty-five, the national card game of Ireland, and we'd play it with my cousins, every summer when we went across for our long holidays with them all. The game is a cross between Trumps and Poker, and tricks are taken with the low cards in black and the high cards in red. Court cards beat pips, the Ace of Hearts beats the court cards, and the Five of Trumps – the Fingers – beats everything. The Ace of Trumps lets you take – 'rob' – the card turned up for trumps and throw one out in exchange, and you play five points a trick to make 'Twenty-five'. 'Play quick and win quick,' my mother used to say, as she dealt out the cards to my cousins and me.

I look at Braddie, and think of how she resembles my mother, her looks, her spirit, and recite the poem from memory.

> Twenty-five
>
> My mother first taught me Twenty-five,
> That intricate game of sixpenny tricks,
> Dealing quick hands in a sneaky skive
> From milking the goat, stooking the ricks.
>
> She taught me how to rob and renege, saving
> The Knave 'til the Fingers had fallen,
> To play Ace of Hearts when battle was raving,
> To not be at home when court cards came calling.
>
> 'The lowest in black, the highest in red'.
> Dark colour of mourning, bright colour of blood.
> Deal in the angels, the quick and the dead:
> None of her cards will ever be dud.

There's a moment of silence. Then Braddie downs her pint in one great gulp.

'Come on,' she says, banging her empty glass on the table. 'Drink up.'

'Where are we going?'

'My room,' she says. 'In the nurses' home. I have some etchings of my own to show you.'

'They bought it for £200,000 in the morning and sold it for £400,000 the same afternoon.'

Toby, Tiffany's boyfriend, is sitting in the living room, tie loosened, his chalk-stripe suit slightly rumpled after a hard day's broking in the City.

'A penthouse flat in Chelsea. It's unbelievable the money you can make in property right now. Tiffers – could you bring me another gin and tonic, darling?'

He picks his up his glass from the Heal's coffee table and rattles the ice in the bottom of it. He gives Tiffany a big smile.

'There's a good girl.'

She takes his glass and heads off to the kitchen.

'What about you, John?' he says. 'Still at the hospital?'

'Yes,' I say. 'But there's only another couple of weeks to go.'

'Oh?' says Toby. 'Are they shutting it down?'

'No,' I say. 'The job was only for six months. In two weeks' time my six months is up.'

'What will you do then?' asks Toby.

'I don't know,' I say.

Tiffany walks in, carrying Toby's gin and tonic.

'Gosh, John. I hope it all works out. Anyway, bottoms up, you lot.'

EastEnders is starting on the television and everyone settles down to catch up with life round Albert Square.

I leave them and go upstairs to my room. I shut the door and stand by the window, gazing down on to the back garden.

Two more weeks.

What am I going to do?

*

247

Monday comes round and I go straight to George's ward. He's there, sitting in his wheelchair, a brown cardigan over his pyjamas, carpet slippers on his bare feet.

'Hello, George,' I say, coming alongside him. 'How are you?'

'That you, son? Not too bad. The quack says I had a problem with my ticker, so they sent me up the Whitechapel.'

'You OK now?'

'Nothing a smoke wouldn't cure. You ain't brought me any, have you?'

'I've got them right here, George. Come on, let's get some fresh air.'

There's a packet of Castellas in the inside pocket of my jacket. They're about the only pleasure George has left. I know they're not good for him, but neither is a life without anything to look forward to. I smile at the nurse as I wheel him towards the door out to the courtyard, my heart soaring. George is OK. I want to find out his daughter's married name so that I can write to her, phone her, see if I can get her to come and see him. He looks the same as ever, the same gnarled face, the same dark blue glasses, the same gruff Cockney voice.

We sit in the sunshine, the warmth a luxury we share, an easy silence between us.

'Well, come on, son,' says George. 'I've been gasping for a good smoke all week.'

I take a panatella out of the packet, and hand it to George. He sticks it in the corner of his mouth and I light it with a red-tipped match. He pulls deep on the cigar and blows out plumes of heavy-scented smoke. He grins a big rogue's grin and starts to chuckle.

'If they could see me at the Whitechapel now. They'd have bleeding fits! Gawd, it was murder there, son. Like a month of Sundays up north.'

'But they reckon you'll be all right?'

He takes another big pull on the panatella.

'They don't tell me nothing, son. But I said to them, if there's anything wrong with my old ticker, can I have a new one, please.'

'What did they say?'

'They said of course. So then I says I want one in particular.'

'Oh yes?' I say.

'Yes,' says George. 'I want Margaret Thatcher's.'

'Why's that?' I ask.

'I want one that's never been used, don't I?'

George laughs in the sunshine, a gravelly, rough old laugh. The sound echoes across the courtyard and floats away with his cigar smoke up into the sunny blue skies of London. George finishes his cigar and after a while we go back inside.

'Thanks, son,' says George. 'You wouldn't get me a paper, would you? I feel like picking a few winners today. About time my luck turned. You can help me choose them if you like.'

'OK, George,' I say. 'Wait there. I won't be long.'

I pass the Bethnal Green Museum of Childhood on my way to the Tube station. It's on the corner of Cambridge Heath and Roman Road, a short walk away. There's a little kiosk inside the ticket hall, where I get the *Daily Mirror* and set off back for the ward.

I think about George as I come to the gates of the hospital. He won't like me asking about his daughter, but I can't just duck it. Perhaps the ward sister might let me have a look at his records. There should be a note of his next of kin, of his daughter's name and address. I walk down the long hospital corridor, looking forward to discussing form with George, hoping that Lady Luck will smile on him.

On the ward something's going on. There are curtains round George's bed. A doctor and the ward sister part them, then draw them across again. The ward sister sees the look on my face and walks over towards me

'We lost him,' she says softly. 'It was his time. There was nothing we could do. You were fond of him, weren't you?'

I nod, staring at the curtains.

'Did he ... did he say anything?' I ask. 'Before ... before ...?'

I can barely speak.

'He said something about Mary,' she says. 'His daughter. She lives in Harold Wood. If you'll excuse me, I have to inform her.'

She walks quickly off towards the nurses' station. Her footsteps echo down the ward's parquet floor. They sound as if they come from a long way away, as if the Earth beneath us was suddenly hollow, as if it was huge and deep and empty.

As if there was a great big hole at the heart of it.

I phone the nurses' home from the phone box outside Bethnal Green Tube Station and ask for Braddie. After a few moments her voice comes on the line.

'Hello,' I say. 'Are you busy tonight? I need to see you.'

The line goes quiet.

'Hello?' I say. 'Are you still there?'

'I'm with Mick,' she says. 'He's in my room at the moment. He's paid me back what he owed me. He got into debt with a few of the lads. Poker. Not the sort of guys you'd want to cross. That's why he didn't turn up that night. They weren't too pleased to be kept waiting for their winnings. So he sent them the money and went over to Ireland until things cooled down. I'm sorry, John.'

I put the phone down. I walk in a daze to the bus stop,

London and the rush hour all round me. But I can't really see any of it, hear any of it.

What is there to see, to hear?

There's a letter for me when I get in. It's on the cork noticeboard in the kitchen. I open it, wondering who it could be from. I don't get a lot of letters.

It's from the City of London Festival. Alan Brownjohn has awarded me a prize in the poetry competition. Could I ring them to let them know what I'd like? Would a bottle of wine or a book be suitable? I walk upstairs to my room, lie down on the futon, and pull the sleeping bag up over my ears.

The Dread is back.

I'm losing it, all over again. I had a girlfriend, now she's gone. I had a job, a job that gave me a purpose in life, and in a few days' time that'll be gone as well. And George, George has gone too. Next I shall lose this house. And then where will I be?

I'll be out.

Archway Tower stands black and bleak against the sky. It's 200 feet tall, the tallest building for miles around. It looks evil and menacing and oppressive. I go inside and take the lift up to the floor dealing with my claim. It's been two weeks since the job at Bethnal Green Hospital ended, and I've had no money since then. I've signed on but nothing has come.

I go through a pair of heavy industrial doors to a room thick with cigarette smoke. The seats are fixed to the floor and mums and their babies, men with tattoos and scrawny forearms, teenagers with Morrissey quiffs and black jeans and silver belts, all sit on the hard seats and stare straight ahead at the perspex window in front of them.

A bald man in a charity shop sports jacket is talking to the clerk behind the glass. Above him is a number – number 35. I walk over and take a ticket from the red dispenser on the wall. I'm number 53. That means there are eighteen people before me. I settle down for the long wait ahead.

The man sitting beside me, the one with the tattoos and scrawny arms, suddenly gets up and walks quickly towards the perspex window.

'When the fuck am I going to get seen?'

He starts banging on the window with his fist.

'Oi! When am I going to get seen? You fucking bastards! I've been here all morning!'

He bangs on the window again, leaning over the bald man in the sports jacket, who remains where he is. He's not giving up his place in the queue. He's probably been here all morning as well.

'This place is doing my fucking head in!' shouts Tattoos. He storms out of the room and everyone has the same thought: we're one closer to getting seen, one closer to getting out of here.

We just have to sit and wait.

I haven't eaten properly for a week. I open the kitchen cupboards, where everyone keeps their bits and pieces, bags of muesli, Baxters soups, jars of Whole Earth peanut butter. A little bit here and a little bit there, and no one will notice. And anyway, the Bible says that the Early Church kept all goods in common. The Lord knows His own.

Up in my room I lie on my futon, the sleeping bag pulled up over my head. I know that I am two people, the well me and the sick me. And I know that the sick me is taking over again.

Most of the time, the sick me lies dormant, sleeping, in that secret dreamworld of night and stars and darkness. But sometimes the sick me wakes up, startled, out of the mysterious place sickness comes from. Then it's as if I've never been well, as if I have a different history, a history where sickness alone is the truth and everything else is part of the Lie, the conspiracy that keeps the sick me at bay.

When I'm sick these are the times when my true nature is revealed, when I am transfigured, when I have vanquished my false self. I become delusional, psychotic, manic, but these states of mind are actually real, are the glimpses into a dimension the mundane, normal world tries to stifle. I enter true conscious-ness, the consciousness civilization has taken from us. That's why mad people are punished. What they experience is true, is truer than true, it threatens those who want to keep the Lie in place.

Then when the well me eventually comes back and I return to sanity I hear whispers from the sick me, asking if I was really ill at all, if I had not looked for a moment into some deeper, holier universe.

For what if I was tormented by devils? What if I could look into a reality others couldn't see? What if I was psychic, a prophet, chosen?

What if the sick me is the real me?

Jones Bros department store down the Holloway Road has the white trousers I'm looking for. The Lord is coming, coming to judge the living and the dead. I must prepare. The white trousers will match the white t-shirt I have.

I take the trousers off the rail and ask the assistant if I can use the fitting room. He points me in the right direction, and I go off to the cubicle. I put them on under my jeans, and come out of the fitting room. I head out of the store and on to the Holloway Road. As soon as I step on to the pavement I feel a hand on my shoulder.

'Can you step back into the store please?'

I'm led to an office in the basement. I'm too shocked to answer any of the store detective and the floor manager's questions. The police are called and they drive off with me.

I look out of the window and feel my life slipping quickly away. We arrive at the police station, and the car pulls up before the blue lamp, the steps leading up to the doors.

I get out of the car and they lead me inside.

XV

Pentonville, Autumn 1987

The doors open and we walk into the reception area. There are three other prisoners, all in their mid- to late twenties, and we're escorted to the counter by two prison officers. Another prison officer behind the counter checks us off on his clipboard, and then a door opens on the left-hand side of reception and we're led into the main part of the prison. The door shuts behind us and I suddenly feel like I felt on the Locked Ward in Banstead.

They could throw away the key and who in the world would care?

Highbury Corner Magistrates Court is busy this morning. There is the same restless static in the air there was up Archway Tower, the same people more or less. I wait with them in the lobby until my case is called. The words of the Co-op manager still ring in my ears.

'This is theft. This isn't someone who's hungry coming in here and nicking a loaf of bread. This is just plain old-fashioned theft.'

Angela sent me out for bin-liners. She'd moved into Fairmead Road a few weeks before, just as everyone in the House was starting to suspect me of pinching their food. I tried to tell Gregory about my claim, the trouble I was having.

'Get up there and sort it out!'

Gregory was sitting his Finals at North London Poly and didn't have much time for me. But I was slowly going mad. I was sure Jesus was coming any day now, and that I had to be ready. I was fixated on money, on how it had destroyed England, the England I had grown up in, that the government and the yuppies were doing the Devil's work, that if we all kept our goods in common we could overcome strife and greed and hatred.

So when I tried to walk out of the Co-op on Junction Road, a roll of bin-liners stuffed down my jacket, I thought I was doing God's work.

'John O'Donoghue!'

They're calling me. I stand and follow the usher into court. The doors close behind me and I walk towards the dock.

———

At the police station it all happens very quickly.

I'm photographed, front and sides, a flash going off in my eyes every time the camera clicks. Then I'm fingerprinted, each finger and thumb pressed by a fat, heavy-handed policeman into a small tray containing a dark, moist sponge. He lifts them out again one by one, and rolls them on to a piece of white card divided into panels for each black print.

'You'll get a summons,' he says, 'and then you have to attend a hearing. Make sure you go, otherwise the court can issue a warrant for your arrest.'

They let me out and I thank God that I'm a free man.

As I walk down the road I think about white trousers, where I can lay my hands on some. I have to hurry.

Jesus could come any day now.

———

The water falls in needle-thin jets, hot and steamy, as I stand naked in the showers. There's a chemical smell, something they put in the water, something to delouse us.

We all finish under the shower heads and grab the rough white towels on the benches. Another line of prisoners, already naked, some holding their hands over their private parts, step across the tiled floor to take our places. We sit on the benches and dry ourselves quickly, then wrap the towels around our midriffs. Prison-issue clothing lies in folded piles on the benches and we change into the gear and lay our old clothes neatly beside us.

I look down at myself and around at the others. We're all in royal blue smocks with matching trousers and blue and white striped cotton shirts, the sort City gents wear, strangely formal with the smocks and the trousers. It's like the Royal Free Hospital porter's uniform I wore when I worked in the post room, like a suit of pyjamas. I'm wearing prison-issue underwear as well, vest and pants, a faint grey crown on the back of the vest. My old identity is gone. The last threads of who I am have been taken away from me.

I am now a remand prisoner of HMP Pentonville.

'Next!'

It's teatime and I shuffle to the front of the line. There are about ten prisoners before me, waiting to get a mug of tea and a plate with two toasts and marmalade. I'm in a big room, bare brickwork painted cream, bars on all the windows, tables in rows where groups of prisoners talk and eat and drink. Prison officers stand around the walls, their white shirts and black ties, black trousers, shiny black boots and big bunches of keys hanging from thick leather belts in marked contrast to our flimsy outfits. The ceiling is vaulted, high, and I think of the sky above us all. I wonder if darkness has fallen, if the stars are out yet.

It could be four, five o'clock, although I'm not sure. I haven't seen a clock in here and I don't have a watch. The prisoner standing behind the metal trolley gives me a blue plastic mug of tea and a matching plate with a couple of thin slices of toast and marmalade. I walk off with it all and sit at one of the tables.

'What are you in for, son?'

A tall prisoner aged about forty with dark hair and a broken nose is standing over me. He sounds like a younger version of George, the same gravelly voice.

'Bin-liners,' I say.

'Bin-liners?' he says. 'What, was it a warehouse job?'

'No,' I say. 'Eighty pence worth from the Co-op.'

'Harry!' he calls out. 'Here, Harry, come and have a butcher's at this bloke!'

Another prisoner comes over. He's tall as well, about the same age, with light ginger hair and freckles, dull brown eyes.

'What is it, Jack?'

'I can't believe it, Harry,' says the first prisoner. 'They've put this geezer in Pentonville for eighty pence worth of bin-liners. It's costing the taxpayer 235 quid a week to keep him in here! Where's the justice in that? Where's the bleeding sense?'

Harry looks disgusted. A bell goes and suddenly teatime is over. The other prisoners rise as one and go up to leave their mugs and plates on the trolley. Jack and Harry stroll off. I wonder where Jack gets his figures from. Two hundred and thirty-five quid. It's about what I'm owed by the dole office.

The bell rings and rings. It's time for lock-up.

My first night in a prison cell.

'I was a member of the Indian hockey team at the Munich Olympics.'

My cell mate is a Sikh, aged about fifty. He lies on the bottom bunk, his big round belly, purple turban and luxuriant beard in stark contrast to the cell's Victorian drabness. There's a table and chair by the wall opposite the bunks, with a big white plastic pitcher placed on the table. A small sink is set into the far corner of the cell, and there's a mirror fixed to the wall above it. I sit on the chair facing him, fascinated by the turban. It's supposed to go seven times around his head, and I wonder what he will do when we settle down for the night. Will he take it off in front of me? Is he forbidden to do so? And where will he put all the yards of cloth?

'Munich?' I say. 'When they killed the Israelis?'

'That's right,' he says. 'A terrible business. Terrible.'

We fall silent.

'I run a cleaning company, out at Heathrow,' he says. 'I employ a lot of Irish people. Very good workers, the Irish. Perhaps you will look me up when you get a chance?'

'That would be nice,' I say.

'Do you smoke?' he says quickly.

'No,' I say.

He smiles, avuncular and warm.

'Well, everyone in here, my friend, is entitled to tobacco,' he says. 'Part of what they call 'canteen'. Perhaps when they come round to take your order you might let me have your allowance? That's if you don't want it yourself?'

'OK,' I say slowly.

'I miss my wife,' he says, sighing. 'And my children. Is there anyone on the outside for you? Anyone you are missing?'

'Not really,' I say.

'Oh,' he says. 'Never mind, my friend. I'm sure they will not keep you here long. You seem like such a nice boy. Well, it will be lights out soon. I think it is time we retired for the night.'

He stands and reaches up to take off his turban. This is the moment I've been waiting for. But he lifts the turban off in one easy movement. His turban is actually some purple silk stuck on to a head-sized loop of cardboard. It's not a proper turban at all. There are no yards of silk, no unravelling, no sense of ritual. He lays it on his bunk and walks the few steps towards the sink. I feel cheated, I don't even think he was at the Olympics. Who knows how long we'll be sharing this cell?

It could be quite a while.

———

'Do you want to go to prison, Mr O'Donoghue?'

The magistrate sits up on his bench. It's really more like a throne, and on the wooden panelling above him is the Royal Coat of Arms, the Lion and the Unicorn holding up a quartered shield of more lions and a golden harp. I thought the magistrate would wear a red robe and a long wig, but he's dressed in a dark blue suit, pink shirt and striped tie, a plump peach of a man, with a soft red face and dark hair.

I'm charged with theft. I should have attended the court after I received the summons for trying to take the white trousers. But I didn't. I was sure Christ was coming well before the date of the hearing. By the time the second summons had come for the bin-liners everyone in the House was urging me to go to court. Christ hadn't come and the delusional fog I'd been in was starting to lift.

I hadn't anticipated going to prison though. But why not? Isn't this what it means to be a follower of Jesus? Didn't He say that those who believe in Him would be brought before judges, kings, high priests? Wasn't this what happened to Him? To the Apostles, the disciples, the martyrs and saints?

'I do, your Honour,' I say.

He bangs his gavel and barks out the sentence.

'Remanded for reports, three weeks. Take him down.'

———

The door opens and I walk in. It's like the cell I shared last night – bunks, table and chair, white plastic pitcher, small sink in the corner, mirror above, the drab cream walls. But I'm on a different landing. I've been moved but no one will tell me why. My new cell mate is lying on the bottom bunk. He's not very tall, about five feet four, with close-cropped dark hair. He stares up at the bunk above him and says nothing.

'Hello,' I say.

He rises on one elbow, cold grey eyes taking me in. His face looks like it's been chipped out of flint, all angles and corners.

'Look, pal,' he says slowly. His accent is Glaswegian, like the boys in Liverpool Road. 'I'm about as happy as you are to be here. But I'm not going to get all chummy just because they've stuck some chancer in my cell. I've been in here six years. You look like you've just arrived from Planet Fucking Zog. You keep to your bunk and out of my way and we'll get on fine.'

I wonder what he's in for. Six years. It must be something bad. I climb on to the top bunk and stare at the ceiling. It's about six o'clock in the evening. I can feel waves of hatred coming from him, like intense white light. I can barely breathe. I don't want to make a sound.

We lie there in silence until it's lights out. In the darkness of the cell I can still feel the hatred rising from him in a thin white beam. I have to keep awake.

I have to watch the white beam.

The door opens and a prison officer stands framed in the doorway.

'Inspection in five minutes. Make your beds and get ready.'

My cell mate is carefully tucking in his sheets and folding

back his blankets. He goes over to the sink and starts to brush his teeth. I take the pot from under the bed and go out on to the landing. I drop my trousers and shit into it.

Groans go up from the other prisoners stood out on the landing, waiting to be inspected.

'Dirty bastard!'

'Send him to the muppet wing!'

'Get him out of here!'

The prison officer who told us to get ready comes back along the narrow landing and sees what I have done. He calls another prison officer over.

'Pull up your trousers,' says the second prison officer.

I do as I am told.

'Right,' he says. 'Let's get you down to the Hospital Wing.'

'Take this.'

The prison officer passes a small plastic beaker of brown liquid through the barred window of the cell. I know what it is: it's Largactyl. I swallow it all down and hand the empty beaker back to the prison officer. He's wearing a white tunic with blue epaulettes on the shoulders over his black trousers and has a kinder face than most of the prison officers I've met. He reminds me of some of the male nurses I knew in Claybury. I watch him walk back down the narrow corridor. There are cells either side, about twenty altogether, and each cell holds just one prisoner. He passes out of my eye line and I hear his footsteps as he goes back to the office and then silence.

I'm in the Hospital Wing, with a cell all to myself. I turn back to the big bed and lie down on top of the pale blue counterpane. The hours drag by. I've refused a visit to the library on the grounds that Jesus wrote nothing down. Writing and reading are temptations I have to resist. So I count the bricks in the wall.

And gradually the Largactyl gets to work.

'I was in the Falklands.'

A prisoner in one of the cells along the corridor is talking to us all. He has a country accent, a soft burr like Keith's Bristol drawl. I can hear him as he speaks, but none of us can see him or each other. We're all locked up and won't be let out until the dinner trolley comes round at six.

'Goose Green. It went on all night and the day after. Those Argies were a lot harder than you'd think. It took a lot of bottle to sort them out. But we did it in the end.'

The corridor falls silent. Then the chatter starts up again.

'Ronnie! Two's me up with a snout when it's dinner. I'm going mental for a fag in here.'

'All right, Steve. I'll see what I can do.'

It goes on all afternoon. Ronnie and Steve brag about the crimes they've committed, the sentences they've served, the prisons they've been in. Their voices are nasal, Cockney, thin, like sparrows chirping by St Paul's. It's like hearing echoes from the past, from Newgate, Bridewell, the Marshalsea.

I close my eyes and try to put faces to all the voices.

It won't be long now.

The dinner trolley is here. We're let out and line up one behind the other. The trusty – another prisoner given the job of doling out the food – stands over the hot plates and the prison officer with the kind face stands beside him. I steal a look at my fellow prisoners as I'm waiting my turn.

The squaddie is at the head of the queue, a tall ginger-blond lad, with freckles and a ready smile. Ronnie and Steve are behind him, two sharp-faced duckers and divers. Ronnie's got acne and long greasy hair down to his shoulders; Steve has blond hair and a scar with livid stitches down his right cheek. There are a few others behind me, but these three are the only ones I've heard all afternoon.

It's my turn at last. Dinner is mince and onions with tiny cubes of carrot chopped into it, mash and a thin greasy gravy. The trusty slops it all on to a blue plastic plate and hands me a plastic knife, fork and spoon. He puts the plate on my tray and dumps a big lump of sponge pudding and custard into a matching blue plastic bowl. I take this from him and put it beside the plate of mince, mash and gravy and carry it all back to my cell. I sit on my bed and eat. I start to look forward to mealtimes, to the pleasure of food, to the break in the monotony of being banged up, to a change from the constant natter of Ronnie and Steve.

Over the next few days I get a round of visitors. First the chaplains, C of E, RC, and Methodist, all on the same morning, each about an hour after the other. They stand by the barred window of the cell and ask me if I'm all right, if I need anything. I tell them I'm OK and say no thanks and then they move on to the next cell. On another day a trusty comes round to take my canteen order. He reads items off a list and I ask for orange squash and a bar of chocolate. The following day the governor appears at my cell window, an austere man in a charcoal-grey suit, accompanied by prison officers on either side of him. He asks me if I've had my canteen, if I've seen the chaplains, if I'm all right. Then it's the doctor's turn.

The prison officer with the kind face opens the door of the cell one morning and takes me down to the office. A middle-aged Indian doctor in a dark suit, grey shirt and blue tie is waiting for me behind a desk. The prison officer stands outside.

'Have you ever suffered from mental health problems?' the

doctor asks me. I tell him about Claybury, Friern and Banstead. He makes a few notes and asks me how I am at the moment, whether I know who the Prime Minister is, whether I'm depressed, whether I have suicidal thoughts.

The interview ends. I leave the office and the prison officer takes me back to my cell.

Pentonville is all straight lines and hard surfaces. A thousand doors bang shut when we're locked up, a noise like thunder from the landings that echoes down to the Hospital Wing. My own cell door bangs with equal fury every time we've slopped out, or had a brief walk around the yard for exercise in the afternoon or after we've collected our meals. The hours drag by. Mealtimes are the only moments of pleasure in the whole day.

Mealtimes, and getting out in the yard.

'Hello, Mr O'Donoghue. I'm a probation officer. I'm here to make a social report on you.'

She's tall with long mousy blonde hair and glasses, in her early thirties, dressed conservatively in a beige jacket and matching skirt. She's the first woman I've seen in two weeks. I steal a look at her legs as she's reading my file, mesmerized by the curve of her calf. She invites me to sit down and asks me questions about where I was living before I was remanded, what my address is, what I'd been up to.

I'm growing more withdrawn. I can barely speak to her. The delusional fog is getting thicker again with every day I spend inside.

I'm becoming a cabbage.

My mother is calling me. I can hear her, but for some reason I can't see her. It must be the snow. It's falling thick and steady, muffling her words. I call out to her, I tell her I'm here, that I'm coming. But as I struggle through the blizzard, the biting wind, the cold, her voice fades. I can just make out the faint sound of her voice.

'John! Where are you? Where are you? Where are you?'

Her voice dies away, echoes in the snow, till finally there is only silence.

Emptiness and silence.

The cell door opens.

'You're getting out today. Come on – they're waiting for you.'

It's the prison officer in the nurse's tunic. I follow him along to the end of the corridor where he hands me over to another prison officer. He takes me through the bowels of the prison, along corridors and through a series of gates. I think about my dream, about snow and wind and cold, about my mother and the sound of her voice. It seemed as real as any of this, more real if anything. If I could have just reached her, just for a moment seen her, spoken to her.

We arrive at a large room where about fifty prisoners are waiting. They're all in blue smocks and trousers except for a few who are in their own clothes. They're remand prisoners who have refused to wear prison gear. We all sit on benches around the wall, the kind you see in changing rooms. There's a sudden air of festivity – we're getting out!

My name is called and I go with a prison officer to a room where I'm asked to sign for my possessions. He hands me my clothes, and tells me to go and change. He opens a door for me behind him and I get out of the prison smock and trousers and shirt into my own clothes.

I come back into the office and hand him my prison blues. He points to a place down the corridor and I go off to join a line of prisoners who are waiting for the doors ahead of us to open.

Suddenly they do and daylight bursts into the dingy air of Pentonville. We surge forward and out to the waiting van.

I smile with the rest of them. I'm a free man.

And I'm still wearing the prison-issue underpants and vest.

XVI

Sunnyside Road, 1988

'The doctor who saw you in prison recommends that you go to a mental hospital, Mr O'Donoghue.'

The magistrate is the same one as before, the soft peachy man who remanded me. I thought I'd be going straight from Pentonville to the House.

'Your honour, Mr O'Donoghue is currently staying at a house run by Patchwork Housing Association in Fairmead Road. I am the housing officer who has responsibility for managing the House, and I want to assure the court that Mr O'Donoghue will be well looked after at this address.'

I turn around. She's standing in the benches behind me. I wasn't expecting this. I was hoping to go to hospital, to start all over again, not to return to the House. Although there are social workers there, there's not much they can do to help me. They can't go to Archway Tower, can't help with my claim, can't talk to me about the sick me and the well me.

'Thank you,' says the magistrate. He turns to the dock. 'I do think it would be best if you returned to Fairmead Road, Mr O'Donoghue. I shall therefore discharge you to the care of your housing officer. Next!'

They all look sheepish when I walk in. I'm still blinking from being out of prison. My eyes are adjusting to distances longer than the walls of my cell, to a world that isn't cream and blue

268

and grey, to traffic and crowds and skies. I've not really spoken to anyone for a couple of weeks, not since I was put on the Hospital Wing, so I'm withdrawn and awkward, a battery hen that's suddenly been let out and doesn't know what to do with its wings.

Gregory gets up off the sofa and comes over to embrace me.

'Welcome home, John,' he says.

I start to adjust to life in the House. It's good to be back in my own room, to be able to walk up and down stairs and go into the garden, to hear silence and birdsong instead of the thunderclap of a thousand doors all clanging shut, to go down to Waterlow Park and see the ducks.

The doorbell rings, long and loud. Everyone's out – there's only me at home. I wonder if it's the postman with a package for someone, or a telegram. I come downstairs and open the door.

'John O'Donoghue?'

A policeman is standing in the doorway. His colleague sits in the driver's seat of a police Rover 3500 parked by the kerb.

'Yes? That's me,' I say.

'We need you to come down the station. Can you get in the car, please?'

'What's going on?' I say.

'Just get in the car, please.'

I shut the door and walk with him towards the Rover. Now I'm really worried. What the hell is this all about?

They drive the short distance to Holloway Police Station and let me out. I go with the two officers through the front doors and we all stop at the counter in reception.

'O'Donoghue, Sarge,' says the driver.

The desk sergeant looks at his ledger from behind the counter.

'Excuse me,' I say. 'I've just come out on remand from Pentonville. I've done my time.'

The sergeant looks up.

'He's not down here,' he says to the two policemen. The sergeant turns to me. 'You're free to go,' he says.

Back at the House I feel dazed. Are the police deliberately harassing me? Have they just made some administrative cock-up? As I turn the key in the lock and open the door I see a letter on the mat in the hall. It's addressed to T. Smythe, Esq. There's no one in the House called Smythe. And yet the letter has the correct address on the front. On an impulse I open the envelope. Inside is a cheque for £200.

Two hundred pounds. I wonder who it's for. The door opens and Gregory walks in.

'God! That exam was really hard. Hello, John – what have you got there?'

I show him the envelope, the cheque inside. He looks at me sideways.

'You know this letter is addressed to Toby. Why did you open it?'

My heart drops into my stomach. Now it looks as if I'm trying to steal Toby's cheque. The rest of the House will think I'm a thief. I've pinched food out of their cupboards, stolen white trousers and bin-liners, done three weeks in Pentonville. I must look like a kleptomaniac, like I've got sticky fingers.

That afternoon the housing officer comes round. She reads me the Riot Act.

'After all we've tried to do for you! And this is how you repay us! This is the last straw. I want you to leave this house immediately.'

My premonition has come true. The fate I've dreaded but known was on its way is here at last. As bad as it is, I'm relieved.

It was hanging over me every day I was in this house. I didn't fit in. I wasn't like the rest of them. And now I can return to what I know best.

Surviving.

The hostel on the Holloway Road is just up from the Odeon. From the outside it looks like the rest of the big houses on this block. White walls, about four storeys high, overgrown front gardens, steps leading up to the front door. But this place is four of those houses knocked together, like a huge B&B. It's anonymous, nondescript, the kind of building that people pass by without looking at twice.

I give in the letter to reception. It's from the council. I went to the Neighbourhood Office, told them what had happened. They gave me a letter and told me to take it to this address. The man behind reception reads the letter and gives it back to me. I sign in and he hands me a key.

There are a few leaflets on a table in the hall. One of them says, 'Come to the Links Club, Islington MIND's Drop-In Centre'. I take the leaflet up to my room and have a closer look. It's on a road where there's a small park just around the corner. I'll go there tomorrow, when they're open. What else can I do? I'm back where it all begins. I'm twenty-nine and starting over again.

I take off my clothes and get into bed.

The Links Club is buzzing. It's 11 a.m. and already the place is full. There's a serving hatch at the far end, and behind this a kitchen. Delicious smells are drifting through the air and I hope lunch won't be long. I look around the big room, tall windows all along one wall, sofas, armchairs and tables, knots of ones and twos talking and smoking, some kind of class going on at the back.

A young blonde woman comes up to me.

'I haven't seen you here before. My name's Anne.' She has an American accent and wears jeans and a blue and white striped cotton shirt.

'I'm John,' I say.

She smiles and leads me past groups of people talking and smoking, over to an orange plastic chair at the side of the room opposite the tall windows. We both sit down and Anne asks me about myself, where I've heard about the Links Club, what I like doing. I tell her as much as I can, about all the asylums I've been in, about Pentonville, about the poems. She asks me to bring a poem next time, that they're thinking of starting a writing group. Someone comes around banging a dinner gong and everyone gets up and moves towards the serving hatch.

'Time for lunch,' says Anne. 'Come on. Let's go.'

Back in my room that evening I eat a Mars Bar and drink a pint of milk. It's cheap and I reckon it'll keep me going till tomorrow. I'll be up Archway Tower, sorting out a new claim. Except this time I'll have a letter from the hostel with me.

Down the hall a row is taking place.

'You fucked him, didn't you?'

'So fucking what if I did?'

'You slag!'

There are bangs and crashes coming from the room. I go downstairs to reception.

'I think you'd better come,' I say to the man behind the counter. 'There's a big row going on upstairs.'

He comes out from behind the counter and goes up to the first floor with me. The bangs and crashes are louder now. We can hear them from the top of the stairs. He walks along the hallway to the room and knocks on the door. Everything goes quiet.

'What do you want?'

The voice is wary, suspicious.

'Can you open the door, please? It's reception. There's been a complaint.'

I wince. Now I'm the one he's going to turn his anger on.

The door opens. It's Ronnie, from Pentonville. He has the same long greasy hair, the same acne he had on the Hospital Wing. Instead of prison blues, though, he's wearing a black Motorhead t-shirt and black jeans.

'A complaint?' he says. 'Who's complaining?'

Then he sees me, standing behind the man from reception. 'You!' he says.

A girl with dark hair and big brown eyes appears behind him in the doorway.

'Sorry about the noise,' she says. 'We were just ... you know ...'

She lowers her eyes and pouts.

'Ronnie gets very worked up.'

She's almost whispering. There's a pause.

'OK,' says the man from reception. 'Just keep the noise down.'

Ronnie looks at me, a hard, cold look, and shuts the door. The man from reception walks back along the hallway and down the stairs. I go to my room. I lie on my bed and think about what's happened. It feels just like being back in the cell with the Glaswegian. I can't stay here. I've got to get away. Before Ronnie knocks on my door.

Before he gets worked up.

Jim Green is showing us how to use a video camera. He's got it pointed at the revolving turntable of a record player at the back of the club. He's slight and spry, with light hair and a Van Dyck beard, tweed jacket and jeans. The turntable goes round and round, mesmerizing us.

273

The Links Club is full again. It's about 11 a.m., and I have a letter in my pocket. The man on reception gave it to me as I left the hostel. It's from the council. They've arranged for me to go for an interview at Sunnyside Road, another place they run. This one is for people with mental health problems. It should be smaller than the hostel. And maybe there won't be anyone like Ronnie there.

Jim finishes filming the turntable. He works here alongside Anne, and another member of staff, Tom. Tom is an O'Donoghue as well, blond and tall, gentle as falling snow.

'Are you all going on the outing next week?' says Jim.

There's a small group of us around him, fascinated by the spinning turntable. He's going to edit the footage and make it dissolve in the film he's doing with us, a film of the outing.

'To the zoo?' asks Mick. He's about my own age, with dark hair, light blue V-neck pullover, jeans and trainers.

'Yeah,' says Jim. 'You up for that, Mick?'

'They'll keep him in,' says Alf, an older man with grey hair, nylon raincoat, carrier bags at his feet.

'It's got to be better than where I'm staying,' says Mick.

Anne catches my eye. She's standing by the door of the kitchen. She smiles and I smile back. I've brought her a poem today. I hope she'll like it.

'I'm thinking of showing the film we make at the MIND Conference this year,' says Jim. 'Is that OK with everyone?'

'You going to make me the next James Dean?' says Mick.

'More like bleeding Torvill and Dean,' says Alf.

The hatch goes up and suddenly it's time for lunch. I queue with the rest, wondering what's on the menu. Anne comes up behind me. I say hello and tell her I've brought her a poem. She asks to see it and I take it out of my pocket and give it to her. She reads it quietly while we wait.

'I really like this,' she says. 'Do you have any more?'

I tell her that I used to have lots, but that I destroyed them all.

'What about you?' I ask. 'Do you write? Are you going to be taking the writing group?'

She tells me that she's just had a poem accepted at the *New Statesman*. She offers to show me a copy when it comes out.

I wonder if I'll ever get any of my poems published. I might do one day, I think.

Once I've got everything sorted.

The hostel on Sunnyside Road is a large building on a small council estate in Archway. It's like a very large council flat, made of sand-coloured bricks with plate-glass windows, about two storeys high, amongst a complex of smaller flats and a big yard where the bins are. I ring the bell and a young man opens the door.

'Are you John? Come in. We've been expecting you,' he says in a soft Scottish accent.

He says that his name is Martin Lunn, that he works here part-time while he studies for his psychology degree at the University of Kent, and leads me to the office. He puts his head round the door and tells his colleague that I'm here. He smiles at me and walks off.

I push the door open and walk in. A dark-haired woman in her early thirties is sitting in a high-backed office chair.

'Hi. I'm Liz. Take a seat. This shouldn't take too long.'

She's Scottish as well and she asks me a few questions: where I am now, what led to me ending up here, if I've ever been violent.

I answer her quietly and tell her that I need to get off the psychiatric merry-go-round, that I've been on it more or less since I was sixteen, that if I do any more turns on it I'll end up like the long-stay patients in Claybury and Friern, like Joey in St Mungo's, like Mitch in the Whittington.

She looks thoughtful.

'You can move in tonight,' she says. 'There's a room going spare at the moment. Take that one. What time do you think you can get here?'

'You going then?'

It's Ronnie, standing in the hallway as I lock my door, all of my gear — such as it is — in a black bin-liner.

'Yes, I'm off,' I say.

'Somewhere nice?' he says.

I don't want to tell him, don't want him anywhere near Sunnyside Road, the future I want to make for myself.

'Another hostel,' I say.

'Ronnie! Come to bed!'

It's his girlfriend, calling him from the room they share. He gazes at me with his cold eyes.

'You take care,' he says. 'There's a lot of nasty people out there. You know what I mean?'

I walk quickly past him and down the stairs. I give in my key at the desk and say goodbye to the man on reception. As I leave, I can hear Ronnie and his girlfriend laughing. But I don't care now. I'm determined. I promise myself I'll never be sectioned, that I'll never see the inside of a prison, a homeless hostel or a squat ever again.

This time I'm going to make it.

Green Ink Bookshop nestles under the shadow of Archway Tower. I'd not noticed it before, but a flyer in Archway Library catches my eye. It says that Green Ink Writers meets fortnightly in the back of the shop.

The night I go along five people have turned up: three men

and two women. They sit round in a circle to read and discuss each other's work, and ask me if I've brought anything. I have a poem, 'What O'Sullevan Said', about a man in a pub puffing away on his pipe. By the end of the poem the smoke drifting up to the rafters has turned to faint music, echoing O'Sullevan's remark at the poem's beginning: 'All music is the friend of silence.' It's a little hallucination of a thing, a giddy turning of sound into image.

In the pub afterwards one of the women tells me that Green Ink has plans to produce a small anthology, funded by Greater London Arts.

'Do you think you could give us a few poems for it?' she says.

I go back to Sunnyside Road in the company of Mad Sweeney, O'Rathaille, and Patrick Kavanagh, and dream about being amongst the Irish poets after my death.

I even think I might be amongst a few of them when I'm still alive.

Sadler's Wells is full to bursting. Michael Clark's ballet *I Am Curious Orange* is drawing huge audiences. I'm working behind the bar in the Upper Circle. I've been at Sadler's Wells for the past couple of months now. I work all over the theatre, in the bars in the evening when the shows are on; in the staff canteen during the daytime, serving the crew, the dancers, the box office and admin staff; stocking up the drinks in the bars in the afternoon; and on the Stage Door at weekends. I've picked up jobs as the weeks have gone by and now I consider myself part of the furniture.

I'm as busy as the wind, and tonight the Upper Circle is packed. There's an usher on duty and she shows the audience into the auditorium as the curtain goes up. There are glasses everywhere, and I'll have to go round and collect them all, wash them, dry them, and get the interval drinks ready. The ushers can be a snooty lot. They like to look down on the bar staff, who are all locals like me. The ushers tend to be students, at Saint Martins School of Art, or some of the drama and dance colleges dotted around London.

But this one is different. I haven't seen her before, and she talks to the members of the audience as they go in with an American accent. She has long blonde hair, wears a white shirt and black skirt and tights, and has something of a dancer's figure herself. None of the other ushers has ever helped me get in the glasses, but now she's going round, collecting them up and leaving them for me on the bar.

'Thank you very much,' I say. 'None of the others does this, you know. It's as if they think they'll catch something if they touch a glass. When the show is over I'll buy you a drink. What's your tipple?'

'I like orange juice,' she says.

'So you're a cheap date,' I say.

'You couldn't afford me.'

By now the house is all in, and her work strictly speaking is over. She's free to go. But I like her spirit and when all is said and done I owe her at least a drink, even if it is only orange juice.

'Meet me in the Harlequin when the show's over,' I say. 'It's pay day and I'll buy you all the orange juice you can drink.'

She smiles, turns on her heel, and is gone.

Work over, I sit in the pub and watch the door. There's a big crowd in, the audience from *I Am Curious Orange*, a few of the stage crew, a few other faces I know from the theatre.

She walks in, long legs, lissom figure, blonde hair down her back. She comes straight up to me.

'Your place or mine?' she says.

*

In the taxi I make an excuse about my new flat. I *am* going to move into a new flat, a council property, very near Sadler's Wells. But it won't be for another few weeks yet. And I can't take her back to Sunnyside Road.

'Egerton Crescent, driver,' she says. I don't recognize the address so I sit back and ask her name, ask her to tell me all about herself.

'There's plenty of time for that stuff later,' she says. And she leans over and kisses me all the way to Knightsbridge.

The taxi pulls up outside an enormous house at the back of Harrods. I reckon she must be an au pair, that she'll have a little room somewhere at the top of the house.

I couldn't be more wrong.

I pay off the taxi and we stand on the street. I look up at five storeys of prime London townhouse. The place is hers, or, at any rate, her father's. She tells me that Daddy bought the house from David Frost, that he was letting it out to students before Pop weighed in. He had it done up, and she has an allowance to buy antique furniture at auction houses for this huge pile in front of me. Daddy is in the States right now and she has the whole place to herself.

She turns the key in the lock and we go inside.

'Daddy, I have a special new friend. His name is John.'

Breakfast the next morning is served by a housekeeper, a dark-haired Englishwoman in her thirties. Miss Hennessey – for that is what I call *my* special new friend – is sitting in the breakfast room with the phone to her ear. She's wearing a man's shirt, open almost to the waist, nothing on underneath. I love her frankness, her freshness, her boldness. She's beautiful and wealthy and a little complicated. She told me last night she was adopted, and I think that though I might be her special friend this morning, by tonight I'll be another notch on her bedpost.

I can't compete with her, her wealth, her family, her connections. All we share is the rootlessness that comes with being in the Big City and having no real immediate family of your own. And I don't relish the role of gold digger. I think Miss Hennessey should be treated with far more respect, far more gallantry, than having some schmuck like me muscle in on her lifestyle.

I kiss her goodbye, as the housekeeper looks on. I have to be back at the theatre. The Saturday matinee will be going up in a few hours and I need to be at work.

As the door shuts behind me I walk down Egerton Crescent singing 'The Fields of Athenry' softly and a little sadly to myself, knowing that it was nice while it lasted.

'You should go to university.'

Martin Lunn is making a big pot of vegetable curry. I'm helping him, in the industrial kitchen at Sunnyside Road. He's stirring in the ingredients, and I'm chopping up mushrooms, peppers and chillis.

'I don't know, Martin. It's for posh people really, isn't it? And I'm not sure I have the qualifications.'

'Ach, not at all,' he says. 'These days lots of mature students are getting into university without any bloody qualifications. Look, why don't you let me help you apply? Just do it to keep your options open.'

That decides me. What have I got to lose? Besides, I can't see myself living in a flat on my own for the rest of my life, even if I am having a blast working at Straddler's Wells as I call it. I'm due to take possession of the new flat any day now. I'll get a little grant off the council to furnish it, and there's a stage hand with a bed and a table he's selling. I'll use the grant to get a telly and a radio, and whatever knick-knacks I might need.

And dream of going somewhere far from the Smoke where I can put everything behind me.

The University of East Anglia is a little like Sunnyside Road. It's got lots of plate glass, buildings made of sand-coloured bricks, concrete, and the kinds of blocks and walkways that went up all over England in the sixties.

I've come up on the train from Liverpool Street to Norwich, and taken the bus out to the campus. I have an interview with Jocelyn Houseman, and have brought *Green Ink 5* with me. It's the anthology Green Ink Writers have published. I've got two poems in the little dark green-covered book, 'What O'Sullevan Said' and 'Forked Tongue', a poem about my father speaking Gaelic, his native language, and the bereft feeling I have in hardly speaking a word of it myself.

We've been shown round the place and given lunch, a granary roll with thick cheddar cheese and lots of cress, and a mug of coffee. Jon Cook, a lecturer in EAS, or English and American Studies to give the school its full name, has given us all a talk about the university, about what we might be able to study here, about life in and around Norwich. He's very impressive, and I'm totally sold on coming to UEA, posh people or no posh people. All I need to do now is impress Jocelyn Houseman in the interview.

I meet her in her office. She's not like Jon Cook. She seems like one of the posh people I'm wary of, a woman from the Shires rather than one of the radical Marxists, the Howard Kirks, the university is supposed to be so full of.

'And who is your favourite poet?' she says.

I tell her I like Dylan Thomas, John Keats, Robert Graves and Patrick Kavanagh. I have some lines of Graves by heart and I recite these as the pale spring sunlight illuminates the room.

She smiles at me and I give her the copy of *Green Ink 5* that

I've brought for her. She says thanks, that the university will be in touch shortly, and wishes me luck.

Mark-Anthony Turnage is rehearsing his opera, *Greek*, at Sadler's Wells. Jonathan Moore is directing, and they're taking the opera to Edinburgh. Nora, the little Irish lady I work with in the staff canteen, gets very vexed by them. The mezzo-soprano and her mate come into Nora's bistro in matching leather mini skirts and white blouses, stockings, suspenders and stiletto heels. They put their feet up on the chairs and flash their legs, their stockings, their suspenders, and take slow languorous drags on enormous king-size fags.

'Would you look at them?' says Nora.

'I'm looking, Nora, I'm looking,' I say.

'They have no shame,' she says, and walks off to rattle away at her cutlery drawer.

Mark-Anthony Turnage is standing at the counter by the till, smiling at me. I see him every day, when they all take a break from rehearsals and he comes down with the singers and Jonathan Moore for a coffee break or for lunch. We've got to know one another a little. His company makes a change from the ballet dancers. The principal gets a little narked when he's got a sweat on after performing at the barre. Mark-Anthony's lot are never like that.

'Have you ever been to Edinburgh, John?' he asks, as I pour him a cup of coffee from the pot.

'No,' I say.

'Well, if you get up there for August I'll save you a ticket. Might even be able to sort you out a floor to sleep on.'

I thank him.

But I have other plans for the summer.

*

There's a brown envelope for me on the mat. It's from UEA. I open it, my nerves jangling. It's an official letter, with the course code of the degree I'd like to do, and in block capitals, 'UNCONDITIONAL OFFER'.

I'm stunned.

'Well?' says Martin. 'What does it say?'

'It says I haven't got in. They've knocked me back.'

He takes the letter from me.

'Och, you big Jesse! Unconditional Offer! It means they're taking you. You don't need A levels or anything else to get in. The offer is UNCONDITIONAL! That's what 'Unconditional' means! Congratulations!'

The boat to Ireland races through the waves. I've been in my new flat for about two months now. But the Neighbourhood Office doesn't have me down as a tenant. The social worker tells me to stick the rent in a drawer until I'm on the system. One day there's £400 lying there.

So I do something I've wanted to do for years.

I book a ferry ticket from Holyhead to Dun Laoghaire and now I'm crossing the Irish Sea. I'll worry about the rent when I come back.

Because soon I'll be off to university and leaving everything behind me.

I walk into the Post Office in Monaghan. My cousin Matt is standing at the far end, behind the counter. He's talking to an old lady who looks like she's come in for her pension. He hasn't seen me yet, and I wonder what his reaction will be when he does.

I walk up behind her as she collects her money. Matt hands back her pension book, and as she walks off he catches sight of me.

'Ach, John,' he says, 'how are you doing?'

He comes out from behind the counter and gives me a big hug.

That summer, the summer of 1988, is glorious. Ireland looks wonderful, green and golden in the sunshine, and I am hailed by my cousins, by Auntie Lizzie and Uncle Tommy, by all around Ballinode, as a long-lost relative finally washed up on to their shores and treated as if I'd never left at all.

Evelyn, who has been working as a nurse at St John and St Elizabeth's Hospital in St John's Wood, tells me she came looking for me the time I was in Friern. I'd given Uncle Tommy as my next of kin, and the hospital wrote to him in Ireland. But by the time he'd got the letter and contacted Evelyn in London, I'd been discharged.

'So what?' I say. 'I'm home now.'

Jim Green helps me pack his Mini. I don't have much stuff, just a few clothes, some books, a bedside lamp.

I've kept in touch with Jim and Anne since I used to see them both at the Links Club. We've become good friends; no cant from them about boundaries and careers and detachment. To them I'm just me, someone they like, someone who likes them.

On the long drive up to UEA Jim tells me about his own time there. After Clare College, Cambridge, he went to East Anglia to do a Master's in English Literature. Kazuo Ishiguro shared some classes with him, and they became good friends. I wonder if I'll meet any writers up there, if my own writing might get recognized by the lecturers or visiting fellows. I can't believe it's actually happening.

We finally pull up at the porter's lodge on the way into campus. They check me off on their list, and give me a key, and tell me where I'll be staying. I'm on Norfolk Terrace, the ziggurats designed by Denys Lasdun at the far end of campus.

Jim cruises slowly down the little roads until we come to the right block. He helps me with my gear down the concrete steps to my room on the ground floor. I put the key in the lock and push the door open.

Through my window at the far end of the room is a view of the sunlit lake and the lush rolling grounds of UEA. The locals used to say it's a third-rate university on a second-rate golf course, but from here it looks like paradise.

After where I've been, what I've come through, where I've gone, I'm glad that this at last is where I've finally arrived.

Epilogue

Organ music fills the air. It feels like the whole church is lifting off, up, up to the stars and into the heavens beyond. I march on the double down the aisle, my beautiful bride on my arm, the proudest man in England, in Europe, on Planet Earth, in the whole wide and wonderful universe.

The doors of St Martin-in-the-Fields are open and we come out into a glorious late summer day. London erupts around us. The buses, the traffic, the people going into the National Gallery, the pigeons around Trafalgar Square, Villiers Street, the Embankment and the Thames a few hundred yards away, the vast metropolis stretching for mile after mile – it all seems to be in a tumult of joy.

Today we are married, and as I look out on the streets of the capital, the streets that only a few years earlier were so hard and so cold, I stand on the steps of St Martin's and I give thanks.

I met Bernadette at a student party in Norwich. It was the start of my second year, 1989, and we started going out together soon afterwards. We moved to London and I arranged to take a break from my degree. We lived in a flat in West Hampstead, and spent those early days walking over Hampstead Heath, or taking the North London Link Line to Richmond, swimming in the big pool there, exploring places I'd never really been to: Kensington, Chiswick, Kew Gardens. I still had some money from my grant and Bernadette had some savings so we went to Corfu. It was like having a honeymoon before the wedding.

When we came back I landed a job working in a residential home in Highgate, poacher turned gamekeeper. The old Victorian asylums I'd known so well were closing down and Community Care was coming in to replace them. The doors were opening. People who had been in hospital were no longer excluded from working in 'mental health'. In many ways, it was the job I was best qualified for. I could now think about the future, about settling down, making a life together with Bernadette. One day in the early summer of 1990 I asked her if she would marry me.

We planned the wedding as Italia 90 got under way. Love had the world in motion, and when Ireland reached the quarter-finals of the World Cup we turned off the box and took a walk up to Kilburn High Road. The whole place was a sea of green, cars sounding their horns, the pubs all empty as Jack's Army came out on to the pavements, wrapped in tricolours, singing their heads off. Then when England got to the semi-finals the country held its breath. Gazza's tears, Chris Waddle's penalty, the heartbreak of losing to Germany ... What a summer!

That winter Geoffrey Howe, the Deputy Prime Minister, made a speech to the House of Commons resigning his position. He asked for 'others to consider their own response to the tragic conflict of loyalties' he'd wrestled with for too long. It was an electric moment. Soon after, Michael Heseltine challenged Mrs Thatcher for the leadership. By the end of the month she'd resigned.

Mrs Thatcher left Downing Street on 28 November. A few days later I strolled along Birdcage Walk towards the Sanctuary at Westminster Abbey. I had to go there to arrange a Special Licence for our wedding at St Martin-in-the-Fields. As I came to Parliament Square I wondered what life would be like now that Mrs Thatcher had gone. It had been a mad decade. Perhaps now things would get better.

I came at last to the Gothic splendour of the Sanctuary and I thought about the letter the vicar of St Martin's had written to *The Times* when I'd been in St Mungo's. He called the spectacle of people sleeping out on the Embankment a 'disgrace to humanity'. It was a rebuke not only to society in general but to Mrs Thatcher and her government in particular.

I looked down the road towards Big Ben and the Houses of Parliament. What had William Blake said? 'I will not cease from mental fight, nor shall my sword sleep in my hand, till we have built Jerusalem, in England's green and pleasant land.'

As I entered the Sanctuary that day England never looked greener or more pleasant, nor London more like Blake's golden vision of Jerusalem.

A white London taxi is waiting for us. Bernadette and I walk down the steps of the church and get inside. We drive off to the reception at Max's Wine Bar off Tottenham Court Road, and greet everyone as they arrive. John Knight, my Best Man; Ian Berry, who has designed the Order of Service; Jim Green, who is shooting the wedding video; Lorna O'Connell who was at my twenty-first birthday; the Macpherson sisters and their mother; people I work with, residents and staff; friends from university; friends of Bernadette; her family. There are speeches, laughter, champagne, toasts, then the image suddenly flickers and dissolves.

In its place is Jack Nicholson, on a boat with the patients from the acute ward. Jack is speaking to the harbour master, telling him that he's taking the boat out on a fishing trip. He starts introducing the patients one by one, Dr Cheswick, Dr Martini, Dr Harding, and so on.

Jim Green has shot the wedding video over a copy of *One Flew Over the Cuckoo's Nest*. I sit on the sofa with Bernadette and the children, all these many years later, and we laugh. Cheswick, Martini, Harding and all the rest really do look like doctors! They look like almost every psychiatrist I've ever met – bearded, bespectacled, eccentric.

'Where did you go on honeymoon?'

'Where did you get the ring?'

'And where did you buy that lovely dress, Mummy?'

My marriage marked another turning point in my life. I've had my share of ups and downs, but I have a much more stable life than I ever knew when I was single. I don't take medication and I haven't been sectioned since I met Bernadette. If sometimes my mood darkens or I buckle under the strain, I have the love of my family to get me through the worst of it. I'm more resilient now, stronger, aware of trigger factors and how to avoid them, of how to deal with my problems as they arise.

Manic depression? The victim of circumstance? A casualty of Thatcherism? I'll pass no remark, as my cousins would say. Let's just say I feel lucky to be here, and leave it at that.

We answer all the children's questions, and I think back to St Martin-in-the-Fields, to all the people who came to the wedding, to those who weren't there. I think especially of my mother and father, and feel sure that one day I'll meet them again, that I'll turn a corner and they'll be there, walking along in bright sunshine, my father in his dark blue double-breasted suit, my mother in a summer dress.

'Hello, John Boy,' he'll say.

My mother will smile at me, her smile of old, and we'll all stroll off together, along by the winding river, following the dapples of light glinting on the water's wavy surface, away to fields where the sun meets the sky, as if we've never been apart, as if at last we'll always be together, as if we'll never again be interrupted.

Acknowledgements

I would not have been able to write *Sectioned* without the kindness, the support and the encouragement of a large number of people. I'd like to thank them here at the end of this book – many of them were there at the beginning and along the way, so this seems the most fitting place to record my debt to you all.

Fatema Ahmed and Sara Holloway both showed early interest in and enthusiasm for *Sectioned*, and made me believe in my writing; Bridget Whelan opened the door for me at MCA; Jonathan Conway and Ivan Mulcahy did far more than merely represent me – they made *Sectioned* possible and offered their expertise at every stage of the book's production; Eleanor Birne, Helen Hawksfield and Bernard Dive at John Murray were passionate, patient and professional as I shared my story with them – being published by John Murray is a dream come true; Jane Housham at the University of Hertfordshire gave me the benefit of her wisdom, experience and friendship. My thanks go to Dr Andrew Maunder at the University of Hertfordshire, for giving me my start as a Visiting Lecturer; Dr Andrew Caink at the University of Westminster, whose quiet encouragement and support is typical of him; Dr Paula James and Lucy Cradduck, and all my students at the Open University; Neil Swire, whose generosity and friendship helped me through some dark times; Jacqui, for her hospitality, warmth and kindness; all at Waterloo Press and The South who have made the lonely business of writing so much less lonely; Anne Rouse, for that long conversation since we first met at the Links Club; Jim Green, for his tireless dedication to helping the likes of me; Mark Fahey, for passing no remark; John Knight and Ian Berry, my two oldest friends, who never judged me, and always subbed me; Pam Sexton, a precious boon, even after all this time; Lorna O'Connell and her mother Margaret, for the days that were in it, and are still to come; Matt Murphy, my cousin, and all my other Ballinode cousins: Geraldine, Mary, Evelyn and Anna, and all of their families – John Kevin sends his love; Matt's wife Eileen and her sister Patricia for being such good sports; and my cousin Mary O'Donoghue for welcoming home a Prodigal Son. Thanks too to St Martin-in-the-Fields and all who help those on the fringes of society. Martin Lunn and Jocelyn Houseman also made this book possible, and I owe them a tremendous debt, for which I hope *Sectioned* is some small recompense. To each and every one of you I send my heartfelt thanks.

I'd also like to thank Keiren Phelan at the Arts Council for his assiduous help, and the Arts Council's generosity in awarding me a grant during the writing of *Sectioned*; and the Oppenheim-Downes Trust for a similar award. Awards mean more than money to writers: they offer recognition when it's easy to lose confidence, so many thanks for your support and encouragement.

Finally – to my wife and children: I am truly blessed and it's in all of you that my blessings are made known.

Read more ...

Sameem Ali

BELONGING

One woman's shocking account of forced marriage

Abandoned by her parents, Sameem Ali grew up in a children's home. When her family took her back she was beaten and treated like a slave. Sameem was excited when she visited Pakistan for the first time, but she soon realised that she wasn't there on holiday. Aged just thirteen, she was forced to marry a complete stranger. Two months later, she was pregnant.

As a young teenage mother, Sameem suffered further abuse from her family. After finding true love, she ran away from home in order to keep her child safe. But she was about to pay the price for violating her family's honour.

Order your copy now by calling Bookpoint on 01235 827716 or visit your local bookshop quoting ISBN 978-0-7195-6462-8 www.johnmurray.co.uk